CULTURE, PLACE, AND NATURE

Studies in Anthropology and Environment

K. Sivaramakrishnan, Series Editor

Centered in anthropology, the Culture, Place, and Nature series encompasses new interdisciplinary social science research on environmental issues, focusing on the intersection of culture, ecology, and politics in global, national, and local contexts. Contributors to the series view environmental knowledge and issues from the multiple and often conflicting perspectives of various cultural systems.

Roses from Kenya

LABOR, ENVIRONMENT, AND THE GLOBAL TRADE IN CUT FLOWERS

Megan A. Styles

UNIVERSITY OF WASHINGTON PRESS
Seattle

Roses from Kenya was made possible in part by a grant from the College of Public Affairs and Administration at the University of Illinois Springfield.

Composed in Warnock Pro, typeface designed by Robert Slimbach
Printed and bound in the United States of America
23 22 21 20 19 5 4 3 2 1

UNIVERSITY OF WASHINGTON PRESS
uwapress.uw.edu

LIBRARY OF CONGRESS CATALOGING-IN-PUBLICATION DATA
Names: Styles, Megan A., author.
Title: Roses from Kenya : labor, environment, and the global trade in cut flowers / Megan A. Styles
Description: Seattle : University of Washington Press, 2019. | Series: Culture, place, and nature | Includes bibliographical references and index.
Identifiers: LCCN 2019023571 (print) | LCCN 2019023572 (ebook) | ISBN 9780295746517 (hardback) | ISBN 9780295746500 (paperback) | ISBN 9780295746524 (epub)
Subjects: LCSH: Rose industry—Social aspects—Kenya—Naivasha. | Rose industry—Environmental aspects—Kenya—Naivasha. | Floriculture—Kenya—Naivasha. | Naivasha (Kenya)—Social conditions—21st century. | Naivasha (Kenya)—Economic conditions—21st century.
Classification: LCC HN793.A8 S73 2019 (print) | LCC HN793.A8 (ebook) | DDC 306.0967627—dc23
LC record available at https://lccn.loc.gov/2019023571
LC ebook record available at https://lccn.loc.gov/2019023572

Cover photograph by Emily Fletke, Unsplash
Interior photographs are by the author unless otherwise noted.

The paper used in this publication is acid free and meets the minimum requirements of American National Standard for Information Sciences—Permanence of Paper for Printed Library Materials, ANSI Z39.48–1984.∞

CONTENTS

FOREWORD

The examination of commodity agriculture and the associated field of commodity chains has been a staple in agrarian studies and environmental anthropology since the mid-1980s with the publication of Sidney Mintz's (1985) foundational work. Much of the subsequent scholarship has come from research regionally focused on sub-Saharan Africa. In this book, Megan Styles is thus responding to and building on a vibrant tradition in studies of postcolonial agricultural and social development. Coffee, cocoa, peanuts, and maize, among other crops, have centered such research in eastern and western Africa—work that has established a high standard for new scholarship on commodity agriculture in African contexts of the twentieth and twenty-first centuries.

However, Styles is also at the leading edge of new interest, especially among anthropologists and human geographers, in what scholars identifying these processes have called "startlingly close connections" between farmers in the global South and markets in the global North (Stone, Haugerud, Little 2000, 9). This newer work is sensitive both to the shaping influences of global capitalism in periods of instability in currency values and commodity prices since the 1990s and the historical contingencies that are revealed by the actions of farmers, local governments, and regional enterprises.

Styles enters this field of inquiry with a contribution that is focused on nontraditional agricultural commodities—in her case, fresh-cut flowers, particularly roses. Her work in the Lake Naivasha region of Kenya examines floriculture for export in a place where the freshwater lake was already the object of desires stemming from broader agrarian development and a nascent tourism industry. It has also been the contentious site of, most recently, anxieties around pollution of the lake by effluents and leachates from intensive land use around it. The agrarian question in Kenya and the colonial history that forged it inform what is vitally and vividly an ethnography of roses being grown and shipped to foreign markets, especially in northern Europe. Styles reveals the distinct postcolonial trajectories of development in agriculture that were born from structural adjustment schemes introduced in rural eastern Africa in the last few decades.

A notable contribution to the study of commodity chains emerges from her subtle understanding of diverging and conflicting perspectives on floriculture as a wellspring of aspirations for farmers, workers, business entrepreneurs, government regulators, and environmentalists. The book brings to life the hopes and struggles of a range of participants in Kenyan floriculture by sequentially focusing on different sets of actors. This approach moves away from a tendency in commodity-chain research to document how local resources, sensibility, and imagination—each viewed through a monochromatic lens—are commandeered to serve global designs. Instead, Styles is attentive here to the conflicted feelings of the people situated in different points of the chain as primary producers, processors, suppliers, promoters, and managers. She examines their location in a complex field of relations to each other and to the export product: roses.

Styles describes the cut flower industry around Lake Naivasha as a nerve center of active economic organization, human agency, and animated social imagination where various Kenyans join each other as they take pride in their accomplishments and aspire to better lives and a place in the sun. This happens, she argues, in full awareness of hardships, injustice, and environmental hazards brought by the flower export economy. Development, as she shows, and as studies from other parts of the world continue to demonstrate, retains its power to enchant its subjects precisely because they are agents in delineating the cultural and economic horizons it brings into view. Even though perilous in the making and often harsh in outcome, connections to global capitalism—the form development has mostly taken in recent times—inform an imaginary of possible prosperity and new adventures for the rural poor in many parts of the world (a point made well by Gardner 2012).

The nerve center, rather than node, that Lake Naivasha becomes in rose export recognizes the coexistence of export-commodity production with other claims on land and lake. The cut flower industry becomes, thereby, a flashpoint for competing ambitions and contrary visions of this bountiful terrain and the industry's potential to bring economic advancement to Kenya. Lake Naivasha is a nerve center because it is simultaneously a political space of contested regional history, a transnational space of interconnections, and a creative space of national experiments in agrarian socioeconomic development. The book delivers a riveting account of the multiple ways that

Lake Naivasha and the flower industry constitute a nerve center. In doing so, it brings fresh and welcome perspectives to anthropological study of global connection through the production and circulation of agrarian commodities.

K. SIVARAMAKRISHNAN
Yale University

PREFACE

This book is based on ethnographic fieldwork and archival research conducted in Kenya between 2004 and 2014. During this time, much has changed. Kenya has had two presidents and adopted a new constitution. Two of Naivasha's three largest flower farms have changed ownership, and one has descended into what will probably become a permanent state of receivership. Thanks to major cash infusions from the World Bank and foreign direct investment, geothermal power production has also expanded rapidly in the Naivasha area; undeveloped land near Hell's Gate National Park is now dotted with geothermal wells, networks of aboveground pipes, and several new state-of-the-art geothermal power plants. These dramatic shifts speak to the constant presence of change and the degree to which Kenyan communities and environments are embedded and entangled in global processes.

When I first began working in Naivasha, press coverage made it clear that cut flower farming had generated significant conflict and debate in Kenya and abroad. Previous research had focused on assessing working and living conditions for farm laborers (e.g., Dolan, Opondo, and Smith 2002; Hale and Opondo 2005) and determining the ecological effects of floriculture and rapid urban development on the lake as an ecological and hydrological system (e.g., Becht and Harper 2002; Harper, Mavuti, and Muchiri 1990; Everard and Harper 2002). While these studies described patterns of social and ecological change under way in the lake area, they provided little sense of what these changes actually *mean* in the contexts of peoples' everyday lives. Although news articles suggested a rich undercurrent of political activity in the lake area, little had been written about the role played by Kenyan civil society, especially environmental organizations, in the struggle to reform floriculture. In most studies and in the media, a detailed description of Naivasha's present was set against a generalized and comparatively thin depiction of the past. My goal was to fill in these gaps.

This book is based on interviews with more than 175 people living and working in Naivasha. I conducted most interviews alone but worked closely with a local research assistant when interviewing farmworkers in Swahili. Whenever possible, I illustrate arguments with quotes drawn directly from these interviews. I also attended more than forty meetings and seminars focused on social and environmental regulation in Naivasha, and regularly accompanied farmworkers, managers, and labor and environmental advocates as they went about their daily lives. In keeping with ethnographic tradition, I have assigned all of my research collaborators pseudonyms. I have also altered the names of the flower farms where I conducted participant observation activities.

I conducted the bulk of my interviews between May 2007 and May 2008, a span that included the three-month period of protracted violence and uncertainty following the disputed results of the December 2007 Kenyan presidential election. I left Kenya on January 15, 2008, amid signs of escalating tensions at the national and local levels. For three weeks, I stayed in London, where I remained in daily contact with friends and colleagues in Kenya. When violence spread to Naivasha and it became clear that I could not return to Kenya as planned, I traveled to Arusha, Tanzania, where I remained until shortly after a peace accord was signed in Kenya.

When I returned in March 2008, I found a changed Naivasha. A week-long wave of violence left at least twenty-three dead, thousands of ethnic-minority residents and farmworkers displaced from their lake area homes, and property worth millions of shillings destroyed. To shelter internally displaced persons from Naivasha and elsewhere in the Rift Valley, the Red Cross constructed two refugee camps in the lake area. In an effort to piece together what happened here during the postelection violence, I volunteered at one of the Red Cross camps and listened while friends and acquaintances shared painful experiences from the period when I was away.

Local manifestations of the postelection violence revealed moral legacies, historical memories, and terrains of power in Naivasha (and in Kenya more generally). These events colored the perspectives expressed by many of the people I interviewed. I discuss these events in more detail in chapter 1 and, where appropriate, make allusions to them throughout the book. Although this postelection violence in Naivasha lasted only a few days out of the hundreds that inform my research, the memories and meanings associated with these events remain potent. This was a jarring reminder of the precarity and contested nature of many elements of Kenyan social, political, and economic life.

In 2014, I returned to Kenya to interview many of the same people with whom I worked in 2007 and 2008. The intervening years had been kind to some, especially the middle-class professionals who had worked so diligently to advance their careers through floriculture. Others had suffered profound professional and personal losses. I compare their rosy aspirations in 2014 to those they expressed in 2008. Their updated perspectives provide insight into Naivasha's evolution as a nerve center.

Throughout the book, I also draw on historical materials from several repositories and private collections in Kenya. In the Kenya National Archives in Nairobi, I discovered a wealth of material related to the agrarian and environmental history of the Lake Naivasha area. Files from the Department of Fisheries and the Ministry of Tourism and Wildlife covering the time period between 1927 and 1975 provide a window on the ways that colonial and postcolonial officials viewed Lake Naivasha as a resource and the environmental management strategies that they employed. These sources and other files (e.g., annual district-level reports, minutes from colonial-era farmer's association meetings, and documents describing land transfers) also include correspondence between government officials and European settlers, who write of their agricultural activities in the lake area, their conflicts with so-called local poachers and squatters, and their aspirations regarding control of the lake and the land surrounding it. Elite actors in Naivasha have tried on several occasions to control or restrict development in the lake area in response to an evolving set of perceived threats.

I use these sources to historically contextualize contemporary forms of agricultural development and ecological politics in the lake area. A list of these sources is included in the bibliography. I also located materials related to the history of both Lake Naivasha and the Kenyan flower industry in the Nairobi archives of the two major Kenyan newspapers, the *Daily Nation* and *East African Standard*. Newspaper articles on these topics cover the time period from 1963 to the present. These sources have helped me piece together a chronology of important events related to the rise of floriculture, and they provide the basis for a discursive analysis of how attitudes and policies concerning both the cut flower industry and environmental issues in the lake area have shifted over time.

In Naivasha, I was also given access to historical materials in the possession of the Lake Naivasha Riparian Association, a local organization that currently plays a leadership role in attempts to design strategies for community-based, cooperative management of Lake Naivasha. These materials included meeting minutes and correspondence between members dating from the founding of the organization (originally an interest group for European settlers owning land adjacent to the lake), in 1929, to the present. Combined with sources found in the National Archives, these materials provide a nuanced picture of the history of the area before and after the advent of intensive floriculture.

ACKNOWLEDGMENTS

I am deeply grateful to everyone in Kenya who shared their stories, lives, and expertise with me. Thank you for your patience, your trust, and your hospitality. Writing about floriculture from many different perspectives has required me to present voices that are sometimes contradictory. There are no heroes or villains in this book, only complex human beings living and working together in a particularly dynamic and provocative place. Thank you for teaching me about the history, beauty, and complexity of Naivasha. The portion of this book based on archival resources was made possible by the wisdom and kindness of the librarians at the Kenya National Archives, the staff who archive newspaper articles for the *Daily Nation* and *East African Standard*, and the leadership of the Lake Naivasha Riparian Association, who graciously granted me access to the organization's private library.

Many inspirational teachers have shaped this research project at every stage. Thank you to K. Sivaramakrishnan, Lynn Thomas, Daniel Hoffman, Lucy Jarosz, Mimi Kahn, Eric Smith, Gene Hunn, Stevan Harrell, and Devon Peña for your guidance and mentorship during my time at the University of Washington and beyond. Thank you to Angelique Haugerud, Maggie Opondo, Katherine Snyder, and Catherine Dolan for providing me with indispensable advice about working in Kenya and for mentorship at key junctures in my research. Thanks also to the members of our UW anthropology hive mind, especially Heather Lazrus, Courtney Carothers, Laura Zanotti, Amanda Poole, Brooke Scelza, Sara Breslow, Melissa Poe, Andi Duncan, Catherine Ziegler, Joyce LeCompte-Mastenbrook, Ismael Vacarro, Karma Norman, Aksel Casson, Tapoja Chaudhuri, and Lisa Meierotto.

Early drafts of material incorporated in this book also benefited from the advice and expertise of mentors and colleagues at Yale University and at the University of Cambridge, where I spent time as a visiting scholar and research fellow in 2008 and 2009, and participants in the Harvard University African Studies Workshop, where I was graciously invited to present my work in 2015. Thanks also to my wonderful colleagues and students in the UW Program on the Environment and at the University of Illinois Springfield. Special thanks to Dakota Kobler for creating the map of Naivasha, to Lorri Hagman and the editorial staff at the University of Washington Press for all you did to improve my manuscript, and to Bonita Hurd for her expert copyediting. I am also grateful to the anonymous reviewers who provided me with invaluable comments and suggestions on the developing manuscript.

My research was made possible by generous financial support from the Wenner-Gren Foundation, the US Department of Education Foreign Language Areas Studies (FLAS) Program, the University of Washington Chester A. Fritz Fellowship, the University of Washington Pembroke College Fellowship (for study at Cambridge University), and a Competitive Scholarly Research Grant from the University of Illinois Springfield.

My many wonderful friends and family members provided humor, companionship, and frequent karaoke breaks throughout the long writing and research process. Thank you to the members of my Seattle family, especially Mel, Laura, Emily, and Kristin, and my friends in Cambridge, especially Bex, Suz, Miriam, and Liz. Thank you to Mom, Dad, and my brother Todd—and all the members of my extended family—for always loving, encouraging, and inspiring me. Adena, thank you for being my heart and my home in the world.

ABBREVIATIONS

CDC	Commonwealth Development Corporation, United Kingdom
CSR	corporate social responsibility
DCK	Dansk Chrysanthemum Kultur (Danish Chrysanthemum Cultivators)
EU	European Union (including the United Kingdom)
KENGEN	Kenya Electricity Generating Company
KFC	Kenya Flower Council
LANAWRUA	Lake Naivasha Water Resource Users Association
LNGG	Lake Naivasha Growers Group
LNR[O]A	Lake Naivasha Riparian (Owners) Association (*Owners* removed in 1995)
NAWACOMP	Naivasha Watershed Conservation and Management Project
NEMA	National Environmental Management Authority
NGO	nongovernmental organization
SACCO	Savings and Credit Cooperative Organization
WRMA	Water Resources Management Authority
WRUA	Water Resource Users Association

ROSES FROM KENYA

Introduction

Place, Power, and Possibility in a Kenyan Nerve Center

THE street corner near the *matatu* (minibus) depot in Naivasha Town is bustling on a hot, dusty day in 2007 as patrons rush in and out of the Naivasha Supermarket, one of two large stores in town that sell processed and packaged foods, housewares, and clothing. Small shops in a row peddle mobile phones, televisions, radios, and other electronic devices. A pharmacy displays an impressive array of human and veterinary medicines, and a photo shop advertises a reduced price for developing color prints. Hawkers on the street press their wares against the windows of stopped vehicles—packets of peanuts, mentholated pain balm, sweets in cellophane wrappers, fresh sausages. Much of this social and economic activity is fed by the local cut-flower industry. When I board a *matatu* on my way to meet with a flower farm manager at a restaurant near the lakeshore, the rear of the vehicle is crowded with bags of clothing and foodstuffs, which traders hope to sell to flower farm workers.

The conductor comes to collect our fares, issuing us stamp-sized receipts printed on soft yellow paper, and we depart, slowing as we cross over the railroad tracks that stretch to Nairobi in one direction and Nakuru in the other. A ready supply of freshwater from nearby Lake Naivasha, suitable growing conditions, and a relatively short drive to the Nairobi airport make this area one of Kenya's premier flower-producing regions. Each day, workers in Naivasha's greenhouses cut and pack millions of roses and other flower varieties bound for supermarkets and florists overseas. Kenya supplies more than 35 percent of the flowers sold in the European Union, and more than 50 percent of those fresh blooms are grown here on the shores of Lake Naivasha (map I.1). Fresh horticultural products (including vegetables and flowers) are one of Kenya's top earners of foreign exchange, and the industry is

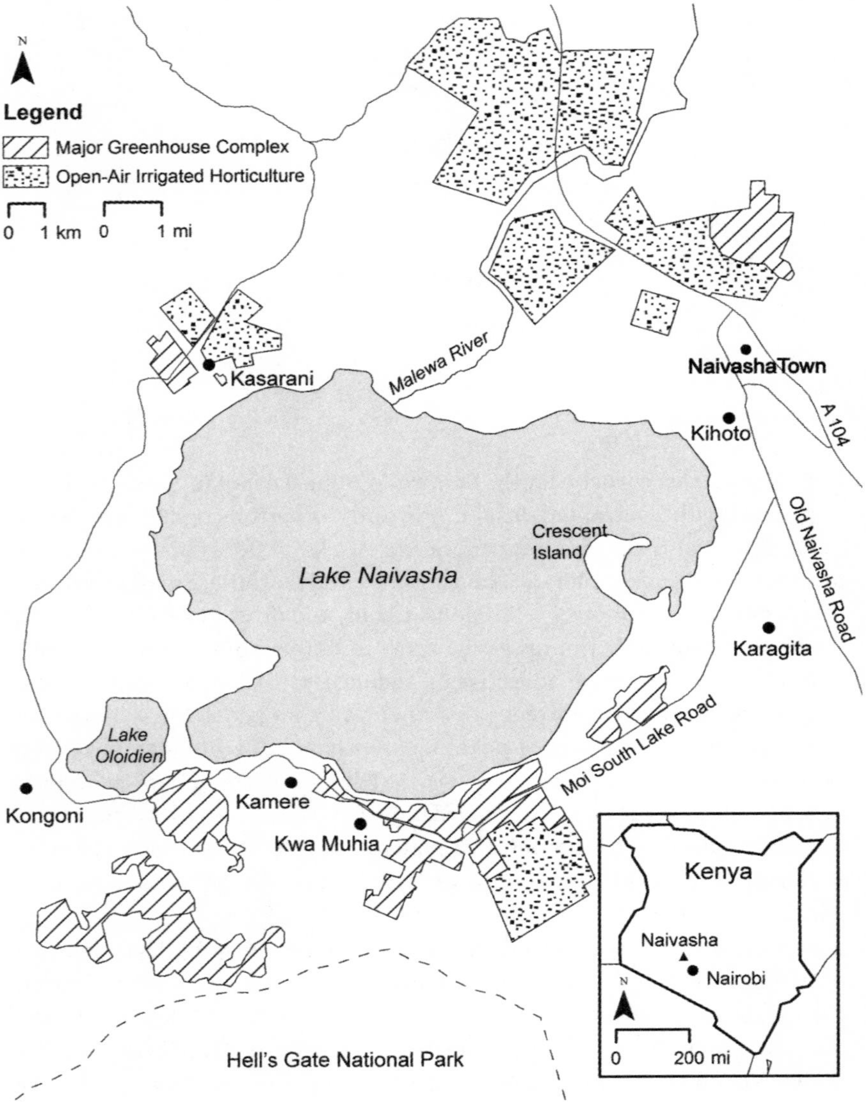

MAP I.1 Lake Naivasha, Kenya. Floriculture has transformed Naivasha ecologically, socially, and politically.

regarded as a cornerstone of the nation's export agricultural sector. At least ninety thousand people are directly employed in floriculture, and an estimated 65 to 70 percent of these workers are women. Despite these economic successes, however, Kenyan floriculture is also controversial.

As the vehicle turns onto the road that follows the south edge of Lake Naivasha, I am reminded of why floriculture generates controversy as well as profit. Through the dust-coated windows, I can see that we are passing one of the six lakeside shantytowns (locally called "villages") where the bulk of Naivasha's residents live. The steep streets are muddy after a recent rain. Since the cut flower industry became successful here in the 1990s, Naivasha's population has ballooned from around thirty thousand to more than three hundred thousand, spurring rapid, unplanned development. Living conditions vary widely depending on how much residents can afford to pay in rent; some houses are made of stone, others wood, and others sheet metal over wooden frames. Most live without access to electricity, running water, or formal waste disposal services. Critics allege that the majority of flower farm employees are underpaid and work in poor conditions. Many flower farm workers find only temporary employment in the industry and never qualify for the benefits that farms provide full-time workers.

A small boy tugs on my sleeve and forms the shape of a camera with his hands. "You're here to take pictures of the animals?" he asks in Swahili. The other passengers laugh. "Not today," I answer. In Naivasha, floriculture sits in awkward juxtaposition with another successful Kenyan industry—tourism. The lakeshore is lined with luxury resorts, budget hotels, and campgrounds that host domestic and foreign visitors. Several of these are explicitly marketed as eco-lodges. Lake Naivasha is designated under UNESCO's Ramsar Convention as a wetland of international importance, and it is one of only two freshwater lakes in Kenya's Rift Valley; the others are soda (saline) lakes. The lake provides seasonal respite to many migratory birds and is a contested space that many human communities lay claim to for subsistence and commercial purposes. The environmental sensitivity of this particular landscape makes floriculture in this area ethically and ecologically challenging. Heavy abstraction of lake water for irrigation, the clearing of vegetation along the lake edge, and pollution from multiple sources arising from rapid, unplanned development threaten water quality and the integrity of the lake's ecosystem.

At last, we reach one of the largest of Naivasha's nearly sixty flower farms, a long stretch of greenhouses made of plastic stretched over rounded metal frames. I alight and present myself to the security guard. Access to these farms is strictly controlled; appointments are made in advance, and taking photographs is rarely allowed. Between 1998 and 2002, the Kenyan flower industry was subject to a wave of intervention and political activism by nongovernmental organizations (NGOs) designed to improve labor conditions and ecological practices in the industry. Kenyan and international activists organized boycotts of Kenyan flowers, lobbied supermarkets to impose regulations on suppliers, and worked with the press to publicize poor living and working conditions of flower farm workers. As a result of this activism, the flower industry is currently regulated using retailer-defined codes of practice. To access a particular market (e.g., to sell to a specific supermarket chain in the United Kingdom or to sell via the Dutch auction system), flower producers must agree to specific labor practices and environmental standards. Farms are often signatories to several codes, and they are audited multiple times a year to ensure compliance. Despite marked improvements in working conditions and environmental practices over the last two decades, the industry remains a target of continued pressure for reform. Farm owners and managers remain wary of journalists and activists posing as researchers.

I am given a visitors badge, and I walk to the farm restaurant where I've arranged to meet my contact for an interview. Dennis laughs and shakes my hand as I enter, "So you have some questions for me about floriculture." He removes his hat and lays it down on the table, ordering a warm soda and a plate of chips. He smiles. "Even I have some questions about these flowers!" Dennis works as a production manager for a Naivasha flower farm, and he has recently returned from an international floricultural trade fair in the Netherlands, his first trip to Europe. While attending the event, he stayed for several days in the home of a Dutch colleague. "You know, I had some idea that flowers are used for beautification and for gifts. But, imagine, I did not know how the Dutch love these flowers until I saw it with my very own eyes." He laughs again, shaking a copious amount of salt onto his chips. "Imagine, that house was covered with flowers. Completely. Even there were flowers in the bathroom. Pictures of flowers in frames. Flowers on the duvet. Flowers on the curtains." He sweeps his hands in front of him. "I think maybe when a Dutchman lays his head on the pillow at night, he is only dreaming of flowers." His comments invite laughs from some of the other café patrons, encouraging him to continue. "Even the Dutchman's dog. When he closes his eyes, he is also just dreaming of flowers."

Dennis has an advanced degree in horticulture and has worked for a Dutch-owned Naivasha flower farm for five years. In recent months, he has traveled to the Dutch trade show and to a sister farm in Uganda, where he met with his counterpart to discuss ways of improving production volumes. In his midforties, Dennis supports a wife and two children, the eldest of whom is attending secondary school. We spend the next hour discussing his aspirations in floriculture. He speaks in excited tones of some of the technologies that he saw at the Dutch expo and the differences between the Kenyan and Ugandan farms. He describes his plot in western Kenya, purchased using a loan against his salary, and his plans to build a house there. He looks out at Lake Naivasha, visible in the distance through a line of acacia trees. "Floriculture has really brought me some success," he says. "And now that I've seen the scale of this thing, maybe I am also going to start dreaming of flowers." He shakes his head and laughs at the idea.

My conversation with Dennis was a watershed moment in my research. Until then, I had focused mainly on the problems and conflicts associated with this form of industrial export agriculture; but in all of my interviews, there was also an aspirational undercurrent, a sense that this place was also a locus of *possibility*. To borrow Dennis's phrasing, I began to more seriously investigate both what it means for different actors living and working in Naivasha to "dream of flowers" and the strategies that they use to achieve these goals. For most of the people with whom I spoke, flowers are a strategic means to many alternative ends. Working in this industry involves much more than growing roses: these actors are also cultivating an interlinking set of aspirations for national development, environmental and social control, and socioeconomic security and prosperity. These aspirations are rooted in their perceptions of floriculture, and they are also intertwined with their perceptions of Naivasha more generally.

Unlike Darjeeling tea or Kona coffee, Kenyan flowers are not marketed with a geographical indicator. European consumers may discern from the packaging that a bouquet of roses was grown in Kenya, but the specific place of production is generally erased in the journey from farm to market. Naivasha does, however, appear regularly in popular and academic articles focused on the impacts of Kenyan floriculture. Both journalists and academics tend to describe Naivasha as emblematic of the paradoxes produced by the expansion of global capitalism and neoliberalism. *New York Times* columnist Alan Cowell (2003) describes Naivasha as an "awkward point of collision between rich and poor, north and south[, that] offers a gritty counterpoint to all the optimistic talk of a globalized economy that will magically raise the destitute and spread prosperity." Anthropologist Catherine Dolan writes of Naivasha, "The cut flower industry is considered a testament of neoliberalism, a panacea for Kenya's privations. . . . [Y]et accompanying the fresh tracks of global capital on Kenya's flower farms is the familiar paradox of the neoliberal model—booming economic growth side by side with human immiseration"

(2007, 240). These descriptions are accurate but incomplete. My interlocutors recognized these contradictions, but they also described Naivasha as a complex, transnational space where they could work collaboratively to generate desirable forms of change. No one I interviewed expected floriculture to be a panacea for anything, but they did see this industry as a useful tool for advancing their complex (and sometimes conflicting) agendas for personal and national development.

I struggled to find a way to accurately describe what I saw happening here until August 2012, when I read an article published in the *East African Standard*, one of Kenya's two major newspapers. In a piece titled "Naivasha's Changing Fortunes," journalist Peter Muiruri wrote, "Naivasha has had its fair share of bad history. But now it appears to have everything in its favour. The highway, lake, land and geothermal exploits make it a potential nerve centre for the entire county come the devolved governance." In a single sentence, Muiruri captured the complex essence of this complex, contradictory, and transnational place. Naivasha has become a "nerve center" in a triple sense. First, this is a politicized place that touches nerves, sparking moral concern on the part of Kenyan and international actors alike. Second, it is also a hub for Kenyan development, a place of global connection and social, political, and economic possibility. And third, in the context of the ongoing neoliberal reorganization of Kenyan regulatory processes and structures, Naivasha is a place where new or alternative forms of governance—including industrial self-regulation and devolved governance, the delegation of powers and responsibilities formerly associated with a central government to regional or local levels—are developed, tested, and potentially expanded to other regions and other economic sectors. Floriculture in Naivasha both aggravates (by touching nerves) and *innervates*, in the sense that it stimulates and energizes Kenyan aspirations for global connection, prosperity, and control over the direction and character of national development.

Many actors living and working in Naivasha—including those whose ambitions have been partially realized through their labor in this industry—remain aggravated by what they describe as the "slippery" nature of floriculture, the ever-present risk of loss or failure. In other words, they recognize what scholars call the "precarity" (cf. Kasmir 2018) that accompanies neoliberal capitalism, the vulnerabilities associated with unstable work, the erosion of class-based identities, and the mobility of global industries. Rather than seeing this as a development mirage, however, they work diligently to glean all they can from floriculture—knowledge, connections, regulatory reform, money, power, and influence—and redirect these gains toward other projects and goals. Some of these goals are personal, but many are also attached to postcolonial ambitions for self-governance and a desire for Kenya to escape what anthropologist James Ferguson (2006) calls the "global shadows," discourses of failure and corruption that relegate Africa and Africans to a permanently marginalized role in a global system. Naivasha is indeed a synergistic nerve center where many actors seek the opportunity, the power, and the right to participate productively in the creative and collaborative construction of Kenya's future. They do so using the global flows of people, information, and money generated by floriculture, but roses are not the endgame. They are a complex means to many other ends.

This book tells the story of Kenyan floriculture from the point of view of people living and working in Naivasha, providing an ethnographic portrait of how this industry shapes Kenyan livelihoods, landscapes, and politics. It also situates floriculture within the deeper social and environmental history of the Lake Naivasha region. How has cut flower production transformed this place socially and ecologically? What has been done to resolve conflicts and concerns about the unintended and problematic consequences of floriculture? Many actors influence the production and regulation of cut flowers in Naivasha. Low-wage laborers form the bulk of the floricultural workforce, but the industry also depends heavily on the labor and expertise of middle-class black Kenyan professionals like Dennis, white Kenyan and expatriate farm managers and owners, elected and appointed Kenyan officials, and human rights and environmental activists who lead the struggle to reform and regulate floriculture. These actors seek different things from floriculture, and they experience the industry's effects, positive and negative, in disparate ways. Cut flowers connect Kenya to the world, and these actors perceive different possibilities in these connections. Their lived experiences and perspectives represent the complex and contradictory ways in which flower farming shapes livelihoods and environments in contemporary Kenya.

Previous research on Kenyan floriculture has focused on "humanizing" (Hale and Opondo 2005) the global trade in cut flowers by improving working and living conditions for low-wage laborers. A rich body of research explores how and why these workers are vulnerable to exploitation and offers concrete recommendations for improving retailer-defined codes of ethics so that they better meet the lived realities and concerns of these workers. Workers' perspectives are especially important, given the geographic, economic, and political distance between producers and consumers in global networks of exchange. European consumers and retailers define the parameters of ethical practice in ways that fit their own "moral affectations" (Dolan 2005b) and concepts of justice (Besky 2014), but these definitions are often at odds with the actual needs and desires of the people who produce commodities like coffee, tea, and flowers.

The Kenyan flower industry can be humanized through investigation of the perspectives of low-wage workers and the enduring forms of exploitation rife within this industry. However, the experiences and perspectives of the more powerful actors who populate this particular commodity chain—including the expatriate farm owners and managers who are often villainized in popular depictions of the industry's effects on Kenyan communities and environments—are also worthy of ethnographic consideration. Despite persistent calls for anthropologists to research the actors who form the middle portions of global commodity networks (e.g., West 2012), ethnographers still tend to focus on the perspectives of subaltern actors, those with less power and the least access to political representation. As a result, some actors emerge as richly complex, while others (especially the most powerful) remain shadowy figures whose principle motivations and aspirations are often depicted as relatively mysterious, static, and/or monolithic.

By analyzing the aspirations of different actors in relation to one another, and by allowing members of each group to speak for themselves, this book reveals the many, messy ways that actors working in floriculture try to repair the aspects of floriculture that they (nearly universally) recognize as problematic, and the ways that even the most powerful wrestle with the nerves exposed by this industry. "Humanizing" a global commodity chain is not just a matter of making it less exploitative: it means exploring the many, conflicting emotions and aspirations that different actors bring to their work in commodity production, exchange, and regulation. Many people living and working in Naivasha, especially educated middle-class actors, see their work as involving much more than growing flowers. They see themselves as harnessing the possibilities in floriculture as part of an ongoing process of statemaking and nation building. This book explores the many forms of agency and power at work in floriculture at local and national levels.

NERVE CENTERS: AGGRAVATION AND INNERVATION IN THE NEOLIBERAL ERA

The concept of a nerve center is useful for thinking about industries other than floriculture and places other than Naivasha. Since Sidney Mintz's (1985) groundbreaking research on sugar, anthropologists have traced the circulation of agricultural commodities to understand how globalization shapes human lives. We are especially fond of researching agricultural commodities like tea, coffee, and chocolate produced in the global South for primary markets in the global North.[1] In the journey from farm to market, these commodities crosscut multiple categories of human difference, revealing the intimate but often hidden connections between people living in geographically distant locales. Ethnographers investigate the values that people assign to these things and the relationships, moral and material, established between actors in these networks of exchange.

We also expose the profound inequalities, injustices, and contradictions created by the expansion of global capitalism and the advent of neoliberalism, the dominant political ideology of our times. In the words of one set of researchers, "a commodity focus offers a window on large-scale processes that are profoundly transforming our era" (Stone, Haugerud, and Little 2000, 1). Since the 1970s, neoliberal policies have focused on deregulating markets, privatizing state-run services (e.g., education and health care), and creating what proponents view as ideal conditions for economic growth. Supporters see neoliberal policies as creating the best possible conditions for development and enhancing global prosperity and security. Critics allege that neoliberalism allows the few to accumulate wealth at the expense of the many, exacerbating global inequality, endangering democracy, and eroding the vitality of earth's ecological systems.

Anthropologists tend to be scathingly critical of neoliberalism, and the literature on African horticultural commodities reflects this oppositional stance. Roses are part of a suite of nontraditional agricultural commodities, mainly fresh vegetables and fruits, promoted by development agencies as a means of helping rural farmers in Africa and Latin America connect to global markets. However, decades of research suggests that structurally embedded limitations make it difficult for low-wage workers or smallholder farmers to benefit in profound or long-lasting ways from their involvement in horticulture. Market-based attempts to improve working conditions and environmental practices on these farms have also met with limited success. Commodity chains linking Africa and the European Union are regarded as buyer-driven (Gereffi 1994), with retailers and consumers playing a dominant role in determining the agenda behind the regulation of horticultural production (Dolan 2004; Dolan and Humphrey 2001; Hughes 2004). Since European consumer politics often draw on problematic, colonial discourses (Freidberg 2003, 2004) or patronizing notions of a moral obligation toward African farmers (Dolan 2005a, 2005b), regulatory codes designed to meet retailer specifications and consumer desires rarely meet the actual needs of laborers, especially women, working in these horticultural industries (Barrientos, Dolan, and Tallontire 2003; Dolan, Opondo, and Smith 2002; Hale and Opondo 2005). Code-based systems of regulating floriculture can ameliorate, but never eliminate, structural inequalities in the global economy (Blowfield and Dolan 2008, 2014).

Although commodity research in anthropology has grown more nuanced over time, most ethnographers still tend to focus on the ways that local processes and lifeways are disrupted, reorganized, or eroded as a result of these connections to global flows. We also primarily research *international* strategies for regulating commodity production (e.g., fair trade and code-based regulations designed and enforced by retailers). This focus on top-down strategies may overaccentuate the role of retailers and consumers, obscuring the efforts of people living and working at sites of production to reform working and environmental conditions (Barrientos, Dolan, and Tallontire 2003). People living and working in Naivasha strategize to reform the "bad" and redirect the "good" that comes from this industry. Rather than portraying neoliberal policies and governance strategies as structures imposed on these actors from above, this book explores the ways that people living and working in Naivasha attempt to use neoliberal concepts and technologies of governance to bring about long-desired forms of socioeconomic and political change.

Many of the dreams of such actors are unique neither to floriculture nor to Naivasha. Anthropologist Paige West writes that, "for rural villagers [in Papua New Guinea], coffee allows access to the riches of globalization and lets them seek relationships with others (what they want and need to make self) . . . [; and] for urban dwellers coffee materializes the nation in important ways" (2012, 31–32). Having documented in detail the forms of marginalization and misery that accompany global commodity production, anthropologists need to pay closer attention to what local actors do with the riches of globalization (real or perceived), the relationships, and the tools of governance (however neoliberal) that they encounter while working in these industries.

Thinking of Naivasha as a nerve center helps us see this place (and others like it) in a different light. Instead of focusing mainly on the human and environmental misery that results from uneven or predatory capital development, it reminds us that commodity production can also energize and innervate complex political, economic, and ecological ambitions new and old. By conducting research in places like Naivasha—locations that are less isolated and less dependent on a single form of commodity production than the rural areas we tend to work in—we can also avoid automatically dismissing "dreams of flowers" (or other commodities) as false expectations. Actors in peri-urban places like Naivasha are better positioned to make industries like floriculture work in their favor. Some of their hopes will almost certainly remain hollow, but their aspirations are also powerful visions of alternative futures that anthropologists should take more seriously. By thinking of the places we work as potential nerve centers, anthropologists can better understand how our interlocutors envision the future and attempt to work with neoliberal tools as they seek to generate structural change.

For actors living and working in Naivasha, the regulatory institutions that accompany floriculture are a potential means of "materializing" the nation in much more literal ways than the consumption of a locally grown product. Peter Little and Catherine Dolan (2000) write that, in the 1990s, horticulture in the Gambia provided a window on "what it means to be restructured" in the wake of development policies and programs that dismantled the state and encouraged farmers to grow nontraditional commodities for export. In the contemporary moment, floriculture in Naivasha provides insight into what it means to be structurally (re)constructed in the midst of changing geopolitical power relationships (e.g., Kenya's deepening relationship to China), a global economy faltering the wake of the 2008 financial crisis, and rising concerns about the availability and quality of the natural resources on which floriculture depends. Naivasha has become a crucible for what geographers Jamie Peck and Adam Tickell call the "creative," or "roll-out," phase of neoliberalism in which "the agenda has shifted from active *destruction and discretization* of Keynesian-welfarist and social-collectivist institutions (broadly defined) to one focused on the purposeful *construction and consolidation* of neoliberalized state forms, modes of governance, and regulatory relations" (2002, 384, emphasis in original).

Code-based reforms have greatly improved labor and environmental conditions, but they have also made flower growers resentful of the expense involved in caring for their labor force. Growers are also hypercognizant of the shortcomings of a Kenyan state that is ill equipped, in the aftermath of structural adjustment, to provide social services and has no authority to track or limit resource use. In this context, they have taken an active role in devising new policies and initiatives that (re)construct a more prominent role for the state in controlling resources and providing services to workers. Naivasha helps us understand what the rollout phase of neoliberalism looks like in practice, but most importantly it also reveals *who* plays a key role in this process and how they understand and shape the process of structural reconstruction. Actors living and working in Naivasha participate in forms of cooperative environmental governance designed to harmonize the conflicting interests and perspectives of people with different attachments to this particular place. While these strategies conform to neoliberal policy prescriptions, the design and implementation of these initiatives reflect complex forms of local agency and a desire on the part of many Kenyans to decolonize this space and reconstruct a more prominent role for the state in regulating the human and environmental resources on which floriculture depends.

People living and working in Naivasha are always of two minds when it comes to floriculture: they recognize and describe in great detail the inequities and despair rife in Naivasha's shantytowns, but they also describe their work as meaningful and necessary, a sacrifice made in the present to bring about a better future. Thinking of Naivasha as a nerve center helps bridge the distance between these two Naivashas and allows us see "dreams of flowers" in a less patronizing and dismissive light. These aspirations provide a window on the Kenyan political imagination, illuminating the ways that even exploitative industries like floriculture create connections and possibilities that intersect with postcolonial desires for development, self-governance, and political and economic power. The futures that people living and working in Naivasha imagine are not postcapitalist (Gibson-Graham 2006), but they are fundamentally postcolonial. They envision a global economy that has shifted on its axis, with African nations no longer dependent on Euro-American aid and investment. To see Naivasha as a nerve center is to see its future *beyond* flowers, to see Kenya as a catalyst for innovation and economic development (rather than a recipient of aid), to see Africa as a place of possibility and increasing institutional security (rather than a loose cluster of states whose methods of governing have failed to meet Western definitions of what constitutes good governance).

CULTIVATING PLACE: ENVIRONMENTAL IMAGINARIES IN HISTORICAL CONTEXT

Thinking about Naivasha as a nerve center requires an engagement with both "rosy aspirations" for the future and the ways that people living and working here understand the *past*. Naivasha is a contested place, with a complex social and environmental history that remains relevant in the contemporary moment. Actors living and working here conceptualize the nature and significance of the changes induced by floriculture in light of their understanding of the history of this place and the value of this landscape. Rosy aspirations and dreams of flowers are not the only agrarian ambitions that animate sociopolitical life in this locale. The identity of Naivasha, like that of all places, is always in flux, always in the making.

In precolonial times, Maasai pastoralists utilized the lake area as seasonal pasture; their descendants still lay claim to the area as ancestral territory today. During the colonial era, white Kenyan settlers established mixed farms and tourism ventures in the area, imagining it as a peaceful rural, residential retreat. Floriculture dominates the local economy today, but the Kenyan government has also invested heavily in geothermal energy production, imagining Naivasha as a future hub for both agricultural and industrial development. Actors living and working in Naivasha disagree about the value of this place, the "proper" ways to manage it, and who has the right to do so.

Floriculture has created new forms of connection to global flows and processes, and it has catalyzed transformations in local social and ecological relations. However, floriculture also remains deeply embedded in Kenyan social and political practices, and conflicts over the effects of floriculture reflect local desires to maintain the possibility for alternative development trajectories in this place. Conflicts surrounding this industry involve much more than disagreements over working conditions and the control of effluents: floriculture both aggravates and innervates debates about the most "appropriate" ways to develop Naivasha's potential without undermining its future. In the words of the feminist economic geographers J. K. Gibson-Graham, "Places always fail to be fully capitalist, and herein lie their potential to become something other" (2006, 33). Attempts to better regulate floriculture are often struggles to maintain the possibility that this place can "become something other"—a rural residential retreat, a sanctuary for wild Kenyan nature, or an emergent industrial center supplying energy to all of East Africa. The politics of place at work in Naivasha have shaped floriculture as profoundly as floriculture has shaped this place.

A rich body of research examining the ways that people form a sense of place is relevant to thinking about Naivasha's environmental and social history.[2] People develop deep attachments to the spaces they inhabit, giving names to physical features on the landscape, deriving sustenance from locally available resources, and forming relationships with other people (and other species) with whom they share these locales. Place is also part of the way that people create a sense of self: living in a particular way in a particular place often forms the basis of shared cultural identity. In the words of the cultural historian Monica Perales, "People make places, but places also 'make' people" (2010, 13). Anthropologists use the term *place-making* to describe the complex processes by which people form deep attachments to particular spaces, infusing them with meaning, forging senses of self and community within them, and developing a sense of moral and ethical responsibility toward them. People often justify their right to occupy, use, or control access to places by *caring* for them in particular ways, and they may censure others (or themselves) for failing to care for these places in the way they conceptualize as proper.

Places are also territories, spaces to which multiple individuals, groups, and institutions may lay formal claim. Territoriality intersects with placemaking but refers more specifically to the ways that people justify their right to occupy, use, or control access to a space using social and legal practices that vary cross-culturally and evolve over time. Geographer David Delaney writes that "territories reflect and incorporate features of the social order that creates them" (2005, 10). When communities clash over who should control places, they may become "violent environments" (Peluso and Watts 2001), contested territories where disagreements over land and resources cause complex, intractable conflicts characterized by enduring forms of physical and structural violence. In order to understand the ways that people cultivate place and the reasons why they "suffer for territory" (Moore 2005), we must examine the historical memories, moral legacies, and contested terrains of power at work within these landscapes (Osterhoudt 2017).

Each chapter of this book explores how a different category of actors understands the history of Naivasha, the attachments that they do (or do not) form to this place, and how they participate in the creation and circulation of "environmental imaginaries" (Peet and Watts 1996)—strategic depictions of the effects of floriculture designed to advance specific political and moral economic agendas. Each set of actors frames the effects of floriculture on Kenyan communities and environments (especially Lake Naivasha) in a different way, and each set offers a different explanation of its own role in regulating floriculture and caring for local communities and the landscape. However, historical memories, moral legacies, and contested terrains of power in Naivasha extend beyond this temporal moment and beyond floriculture. When Kenyan actors celebrate or decry the effects of floriculture in Naivasha or explain what they have done to harness global flows in the service of national development or environmental conservation, the imaginaries that they invoke are not just dreams of flowers. They are also powerful arguments about how they belong in Kenya and in this place, what they see as problematic about the past and the present, and who has the power to direct the future.

Social theorists use the term *moral economy* to think about the ways that concepts of ethics, fairness, and justice complicate economic behavior in capitalist systems (cf. Scott 1976). Because employers and employees, for instance, are relationally dependent on one another, there are mutually agreed upon "moral" limits to the ways that one can exploit the other, regardless of the financial incentives for exploitation. The same is true for relationships with nature and place, especially in agrarian settings; powerful actors are expected to demonstrate moral and ethical behavior in relation to the environment, to care for both their workers and the landscape on which their riches depend. Sarah Besky writes that, in the case of Darjeeling tea in India, "for workers, justice is rooted in ideas of reciprocity between management, labor, and the agro-environment in which they all reside" (2014, 32). The idea of a "tripartite moral economy" helps her explore the "meaningful relationships" that develop between human and nonhuman nature in the plantation system and the ways that the tea plantation worker is "a participant in both a global market and a vestigial legacy of colonial feudalism" (33).

This concept of a "tripartite moral economy" is useful for investigating the relationships that develop between workers, employers, and the agri-environment in an industrialized agricultural industry shaped by different colonial and postcolonial legacies. Floriculture arose in Kenya more than a decade after the nation gained independence from Britain in 1963; and in this sense, these are fundamentally postcolonial ventures. Workers migrate from elsewhere in rural Kenya to fill jobs in this industry, and unlike in the case of Darjeeling tea plantations, they are not given access to land for subsistence production. Some live in on-farm housing, but most live in villages along South Lake Road, where they rent houses from landlords, with whom they may or may not share a kinship or ethnic affiliation. The majority of workers do not view Naivasha as home, and their "dreams of flowers" involve using their wages to invest in places elsewhere. They are not peasants in the sense that anthropologists generally use this word; they are (at least initially) low-paid, landless wage laborers who work in greenhouse settings, where the act of cultivation more closely resembles factory production than colonial feudalism.

In this setting, farmworkers rely heavily on middle-class intermediary actors (e.g., low- and midlevel Kenyan farm managers, NGO workers, journalists, and researchers) to help them challenge aspects of their working and living conditions that they find intolerable. These middle-class actors view moral economic mediation as a critical component of their own work in floriculture. Although these farm managers are more powerful than low-wage laborers, they rely heavily on their own relationships with farm owners and members of Kenya's elite political class to achieve their own aspirations in floriculture. Moral economic relationships in Kenyan floriculture are embedded in complex forms of relational dependency that extend beyond this industry, this place, and this temporal moment.

Anthropologists working in Africa argue that, while participants in industrialized capitalist economies tend to view their wealth in terms of the things that they accumulate, Africans focus on cultivating their "wealth in people" (Guyer 1995), the relationships and interconnections that help them sustain their livelihoods and actualize collective and individual aspirations for the future. Workers, managers, and farm owners are hierarchically connected through their participation in floriculture, but they are also connected hierarchically and laterally to one another and to other Kenyan actors through extensive, off-farm patron-client networks. In a patron-client system, wealthier, more influential actors (patrons) provide material support to less powerful actors (clients); relationships between patrons and clients are hierarchical but also mutualistic, in that patrons also depend on clients for the forms of political and social support that help them gain privileged access to the wealth they then redistribute through their networks.

In the case of floriculture, farmworkers remit their wages (meager though they may be) to family members in their home regions, supporting networks of clients in rural Kenya. Farm managers build alliances with elected officials, promising them political support from farmworkers in exchange for increased pressure on farms to improve working conditions. Elected officials rely on flower farm owners to help them negotiate better trade deals with the European Union and promote the nation as a profitable and safe place to invest. Farm owners in turn rely on workers, managers, and elected officials to ensure that roses are harvested, packed, inspected, and shipped overseas day in and day out. Each of these forms of mutual entanglement involves political, economic, and *moral* expectations. Floriculture also expands these interconnections and patron-client networks transnationally, complicating and multiplying the moral economies at work in Naivasha. People living and working in Naivasha express a profound sense of moral economic obligation to one another and to the local environment. However, they also view the morals that shape local political and economic relationships as existing in a permanent and problematic state of flux.

Code-based regulations prescribe one set of ethical practices. However, the regulatory authority of these codes ends at the farm gate, leaving most of Naivasha's social and ecological landscape subject to other moral and ethical imaginaries. When farms change hands, new owners introduce different management regimes. When these owners are expatriates from geographic contexts that farmworkers and managers view as foreign and unfamiliar (e.g., not from Britain), moral economic expectations are renegotiated. Local actors also point out that moral expectations differ in each of Naivasha's economic sectors. Employees working for the Kenya Electricity Generating Company, a parastatal organization that operates geothermal power facilities in the Naivasha area, live in relative luxury compared to flower farm laborers, and tourists seem to care more about wildlife than they do Naivasha's human communities. In this Kenyan nerve center, moral economic relationships are multiple, contradictory, and evolving. Some see this shifting moral terrain as a way to restructure power relationships and renegotiate relationships of dependency and obligation; others view this as threatening. Many actors seek to (re)direct, formalize, and institutionalize the moral economic relationships they see as most appropriate or advantageous through their work in floriculture. As they work to regulate and reform this industry, they draw on sometimes intersecting, sometimes conflicting, commitments to this place and the many communities that inhabit it.

DEVELOPMENT AS PERFORMANCE: POSTCOLONIAL SUBJECTIVITIES IN A NERVE CENTER

As a nerve center where both neoliberal aggravations and innervations are on display, Naivasha attracts a great deal of international attention. I rarely went more than a few days without encountering another international researcher, volunteer, auditor, journalist, or NGO worker. We would meet at public meetings or in a local café and compare notes on our respective research or development projects. In a sense, Naivasha is under many forms of global surveillance, a fact that is not lost on anyone living and working here. Kenya is often used as "a point of reference against which [Western] scholars assess the successes and failures of other African states" (Haugerud 1993, 6). As they go about their everyday activities, people living and working in Naivasha are acutely aware that they are being watched by members of an international audience interested in assessing Kenya's development progress. These actors go about their work in floriculture with a self-conscious sense that they are performing under the gaze of others—farm managers, investors, Kenya's political elite, on-the-ground international actors in Naivasha, and international actors in faraway places. Different categories of actors conceptualize in distinct ways the benefits and burdens associated with the visibility, or exposure, that comes with living and working in a nerve center.

Literature on postcolonial subjectivities, especially recent research focused on Africa's growing middle class, is useful for thinking about the ways these actors perform their duties in Naivasha. Anthropologists use the terms *identity* and *subjectivity* to think about how people form a sense of self, a sense of who they are and why their lives and actions are meaningful. Identity is something that a person is conscious of and has some agency over, a deliberately constructed and evolving sense of who one is in relation to others. However, the sense of self is also shaped by the forces one is subject to—power relations, historical processes, and discourses over which individuals have limited control. As a system of externalized and *internalized* domination, colonialism involves the seizure of territory and resources, but it also involves the "colonization of the mind" (wa Thiong'o 1986) and of the self. Anticolonial theorist Franz Fanon writes, "Because it is a systemic negation of the other person and a furious determination to deny the other person all attributes of humanity, colonialism forces the people it dominates to ask the question constantly: 'In reality, who am I?'" (1968, 250).

Postcolonial African subjects still confront ongoing processes of systemic negation. In global discourse, Africa is often represented as a foil for the West, as a place that is foreign and inscrutable, a continent full of failed experiments in economic development and democracy where so-called "anarchy" (cf. Kaplan 1994) thrives, presenting a strategic danger to the world. Cameroonian political theorist Achille Mbembe writes that "the African experience constantly appears in the discourse of our times as an experience that can only be understood through a *negative interpretation*. . . . [Africa represents] all that is incomplete, mutilated, and unfinished" (2001, 1, emphasis in original). Kenya's international reputation as an exceptional "point of reference" heightens the sense among Kenyans that, when they interact with transnational actors, what they do, say, and think is being used as evidence of the presence or absence of something that the world perceives as lacking elsewhere in Africa. When I asked people living and working in Naivasha why they came to this place, their answers involved descriptions of who they understand themselves to be, who they would like to become, how others see them, and the complex connections between these different senses of self. Their narratives nearly always referenced the perception that Kenya is "less" than other nations—less developed, less well-governed, less educated, less powerful. However, many also see themselves as instrumental in making Kenya "more." Middle-class professionals in particular saw themselves as responsible for spurring the nation's development progress.

Development aid and donor funds in Africa are often tied to a nation's ability to demonstrate good governance, defined narrowly as policies and practices that promote democratization, administrative efficiency, and accountability. In her cogent analysis of the development, circulation, and impact of "good governance discourse," political scientist Rita Abrahamsen argues that this new development focus emerged in the 1990s as a way to explain the failure of structural adjustment policies to produce predicted forms of economic growth. The problem was not the flawed logic of the policies themselves but rather African governance. This discourse assumes economic liberalization will stimulate the development of an African middle class separate from the state that will "act as the democratisers of their societies" (2000, 63). These assumptions come from a selective reading of European history and are rooted in the belief that democracy and economic liberalization "are historically linked and constitute the two sides of the same coin" (64). Abrahamsen questions whether these members of an emergent African middle class will act in the service of Western concepts of democracy and whether they will agree with the neoliberal consensus that the state is an obstacle to economic growth.

In the decades since good governance discourses became pervasive, economic growth in sub-Saharan Africa has led some nations to the brink of middle-income status, according to the measures developed by the World Bank (Green 2014, 2015). While rural populations in many of these nations remain impoverished, the number of urban, educated, middle-class elites has expanded. In her ethnographic analysis of the cultural logics, everyday practices, and desires that motivate Tanzanian aspirations for "middle-classness," Maia Green argues that, in this temporal moment, "aspiring to be middle class is no longer restricted to the realm of the imagination" (2015, 158). Shifts in the global economic order, including Chinese investment, economic growth, and global demand for natural resources (especially minerals) have repositioned sub-Saharan Africa (in the eyes of international and local actors) as an attractive zone of economic opportunity. Green writes that, in Tanzania, members of the emergent middle class are motivated by desires to reposition the nation in the international economic order. However, they do so in ways that depart from "cookbook" recipes for market reform prescribed by donors and development agencies, incorporating elements of socialist public-sector policies.

Middle-class Kenyans living and working in Naivasha also negotiate contemporary development discourses and express excitement about the opportunities created by an emergent, global "economic reordering" as they build their senses of self and engage in practices of statemaking and nation building through their work in floriculture. In many ways, these actors have embraced the idea that they are responsible as an educated, professional class (and as a generation) for embodying the principles of good governance. They are conscious of the international gaze and attempt to model, through their work in floriculture, a Kenyan capacity for self-governance and accountability. However, they are also very aware of the ways that development discourses subjugate, stereotype, and *constrain* the Kenyan political and economic imagination. Although they are hyperaware of the need to perform to international standards and protect the image of the nation, they view this moment in Kenya's (and their own personal) development trajectory as temporary and strategic. Living and working in a nerve center affords them access not only to floriculture but also to *alternative* political and economic opportunities (e.g., geothermal power generation, the NGO sector, civil service, and elected office), and they remain willing and ready at all times to redirect their labor to processes that can fulfill their aspirations to move Kenya out of the global political and economic margins.

Their approach to actualizing their aspirations, like that of Tanzanian actors, is not like following a cookbook; nor are their aspirations monolithic. Rather than viewing the state as an impediment to economic growth, many hope to (re)center the state as a locus of development, but they disagree about what the state should look like and who should control or direct it. Despite the enthusiasm and sense of possibility that accompanies their work in floriculture (and in Naivasha), they still share a sense that, although being middle class has moved beyond the realm of imagination, it is still not quite real, stable, or permanent. Like low-wage laborers, they described development in Naivasha as "slippery." Although Kenya might gain additional prominence in a global reordering, it is unclear *who* will benefit from this increased power and influence. As they perform their duties, they remain conscious of who is watching and the many ways that their capacity as individuals (and as a professional class) is measured by members of an international audience, Kenya's political elite, and Kenyans who do not have the same access to the resources and opportunities flowing through this nerve center. They must still constantly ask, "In reality, who am I?" Naivasha's status as a nerve center makes them more visible to others, complicating their notions of self; for many, life in Naivasha is a strategic performance.

Members of Kenya's black professional middle class are not the only actors in Naivasha who grapple with questions of their worth, belonging, and positionality in postcolonial Africa. White actors—descendants of colonial settlers, expatriates, and short-term visitors involved in research and development work—also confront issues of postcolonial identity and subjectivity in Naivasha. These white actors must also negotiate circulating discourses about African development, colonialism, and privilege. White Kenyan and European expatriate actors in Naivasha often react defensively to discourses framing them as the faces of enduring (or new) forms of economic colonialism. As David Hughes (2010) has shown for Zimbabwe, environmental politics in Naivasha are central to the way that white Kenyan and expatriate actors, in particular, negotiate the "problem of belonging" in postcolonial Africa. A deep engagement in matters of conservation has helped them establish "a credible sense of entitlement" (2010, 1) to land, resources, and power in this Kenyan locale. Although the question of belonging was particularly acute for white Kenyans and expatriates living and working in Naivasha, black Kenyan professionals who came here from elsewhere also perceived their participation in conservation and community development efforts as a way of legitimizing their right to live and work in this place. Similarly, Naivasha flower farms strategically "green" their operations in order to legitimize their existence in a space that "belongs" to them by deed but not necessarily by public consent. *Environmental,* as well as social, projects have become important spaces where people living and working in Naivasha debate what it means to be *Kenyan* in a moment when local, national, and international power relations seem to be shifting.

Naivasha is a place where the politically ambitious can build a following by working as union organizers or human resource managers. A place where educated middle-class Kenyans can find work as farm managers or representatives of the international NGOs involved in efforts to reform floriculture. A place where entrepreneurs can start successful subsidiary businesses that recycle farm plastics, install irrigation equipment, or market food products to a growing community of farmworkers. And, to some extent, a place where low-level farmworkers can earn the capital to invest in land and businesses in other parts of Kenya—provided they do not get caught in cycles of debt, lose their jobs, or encounter myriad other circumstances that might derail these aspirations. Naivasha is a space of tremendous anxiety, but it is also a space of possibility, a locus of rosy aspirations for personal, regional, and national development.

In this nerve center, dreams of flowers are rarely about flowers at all: they are a window on the Kenyan political and economic imagination. Actors living and working in this postcolonial context are working with the (undoubtedly neoliberal) tools and connections provided by floriculture to (re)make the Kenyan state and reposition the nation in a shifting global political economic order. Their aspirations are myriad, the morals that guide them contradictory, and the immediate future precarious; however, these dreams matter, whether or not they are actualized. Seeing Naivasha (and places like it) as a nerve center reminds us that people act in the ethnographic present in light of their understandings of the past and their hopes for the future. Kenyan floriculture provides insights into both the aggravations and the innervations generated by neoliberalism, and the ways that postcolonial actors attempt to utilize these forms of connection and reinvention to bring about long-desired forms of change.

CHAPTER ONE

Situating Naivasha

A Complex and Contested Place

IN October 2007, Andrew Cole, the long-standing chairman of the Lake Naivasha Riparian Association (LNRA), a prominent local environmental group, announced at the organization's annual general meeting his decision to step down.[1] With his voice occasionally cracking, he urged the gathered crowd to "wake up" and learn to work together as a "community" in order to "discard any elitist image we may have." He warned, "If you want to go on as we are, you might see the death of this organization and the death of the lake." He urged the association's incoming chairman, a prominent local business owner and the organization's first black Kenyan executive officer, to strengthen the relationship between the LNRA and the flower industry, to create the opportunity for "a combination of responsible business and sustainable use of natural resources." He worried aloud that he had wasted the last twenty years of his life. "This is the end of an era as far as I'm concerned," he concluded. "We achieved a great deal, but I believe we could have achieved much more if we had been visionary in our thinking and put aside self-interest." He then took his seat as the honorable secretary turned to the next agenda item.

In many ways, Cole's resignation did signal the end of an era in terms of eco-politics in Naivasha, the center of Kenya's lucrative cut flower industry. After ten years in the making, the chairman's brainchild, the Lake Naivasha Management Plan, a multistakeholder initiative for community-based management of the lake and its catchment basin, had seemingly failed. A lawsuit filed by several local interest groups had blocked the plan's implementation. Attempts to advance the court case by lobbying government had yielded warnings that LNRA officers would be considered in contempt of court for seeking to influence the outcome of an ongoing case. Citing these and other frustrations, the chairman stepped aside to make way for new leadership and what he referred to as a "business-driven" approach that he hoped would encourage flower farm owners and managers to recognize the LNRA-led process as the most legitimate among several ongoing attempts to create a management plan for the lake and its environs. For Cole, the success of this organization was paramount. He believed strongly that Naivasha was at a crossroads, that without regulatory intervention the lake would quite literally die. Perhaps the most remarkable thing about this speech is that Cole's concerns were not new. Since the 1920s, elite actors concerned about various forms of development in the Naivasha area have made dire predictions about the death or serious decline of the lake. Had they succeeded in restricting particular forms of development, floriculture might never have become a dominant local land use.

Although floriculture has solidified Naivasha's reputation as a transnational nerve center, this place has aggravated moral sensibilities and innervated experiments in social and environmental governance in *many* historical moments. Elite actors have attempted on multiple occasions to organize multistakeholder, cooperative initiatives to manage Lake Naivasha and control matters of local development. While none of these has been fully successful in the ways that local actors initially intended, each attempt provides insight into the ways that people living here have conceptualized Naivasha's importance (personally, nationally, and internationally) and forged complex senses of place and belonging in this Kenyan nerve center. Social and environmental politics in Naivasha in several eras are of central concern here—the precolonial period, when Naivasha was recognized as a common property regime under the control of Maasai pastoralists; the British colonial era, when Naivasha became a designated site for permanent white settlement; the immediate postcolonial moment, when Naivasha was especially popular with local and international tourists; and the contemporary moment, when floriculture dominates the local landscape. This is a "moment" in the sense that this place will continue to change. No state is permanent, and the past remains relevant, alive, and contested in every version of the present.

The Lake Naivasha Riparian (Owners) Association (LNR[O]A) has played an important role in local politics from its origins in the late 1920s to the present.[2] While other environmental initiatives and community-based groups have come and gone, the LNRA has remained an important institution that has been reinvented several times in response to emerging environmental and social concerns. The demise of the LNRA's management plan process provides a window on the ways that floriculture has transformed power relations, political possibilities, and moral economic (and ecological) sensibilities in this place. Cole's concerns about the future of the lake were not new, but his resignation hints at the profound ways that floriculture has changed social and political relations in Naivasha, disempowering some and (at least superficially) empowering others.

In 1904, the British colonial government relocated Maasai pastoralists living in Kenya's fertile highlands to make room for white settlement. What had been a common property regime became an area of mixed farms and residential estates privately owned by white settlers, most of whom intended to live in Kenya permanently. These settlers had little trust in the colonial administration, and they used every avenue possible to give themselves greater authority over this space. Citing British law, they successfully lobbied the colonial government to sign a riparian agreement that gave lakeside landowners de facto control over the riparian areas adjacent to their properties. After Kenya gained independence in 1963, the (formal and informal) legal agreements and institutions that white settlers established during the colonial era proved useful as local actors responded to new threats, especially the growth of the tourism industry in the lake area and the specter of land-grabbing by what they perceived as a corrupt postcolonial Kenyan political class. In the era of floriculture, these institutions and agreements were reinvented again, but as the LNRA chairman's comments suggest, flower farming changed the composition of the community, introduced new (neoliberal) logics of governance, and shifted power relationships. Some local actors viewed these changes as alarming and potentially tragic; others celebrated these shifts, viewing floriculture as an opportunity to "decolonize" this space.

In Naivasha, contemporary neoliberal approaches to addressing the environmental and social problems posed by floriculture are intertwined with older or alternative governance strategies that emerged in response to perceived threats that predate (and often coexist with) floriculture. Contemporary actors frequently reference these events in Naivasha's social and environmental history as they explain their perspectives, justify their decisions, and describe their sense(s) of place and belonging. Combined, these fractured narratives help us think about how Naivasha became a Kenyan nerve center, how floriculture has transformed local (and national) social and environmental relations, and why and how these changes matter.[3]

THE VIEW FROM THE DUMP

Some of the best views of Lake Naivasha can be seen from the Naivasha Municipal Dump, an open-air facility not far from Naivasha Town where public and private waste haulers pile trash in mounds. I watch from the passenger window of the Naivasha municipal dump truck as pickers descend eagerly on the pile that we have just discarded. They quickly sort through the material, hoping to earn "small money" by salvaging and reselling items like plastic buckets and bottles. I am struck by the visual contrast between the heaps of garbage in the foreground and the panoramic view of the entire lake in the background. The dump truck driver laughs, saying, "Yes, it's very beautiful from here, except for the smell."

I get out of the truck to snap a few photographs. From this vantage, the environmental stakes involved in floriculture become clearer, not just because I am surrounded by mounds of trash. Lake Naivasha is small and shallow; its surface area fluctuates between 100 and 150 square kilometers during dry and wet cycles, and the average depth is only six meters (Lake Naivasha Riparian Association 2008). Lake Naivasha is a rare freshwater body in Kenya's Rift Valley. Nearby Lakes Nakuru and Elementeita are saline. The lake looks comparatively lush and green in contrast with the dryer surrounding areas, where farmers depend on rainwater or groundwater for domestic and agricultural needs. The Malewa River accounts for 90 percent of the freshwater that flows into Lake Naivasha; the remainder comes from ephemeral streams, groundwater seepage, and rainfall (Kamau et al. 2008, 146).

The water in this lake is a precious resource, and cut flowers are an especially thirsty crop. A single rose requires seven to ten liters of water, and hydrologists estimate that between 1995 and 2005, sixteen million cubic meters of water were "virtually exported" from the Lake Naivasha Basin through the trade in cut flowers (Mekonnen, Hoekstra, and Becht 2012, 3725). Rapid urban and agricultural development in the lake area have contributed to declining water levels (Becht and Harper 2002; Tarafdar and Harper 2008). From the dump, I can see that Crescent Island, so named because it was once a true island surrounded on all sides by water, is now a peninsula.

Water quality in the lake area has also declined precipitously since the rapid expansion of floriculture, mainly owing to nonpoint-source nutrient and sediment pollution associated with commercial agriculture and urban development in the lake's catchment basin (Hubble and Harper 2001). The lake is surrounded by a wide riparian zone dominated by papyrus. The papyrus swamp at the mouth of the Malewa River plays a critical role in protecting the ecological integrity of the lake (Boar and Harper 2002; Hubble and Harper 2001; Morrison and Harper 2009). As more lakeside vegetation is cleared for development, pollutants like sediment, raw sewage, and fertilizers from small-scale farming in the upper catchment basin flow directly into the lake, negatively affecting fish and wildlife (Kitaka, Harper, and Mavuti 2002). Records suggest that Lake Naivasha was once fairly clear, but

FIGURE 1.1 Naivasha greenhouse complex. The plastic accentuates the heat provided by the equatorial Kenyan sun, creating ideal growing conditions for many flower varieties. Some local greenhouses are simple structures, but they can also be advanced, with fan systems to help with ventilation and automated fertilization and irrigation systems.

the water today is murky and dark. Visibility rarely extends beyond an inch beneath the surface.

The north side of the lake, visible in the distance, is less developed, providing a window on what the entire lake area might have looked like forty years ago. Wide swaths of intact papyrus line the shore, serving as a natural layer of protection by soaking up toxins and filtering out sediment. However, the southern edge of the lake is comparatively crowded with greenhouse complexes (figure 1.1) and human settlements. In this particular moment, the area is home to fifty-seven flower farms, with two new ventures under construction. Most of these farms are between fifteen and twenty hectares, but the three most prominent local farms are much larger. Oserian, Naivasha's largest flower farm, produces roses and other blooms on a remarkable 225 hectares, an area equivalent in size to 468 American football fields.

Karagita, Naivasha's largest shantytown village, is also visible from here. Between the tight rows of houses, the streets and footpaths consist of bare, compacted soil. During rain events, these often become deep gullies, sweeping trash, sewage, and sediment toward the lake. More than three hundred thousand people live in Naivasha Town and the six lakeside villages—Kihoto, Karagita, Kwa Muhia, Kamere, Kongoni, and Kasarani. Most area residents live without access to formal waste disposal services, and there are no local sewage treatment facilities. In between greenhouse complexes, comparatively undeveloped stretches mark the locations of Naivasha's many hotels, lakeside residences, and farms where landowners have left trees and wider swaths of papyrus intact.

Many dimensions of Naivasha's beauty and complexity are visible from here—signs of the region's commercial success and evidence of the lake's ecological significance and its decline. However, as I snap a few photographs, I think about how much remains *invisible* in this view of Naivasha from above. Although floriculture certainly dominates this landscape in the contemporary moment, this industry is fairly new. Flowers have been grown in the Naivasha area only since the 1970s. When I spoke with local actors about the social and environmental effects of floriculture in the present, many spoke at length about what Naivasha was (or was not) in the past. Although news articles on the effects of floriculture tend to focus on declining water quality and biodiversity, people living and working here focus on issues of access, ownership, control, and security (personal and national). Floriculture has profoundly influenced power relationships and access to land and resources in this place, creating conflicts over who belongs here and who has a right to govern this space. Historical tensions and conflicts ripple beneath the surface in contemporary conflicts over floriculture, and narratives about the success of floriculture are often set against vivid social and environmental imaginaries of what has been lost or sacrificed to bring about this form of development.

NAIVASHA AS MAASAI TERRITORY

Place-names are often the best markers of who once inhabited a specific locale and the significance that it held for them. Maasai place-names abound in Naivasha. The name *Naivasha* itself is derived from a Maasai term, *enaiposha*, meaning "rustling waters." Oserian, Naivasha's largest flower farm, borrows its name from the Maasai name for this locale, *Ol Oserian* (place of peace; Hayes 1997). One of the earliest written descriptions of Lake Naivasha appears in the journal of Joseph Thomson, a Scottish-born explorer who passed through the Naivasha area in 1883 and 1884. Shortly after reaching the lake, Thomson writes, his party was delayed for five days while Maasai came from near and far to meet them and demand trade goods. Thomson observes, "We made great friends with some of the elders, who delighted to sit and talk with us, showing a frankness and an absence of suspicion such as I have never seen elsewhere among Africans" (1887, 337). He describes these elders as possessing "an admirable knowledge of the geography of an enormous area[, which] they had acquired by their continuous war raids and their nomadic habits." Thomson was surprised that "they imparted their information without reserve," and he developed a respect, albeit a patronizing one, for their knowledge and authority.

Before the early 1900s, the British colonial government considered encouraging Indian settlement or the development of an African peasant economy in what would become Kenya (Sorrenson 1968, 5). However, they eventually determined that white settlement would contribute to the development of a stronger economy and help make the recently completed Mombasa-Kisumu railroad profitable (Winter-Nelson 1995). Officials debated whether to move Maasai residents to native reserves or to encourage peaceful coresidence with a white settler population in the Kenyan Highlands. Colonial correspondence from this time highlights the importance of the Naivasha area to Maasai subsistence strategies. In a letter dated February 22, 1904, Frederick Jackson (deputy to Charles Eliot, commissioner of the British East African Protectorate) wrote to Secretary of State Lansdowne, "The Masai will never give us serious trouble so long as we treat them fairly and do not deprive them of their best and favorite grazing grounds, i.e., those in the vicinity of Lake Naivasha" (quoted in Hughes 2006, 28). In deference to the importance of these grazing lands, Jackson advocated a moratorium on settler land grants between Naivasha and Nakuru. Eliot's successor, Charles Hobley, also favored restricting white settlement in this region, noting that Maasai occupation "had over time greatly improved the grazing and made it sweet" (29). Soon after assuming leadership, however, Hobley reversed his position, concluding that Maasai "arrogance" and settler "belligerence" would inevitably cause conflict. A rinderpest outbreak south of Naivasha in March 1904 also sparked concern that Maasai cattle would spread disease to white-owned livestock.

In August 1904, Maasai *laibons* (traditional political leaders) signed a controversial treaty known as the Maasai Agreement, which surrendered control of grazing grounds in the Central Rift Valley between Naivasha and Nakuru to the colonial government. Between February and June 1905, colonial officials relocated Maasai inhabiting this region to two newly designated reserves. Although officials did not keep systematic records of Maasai resistance to removal, colonial correspondence suggests that they were reticent to vacate the "prized grazing grounds" near Naivasha. Members of both of the dominant Maasai subgroups in the immediate Naivasha area, the Purko and the Keekonyokie, "lodged objections" to removal (Hughes 2006, 35). Some actually stayed in the Naivasha area until they were forcibly moved in 1910. The British colonial government's decision to remove the Maasai from the Kenyan Highlands to make way for white settlement helped transform Naivasha from a space of local significance into a transnational nerve center, challenging moral standards and introducing experimental forms of social and environmental governance.

Physical removal did not sever Maasai attachments to this place, nor did it stop them from using these seasonal grazing grounds. Maasai living in contemporary Naivasha engage in a diverse set of economic activities. Many raise smaller livestock (e.g., sheep and goats) locally and sell these animals to local butcheries. Some also sell handicrafts or work as security guards, and a small number of Maasai work as wage laborers in the flower industry. These commercial activities allow them to support their families in Naivasha and invest in small businesses, livestock, and land in areas they view as home (e.g., the Narok District). Maasai living and working in contemporary Naivasha view their ancestral rights to this space as critical, but they are pragmatic about when they choose to assert these claims. Like other stakeholders in Naivasha, members of the Maasai community view floriculture as potentially positive. However, they vehemently resist the wholesale enclosure of Naivasha's resources for floriculture alone. They make strategic use of their indigenous identity to build partnerships with nonprofit organizations, researchers, and journalists to advocate for their rights to access land and resources in Naivasha, and they lobby farm managers to fund corporate social responsibility projects that will benefit Maasai communities.

As prime grazing land for cattle, sheep, and goats has been enclosed behind flower-farm gates, ancestral Maasai claims to this territory have become increasingly politicized and contested. Many local landowners view Maasai claims to this place as both illegitimate and threatening. While they recognize that Maasai used this space, they refute the notion that they owned it. It is common for landowners, especially white Kenyans and European expatriates, to describe precolonial Naivasha as a no-man's-land. In the words of one small flower farm owner: "It's bullshit that this was Maasai land. . . . [T]hey were never here permanently. I mean, they're nomadic. They never owned it. It was never their land. It was no-man's-land." Lakeside landowners also argue that pastoral lifestyles are environmentally destructive or insist that contemporary Maasai in Naivasha no longer have traditional claims to grazing land because they are no longer living traditional lifestyles.

One local landowner explained, "I have no problem with them grazing their cattle here [on my property], but they're also harvesting trees for charcoal, poaching fish and game, stealing equipment, and setting up *dukas* [small shops]. None of these things are traditional." Other landowners insisted that most of the Maasai families living in Naivasha today are not direct descendants of those who used the area in precolonial times.

The notion that floriculture continues to displace Maasai pastoralists from Naivasha figures centrally in debates about impacts of this industry. The issue of Maasai representation has also been used to legally block and/or delegitimize multistakeholder regulatory initiatives (e.g., the LNRA-led management plan process). Two things are apparent in this regard: (1) nearly everyone working in Naivasha floriculture views Maasai claims to this space as powerful (even when they view them as illegitimate), as these claims hold great rhetorical and political potency; and (2) far from being at permanent odds with Maasai economic strategies, floriculture figures centrally in the political and economic aspirations of actors within the Maasai community. Debate surrounding Maasai claims to this space can be used to spark moral outrage and to innervate (or strategically *dis*connect and derail) particular regulatory strategies in Naivasha. Maasai actors play important roles in determining who controls access to wealth, resources, and power in Naivasha.

NAIVASHA AS THE "WHITE HIGHLANDS" (1904–1963)

White settlers brought new forms of interconnection and new moral economic sensibilities to this Kenyan nerve center. They experimented with commercial agriculture and established new forms of cooperative environmental and social governance in response to what they viewed at the time as threats to their land rights, autonomy, and livelihoods. Colonial policies designed to help settlers recruit farm laborers also profoundly shaped the ethnic makeup of Naivasha's population. The power relationships, governance strategies, and sense of place that white actors (and those who came to work on their farms) established in Naivasha during the colonial era remain salient today. As the floriculture industry has matured and Naivasha has become increasingly transnational, these moral economic and environmental relationships have been challenged and strained, causing many white Kenyan actors to view Naivasha's past with nostalgia and the future with trepidation.

White settlers in Kenya were land rich but labor poor. Crown land ordinances enacted in 1902 and 1915 reserved more than seven million acres, roughly 20 percent of Kenya's total arable land area, exclusively for white settlement (Winter-Nelson 1995, 31).[4] In order to draw African farmers away from subsistence production and create the wage labor force needed to fuel commercial agriculture in the White Highlands, the colonial administration introduced a series of hut and poll taxes, with payment in cash required of all men. They also outlawed the African production of cash crops in the areas bordering the White Highlands. Historian Tabitha Kanogo writes, "Most of the settlers themselves were rather poor and could only afford to hire labor if it was cheap and could be paid for mainly in kind, in the form of land for cultivation and grazing" (1987, 2). White settlers recruited Kikuyu agriculturalists from central Kenya by promising them land for grazing livestock and planting small gardens.[5] The terms of their employment contracts allowed Kikuyu farmworkers to engage in independent agricultural production and herding as squatters on land owned by settlers. Allowing Kikuyu farmers to grow their own produce saved white settlers the expense of providing farm laborers with full board, and it made employees more inclined to stay.

In the immediate vicinity of Lake Naivasha, white settlers engaged in cattle and dairy production and raised fodder crops, mainly lucerne (alfalfa), near the lakeshore. Some also experimented with vegetable crops meant for export and/or regional markets. For instance, the McCrae brothers established an eleven-thousand-acre sisal operation in the lake area in the early 1920s (Hemsing 1992, 29). According to my interviews with longtime area farmers, these experiments in export vegetable production repeatedly failed, owing to inappropriate climatic conditions (in the case of sisal), unpredictable rainfall and fluctuating lake levels, and a general lack of market access. Occasional outbreaks of livestock disease also posed a persistent problem.

Three large-scale estates were recognized locally (Carnelley 1976) as the most productive of the settler farms bordering the lake before World War II: Lord Delamere's Manera Estate, Sir John Ramsden's Marula Estate, and Gilbert Colville's Ndabibi Estate. These farms produced fodder crops and raised cattle for milk and slaughter. In 1927, Lord Delamere provided financing for the Kenya Cooperative Creameries at Naivasha, which solidified the area's reputation as a cattle and dairying center. Nearby Nakuru, which was closer to Delamere's intensive sheep-farming operations at Soysambu and Njoro, became a more important farming center (Hemsing 1992, 31).

While these larger estates met with some commercial success, Naivasha settlers depended heavily on vegetable produce grown by Kikuyu farmers. In an unpublished memoir, one white settler living in the Naivasha area recalled that "large safaris of Kikuyu used to bring head loads of maize, bananas, flour, and beans over the Aberdares to sell, this being the most useful way of feeding the labourers" (Hewett and Denwett, quoted in Carnelley 1976, 22). White landowners also allowed Kikuyu laborers to grow vegetables, such as cabbage and potatoes, on small plots near the lakeshore. The Naivasha District report for 1916–17 indicates that, at the time, there were an estimated thirty-three hundred Kikuyu living in the district. During this period, these "natives" sold 200 tons of potatoes, 180 tons of maize, and 40 tons of beans at markets where transactions were tracked by colonial officials. Europeans initially intended to hire Kikuyu agriculturalists on short-term contracts as a migrant labor force, but many developed long-term connections to their places of employment "evolv[ing] a viable socioeconomic system within the White Highlands" (Kanogo 1987, 3). As Naivasha was becoming a white space, it was also becoming a Kikuyu one.

In the 1920s, Naivasha's white settlers did not trust the colonial government. Like settlers elsewhere, they preferred to remain "administratively autonomous from central state control" (Gordon 1986, 159). In 1928, a drastic drop in the lake's water level exposed large tracts of the foreshore. A handful of anxious lakeside landowners wrote to the colonial government to ask whether their property boundaries extended to the newly receded lake edge.[6] Fearing that the government would survey and subdivide the exposed foreshore, cutting off their lakefront access, these landowners demanded a formal explanation of how to interpret their property boundaries with respect to the lake edge. They hoped for a speedy resolution that would ensure their exclusive rights to any land exposed by future lake-level recession.

At the time, lakeside landowners were also under pressure from colonial officials to allow public access to the lake. As early as 1925, colonial officials noted that newly subdivided lots bordering Lake Naivasha had titles that did not include a riparian reserve, a designated stretch of land surrounding any water body retained as property of the Crown. Captain Archie Ritchie, the newly appointed head of the game department, was especially upset by these developments, which hindered his ability to patrol the lake by boat. Writing to the land department in March 1927, he noted that there were only four passable outspans where the lakeshore could be conveniently reached. Predicting that Naivasha might become an important location for sporting in the colony, he argued, "I am certain that it is in the communal interest for Government to retain as many points as possible on the lake shore for public use, provided that such points have access to the lake itself and not to an impassable swamp."[7]

The Naivasha District Committee balked at this suggestion. J. D. Hopcraft, one of Naivasha's prominent early settlers, replied angrily, "I need hardly to add that if the Government is able at any time to take choice plots of land of this size from settlers in this country, especially in the face of local opinion, no farms will be safe." Another settler worried that public access points would be used by "Asiatic and other members of the community, and that their presence on this farm would be a nuisance in many ways."

Following a period of discussion and debate, colonial officials agreed on a compromise solution. In 1929, white lakeside landowners formed the Lake Naivasha Riparian Owner's Association (LNROA), and in December 1931 they signed a formal agreement, which became fully legal upon the colonial governor's signature in March 1932. This agreement pledged that lakeside property boundaries would be extended to the lake level. The lake's riparian zone would remain the property of the Crown, following British law, but the owners of adjoining property would be the designated caretakers of the riparian areas abutting their land. LNROA members agreed that landowners could cultivate in the riparian area but would refrain from building permanent structures other than pump houses. The riparian line was set using the lake level marked in a 1906 survey, and the signatory parties pledged that the agreement would be binding for their descendants and all future property owners. The Riparian Agreement addressed concerns about property boundaries, but it did not settle the debate about public access to the lake.

This Riparian Agreement is still honored by the contemporary Kenyan state. Formal legal recognition as the rightful stewards of Lake Naivasha has become central to how white Kenyan settlers and their descendants articulate their commitment to this place and justify their entitlement to land and resources in Naivasha. In 2007 and 2008, the LNROA (now the LNRA) remained a significant political and social force in the lake area.

For several decades after the drafting of the Riparian Agreement, the LNROA served mainly as a third-party arbitration organization. Members who wished to dispute their property boundaries could arrange for arbitration through the LNROA. Landowners disputed their shared boundaries, especially during dry years, and argued about the activities of one another's squatters. Letters from members to the organization's secretary suggest that many of these conflicts arose because so much of the land around the lake was in absentee ownership. Squatters gradually expanded their agricultural activities in the riparian zone, infringing on other settlers' property lines, and settlers themselves sometimes overstepped their legal boundaries, which became difficult to discern when the water level rose and fell.

Although members were concerned about their neighbors' activities and frequently sent letters of complaint to the LNROA leadership, they resisted any formal regulations that would limit their ability to develop their land as they wished. They preferred to use peer pressure, through the LNROA and the Naivasha Farmer's Association, to put a halt to activities they deemed troublesome. Two circumstances in particular caused a furor among LNROA members and tested the limits of self-regulation in Naivasha: (1) a proposed large-scale engineering project that would divert water from the lake's feeder rivers, and (2) frequent accusations that the managers of Sir John Ramsden's Marula Estate were drawing borehole water far beyond the permitted levels. Despite these internal disagreements, LNROA members remained committed to informal self-regulation. They vehemently rejected suggestions from colonial officials that they draft formal rules outlining the types of productive activities allowed near the lakeshore.[8]

As lakeside owners negotiated their foreshore rights with the colonial administration, they also lobbied the game department to introduce a species of sport fish to Lake Naivasha. R. E. Dent, the fish warden of Kenya, conducted an initial survey in 1926 and found that the lake was home to only one variety of fish, *Haplochilus antinorii* (reclassified as *Aplocheilichthys antinorii*), the black lampeye.[9] In 1926, *Tilapia nigra*, a species native to Kenya's Athi River, was introduced to establish a food supply for a future sport fish. With the tilapia population firmly established by 1928, Dent introduced fifty-six American black (largemouth) bass in February 1929.

The trustees of the British Museum strongly objected to the introduction of an alien North American species to a Kenyan lake. The trustees argued that P. M. Jenkins, a "lady zoologist," had just been dispatched to survey Lake Naivasha's fauna, and that no alien species should be introduced until native fauna had been fully catalogued and "adequate safeguards" put in place.[10] The colonial government stood by Dent's decision on the grounds that the establishment of a sport fishery in Lake Naivasha would yield significant economic benefits to the colony. In the words of a contributor to a discussion of the matter held by the Linnaean Society of London in November 1929, "Some introductions are necessary if the white races are to occupy the empty spaces of the world."

In 1932, Captain Ritchie began writing letters to the colonial secretary, expressing his concerns about rapid, uncontrolled development in Naivasha following the introduction of tilapia and bass.[11] He warned the secretary that "Lake Naivasha must inevitably become, in ever increasing degree, one of the chief playgrounds of Nairobi; even of the whole colony." He expressed serious concerns about rapid development along the lakeshore. "Land has been cut up into small plots[,] and bungalows, mushroom like, spring up in a night. There are at least 4 hotels at the Lake edge. . . . Enough has been said to make it clear that Naivasha has already developed very rapidly; and it has yet barely started!" Ritchie urged the colonial secretary to act immediately to exert some control over development, arguing that he desperately needed additional personnel and resources. "It is, I think, beyond dispute that there should be some central direction of all development. . . . I feel strongly that Lake Naivasha should be placed under firm control; and that, with the least possible delay. Damp clay can be moulded; but dried, it can only be chipped."

On February 2, 1933, Ritchie wrote to the colonial secretary again, suggesting that a central board of control be established for the management of Lake Naivasha. LNROA members staunchly disapproved of this proposal, arguing that they should not have to share control over the lake with outside stakeholders, especially anglers from Nairobi and the county council. No board of control was established. Instead, LNROA members served as deputized game wardens, and the overextended fisheries and game departments sent copies of proposed rule and policy changes to LNROA leadership for comment. Officials often made extensive changes or abandoned initiatives entirely based on the association's suggestions.

The LNROA became less active during and immediately after World War II. Naivasha District records indicate that absentee land ownership was a problem in the lake area, especially after some settlers left for military service. In 1947, a report issued by district officials indicated that, while the Naivasha area provided good trade opportunities for Kikuyu squatters, unoccupied farms near the lake had become potential "locations for criminals."[12] Although the report does not detail what these "criminals" might have done to disturb the peace, this was a time of escalating tensions over land issues.

As white settler agriculture became more commercially viable during and after World War II, settlers lobbied the colonial government to place new restrictions on the squatter system. The 1937 Resident Native Laborers Ordinance drastically reduced the acreage available for squatter agriculture and placed restrictions on the number of cattle that could be owned by squatters. In the Kikuyu labor reserves, new economic opportunities generated by colonialism had also spurred increased demand for secure land rights. Colonial land laws favored wealthy, male heads of household, helping concentrate land ownership in the hands of only a few elite Kikuyu men (Bates 1989). The consolidation of land titles and power in the hands of these elites made it difficult for Kikuyu laborers returning from the White Highlands to be reabsorbed into these communities. Simmering conflicts over squatter rights and access to land became a driving force behind the Mau Mau Uprising (also known as the Mau Mau Revolt or Rebellion) between 1952 and 1960 (Kanogo 1987). Fighters participating in this loosely organized rebellion used guerilla tactics to resist British colonial control in Kenya, destroying property and engaging in direct confrontation with colonial officials and white settlers.

Colonial officials referred to this period as the "Kenya Emergency," denying that this was in fact a politically legitimate form of resistance. This semantic position also helped waylay fears that the uprising was centrally organized. Historian David Anderson argues that during the worst of the fighting, between 1952 and 1956, Kikuyu districts in Kenya became a "police state" (2005, 5). The Mau Mau Uprising was crushed at great expense by the colonial government and the British Army, which imprisoned a large portion of the Kikuyu population and hanged scores of accused dissidents (Elkins 2005; Anderson 2005). Although colonial officials managed to regain some measure of political control, the uprising helped bring about the end of colonial rule in Kenya as British authorities began to seriously question the economic and political feasibility of maintaining the colony. LNROA records and district-level reports provide a window on how settlers living in Naivasha understood (and contributed to) escalating tensions.

In a series of letters beginning in 1951, Lord Delamere beseeched the LNROA president, Wilfred Hopcraft, to resurrect the "largely moribund" association in response to growing concerns about illegal squatter activity in the riparian area.[13] The letters suggest that, during the war, squatter cultivation had been encouraged by the district commissioner, but that it had "now grown to such proportion that it must be cleaned up." Delamere reported that he had heard from Mr. Wilson, senior labor officer for the Rift Valley Province, that "hundreds of acres" of riparian land were currently under illegal cultivation by squatters. Mr. Wilson, Delamere argued, "was determined to stop what was a serious racket and a menace to the White Highlands and a stronghold of the Mau Mau." The LNROA leadership discussed how to destroy these *shambas* (small farms), a task that they deemed difficult and bound to induce violence. In the end, they passed a resolution holding riparian landholders responsible for illegal cultivation adjacent to their property and encouraged them to address the problem.

Naivasha District Annual Reports from 1953 to 1958 contain frequent references to Mau Mau activity in the lake area.[14] On March 27, 1953, a gang attacked the Naivasha Police Station, killing two constables and stealing "a great deal of arms and ammunition." Farmers in the district were called to active duty, and the report recommended the expulsion of Kikuyu from certain areas. In 1956, Naivasha and Gilgil were both said to be home to "an efficient wing of the Mau Mau organization." Papyrus around the lake edge was cleared to help reduce cover for these "terrorists," many of whom had fled the Central Province looking for sanctuary in the Naivasha District. Settlers erected towers along the southern lakeshore; these were staffed by "farm guards," who ensured that Mau Mau fighters did not steal food crops in the riparian areas. References to Mau Mau activities disappear from these annual reports starting in 1958.

In 1961, J. B. Carson attached a cover letter to the *Naivasha District Annual Report* describing the reaction of district settlers to the 1960 Lancaster House Conference, where British and colonial officials began to negotiate the parameters for Kenyan self-rule. He wrote, "Uncertainty, anxiety, and a large degree of despondency have characterized the European farming community since the fateful Lancaster Conference. On [*sic*] that community, however, there have been no signs of panic and very few departures. In general, the older farmers without children, or with grown-up children, are anxious to stay. Among younger farmers with young families the . . . feeling [is] that it is not too late to start elsewhere and . . . there is no future for their children in this country." He also argued, "Among Africans, the position is in reverse. The older ones express anxiety and fears regarding intimidation and likely reprisals on Government Servants, ex-police, and Kikuyu loyalists. . . . As in Britain about 400 AD, many indigenous inhabitants are not anxious for the legions to depart." His summary of the reactions of younger Kenyans reveals his disdain for their emergent sense of nationalism. "Among the younger element, however, the future is rosy, albeit lazy. An immense surge of self-confidence and African nationalism has percolated the younger set. This might more impolitely, but truthfully, be described as immature political thinking and rank tribalism!"

In a letter dated March 16, 1961, C. T. Todd, a lakeside landowner, wrote to the LNROA chairman, suggesting that, because of the Riparian Agreement, their titles were "irrevocably bound together" and "unique in Kenya, in that such Titles are directly held from the British Crown, and not, as in the case of other land in Kenya, from the Government of Kenya." Based on this assumption, he argued that their property rights were "more secure," and they were entitled to compensation directly from the British Crown.[15] He concluded, "I believe that it might be possible, when Independence comes, [that] the owners of the plots on Lake Naivasha, named in the [Riparian Agreement] would have the right to secede from the rest of Kenya and remain under the Crown as a Colony, unless the Crown would agree with the plot holders to compensate them for change of ownership."

Although LNROA leaders did not pursue the radical suggestion that Lake Naivasha remain a crown colony, they did survey owners of riparian land to gauge their interest in being bought out by the settlement board as a group.

Letters from association members communicated an interest in selling their land in this manner, although many placed caveats on the venture. One wrote that selling was desirable, "tho *[sic]* not at a ridiculous price." Another wrote that he was interested in pursuing an agreement "as long as it is not binding." A few older residents living on small plots expressed an absolute desire to leave Kenya. Only two settlers indicated that their plots were not to be offered for sale or that they were still unsure. On August 29, 1961, the LNROA chairman wrote to the settlement board offering 10,402.79 acres of surveyed land and 2,157.5 acres of riparian land for purchase as a block. Although the settlement board sent notice that they had received and were considering the request, nothing came of it. They did not cite a reason for this decision, but it is likely that they shared the opinion, common among white settlers in Naivasha, that the area was inappropriate for African resettlement.

During the colonial era, Naivasha became a space of white aspirations for agrarian prosperity and racial insularity, which settlers hoped to achieve through mixed farming and tourism. LNROA members worked closely with colonial officials to enforce rules that restricted others from infringing on their property rights. However, they resisted attempts to create formal restrictions on development in the lake area. White settlement in Naivasha did not erase Maasai claims to this space, nor did it prevent Kikuyu workers from forming their own attachments to (and aspirations for the future in) Naivasha.

NAIVASHA IN POSTCOLONIAL TRANSITION

Following Kenyan independence in 1963, a land reform strategy was devised that would "preserve the productive large-farm sector while satisfying demand for broader access to land" (Winter-Nelson 1995, 38). The Kenyan government purchased roughly one-third of European-owned lands and transferred these to African buyers in parcels ranging between twenty-five and thirty-three acres. The largest and most profitable farms were transferred intact to wealthier African elites, many of whom had gained favor with the colonial government by opposing the Mau Mau Uprising (Kanogo 1987). Six years after this program of agrarian restructuring, small-scale farms were producing over half of the value of Kenya's agricultural output (Winter-Nelson 1995). Smallholder farms were soon regarded in development circles as "the heart of the Kenyan model [of commercial agriculture]" (Orvis 1997, 6).

The area immediately surrounding Lake Naivasha was not designated for African resettlement. According to one longtime Naivasha resident, "Africans didn't have any interest in this land. Without irrigation, you could only cultivate in the riparian area, and the lake level was unpredictable. Crops were frequently destroyed." His conclusion contradicts the obvious interest that Kikuyu squatters had in cultivating here, but it is possible that fertile land on the nearby Kinangop Plateau was more attractive to these small farmers. Immediately after independence, land in the lake area remained a patchwork of mixed farms, cattle and dairy ranches, hotels, and residential hobby farms, many of them still in white ownership. In the late 1960s and early 1970s, some white Kenyan landowners sold their acreage (e.g., large coffee estates) elsewhere in Kenya and relocated to smaller farms in the Naivasha area.

After independence, changes in environmental management strategies and power relations in the lake area were gradual, and LNROA members retained their legal right to care for riparian land. A white civil servant was appointed chief warden in charge of the Lake Naivasha region. In September 1967 a group of black fish and game employees wrote to the permanent secretary complaining about the special relationship between LNROA members and game department officials. They complained that the white chief warden did nothing to discourage vigilante policing on the part of LNROA members, who confiscated fishing gear from suspected poachers.[16] Although the permanent secretary expressed solidarity with the racial politics inherent in the fish wardens' letters, he viewed LNROA members as key allies and partners who should not be alienated.

Fisheries files from this period describe a number of start-up industries designed to benefit the "African" population in the lake area. A fish-packing plant bought tilapia from licensed fishermen for sale in Nairobi.[17] In a decision that would have an extremely negative impact on the local ecosystem, crayfish were introduced to Lake Naivasha in 1970. According to ecologists, these crayfish destroyed most of the native macrophytes in the lake, triggering a loss in water clarity and quality (Smart et al. 2002).

The LNROA became dormant again during the mid-1960s, with some minimal activity concerning boundary arbitration. In the late 1960s, however, the association sparked to life again as members debated two "invasive" forces, salvinia (an alien species of water plant that choked out native plant life) and the rapid expansion of tourism. During the 1960s and 1970s, a number of new hotels and campgrounds opened in the lake area. A large marina stored speedboats for weekenders, and waterfowl hunting and fishing opportunities attracted both domestic and international tourists. In the words of one third-generation white Kenyan whom I interviewed: "The water was crystal clear then, and loads of people would come from Nairobi every weekend to fish. They all kept power boats in the marinas here, and the lake would be covered with them on a nice day." Naivasha had finally become the "playground" that Captain Ritchie had foreseen in 1932. LNROA members voted to ban duck hunting and passed new rules for boating and fishing, but they were concerned that the expansion of tourism would remain a threat to both the lake and their control over it.

In the 1970s, LNROA members drafted a proposal to establish the Naivasha Authority "to supervise and coordinate all development around the lake," largely in response to the crisis caused by salvinia and the realization that coordination between landowners and other user groups would be necessary to fight this sort of problem in the future (MacDonald 1970; "Salvinia Weed" 1970). This proposal was presented at the LNROA's annual general meeting on December 3, 1971.[18] While a majority of members approved a statement in favor of creating a central Naivasha Authority, the organization's executive committee later decided to postpone any action, noting that "this was not the right moment to raise such a controversial issue."

In a letter dated December 4, 1971, the LNROA chairman, Roger Mennell, wrote to one of the association's members, Colonel C. M. Cowie, to thank him for speaking "so forcefully about the need for a Naivasha Authority." He regretted to inform Cowie that the board had decided to postpone action. He wrote, "Although they agreed with the idea in principle, they felt that their first responsibility was to the Members of this Association, and for the majority of these people, the most important thing is to retain the right to cultivate their riparian frontage." Mennell argued that LNROA board members did not wish to draw attention to Lake Naivasha at the moment, because "recently there has been a good deal of talk in certain quarters about using this land for settling Kikuyus who have no plots." He noted that, although those present at the annual general meeting had voted "overwhelmingly . . . in favor of urging Government to set up such an Authority[,] . . . this was considered unimportant compared to the dangers of focusing local attention on what is, in fact, still Government land." Having realized that "this Association is bound to be more concerned with the 'rights' of its Members than working for the benefit of the area as a whole," Mennell resigned as honorable secretary.

Given the opportunity to set policies that would shape the future of development in Naivasha, LNROA members again refused to act. Cooperating with the central government might mean sacrificing some of their autonomy. They did not want to limit their ability to cultivate in the riparian area, nor did they desire to call attention to the fact that the riparian reserve was technically government land. Tourists in speedboats were "threatening" but not concerning enough for them to submit to a higher authority that they might not be able to control.

THE RISE OF KENYAN FLORICULTURE (1970S–PRESENT)

In 1969, a Danish millionaire, Jan Nielsen, established Kenya's first large-scale cut flower farm on a six-thousand-hectare estate in Eastern Province. Called DCK (Dansk Chrysanthemum Kultur), the company specialized in growing chrysanthemums for export. The Danish government provided a generous grant that covered one-third of the initial investment costs. The Kenyan government provided inexpensive land lease rates, unrestricted work permits for expatriate employees, exclusive production rights to several flower varieties for the next eight years, and a promise not to revise tax laws for foreign investors for the next twenty-five years (English, Jaffee, and Okello 2006, 139). Within a few years, DCK employed sixteen hundred people and had more than one hundred hectares planted in chrysanthemums and other crops (Jaffee 1994); the farm also featured advanced irrigation and cold storage systems.

DCK expanded in the 1970s, acquiring a second farm near Naivasha for the production of carnations.[19] By 1976, DCK had a total of twenty-three thousand acres under cultivation and employed a labor force of three thousand on its two farms in Eastern Province and in Naivasha (Njururi 1978). To spur the expansion of the floriculture sector, DCK and the Kenyan government lobbied the European Economic Community to allow Kenyan flowers into European markets duty-free. In 1976, the European Economic Community granted the cancellation of all tariffs on Kenyan flowers on the grounds that the industry represented an important development opportunity (Raphael 1976; *Daily Nation* 1976). Officials representing Denmark, West Germany, the Netherlands, and other European centers of flower production protested this agreement.

Shortly after this trade victory, DCK's fortunes began to unravel. In 1976, the farm was put in receivership after Nielsen was indicted simultaneously by the Danish and Kenyan governments for violating foreign exchange regulations by not remitting export earnings back to either nation (Njururi 1978). In 1981, DCK was acquired by Brooke Bond, a British corporation that was, at the time, the leading tea company in Britain. Brooke Bond operated tea and coffee estates in Kenya and also owned shares in a number of smaller Kenyan companies.

In 2008, I interviewed Roger, one of the managers hired by Brooke Bond to operate its newly acquired flower operations in Kenya. He explained that the financial scandal was not the only factor that contributed to DCK's decline. The chrysanthemum operation in Eastern Province was severely affected by an insect infestation, and DCK had difficulty finding markets for the carnations they were exporting to Germany via Lufthansa. Roger explained, "[DCK hired] a German marketing company [that] started a subsidiary called Kenya Flowers, but they didn't really know anything about marketing flowers. . . . Planes were leaving here with nowhere to go. . . . This was the first time anyone anywhere in the world had tried to airlift whole planeloads of flowers, and they basically had to dump them in Frankfurt and then go from there."

Brooke Bond closed the Eastern Province operation completely, selling one of two farms back to the government and the other to another horticulture company. Company executives chose to focus on the cultivation of spray carnations at Naivasha and changed the name of the farm to Sulmac.[20] They gradually diversified and began growing large volumes of statice, alstroemeria, and lisianthus. By 1979, Sulmac had 120 hectares planted in fifty different varieties, and the company produced 90 percent of Kenya's cut flowers (English, Jaffee, and Okello 2006, 140). In 1984, Brooke Bond was purchased by Unilever. According to Roger, "Unilever was surprised to find that they owned a carnation farm at Naivasha. They wanted the tea estates. . . . [However], in one good production year, the carnation operation, which was only 20 percent of Brooke Bond's acreage in Kenya, brought in 40 percent of the profits." Although Unilever executives considered palm oil, coconuts, and tea as the company's core strategic crops, these profits kept them from divesting from flowers for more than a decade (Jones 2005).

DCK/Sulmac's success in Naivasha triggered other experiments in export floriculture in the lake area. One of these early experiments would grow to become Naivasha's largest flower farm, Oserian. In 1967, Dutch expatriate Hans Zwager and his wife, June, a British citizen, bought the five-thousand-acre Oserian estate in cooperation with two other investors, Charles Hayes, founder of the Nation Media Group, and Michael Dunford, a founding partner in Safariland Marina, one of Naivasha's first luxury resorts. At this time, many local residents and officials envisioned tourism as the key to Naivasha's future economic development.

According to a business proposal on file in the Kenya National Archives, Zwager and his partners intended to develop Oserian into a destination for "the permanent tourist—i.e., the retired person who wishes to lie in a pleasant climate with attractions such as low income tax, no death duties, etc." They imagined that these permanent tourists would be elderly people "of considerable means" from Europe and North America "who seek to establish themselves permanently or semi-permanently in a place in the sun where both the political and natural climate are agreeable." If "Project White House" (as they called it) was greenlighted, Kenya could compete with Spain, Malta, and Greece in attracting these retirees.[21] They requested that the Kenya government work with them to provide potential residents with the proper immigration status, ensure that their income generated abroad would not be taxed, and extend key services (e.g., water, electric, telephones, and roads) to the site.

The Project White House proposal notes that "the land has very limited agricultural value. Much of it is rough, rocky, steep and bush-covered and provides a precarious existence for a number of wild animals. There is however a large and attractive residence." The "attractive residence" at the heart of the development pitch is the famous Djinn Palace, of *White Mischief* (Fox 1982) fame, the lakeside residence where, according to legend, Lord Errol and his contemporaries reportedly drank heavily, swapped sexual partners, and nursed grudges that allegedly led to Errol's murder. According to the few surviving pieces of correspondence associated with this proposal, the Kenya commissioner of lands (J. A. O'Loughlin) indicated that the government approved of the plan but could not guarantee the provision of services. Without these guarantees, the investors were not able to obtain financing for the project.

According to his memoir self-published in 2005, Zwager bought out Hayes and Dunford using money from a lucrative career in agricultural chemical sales and financing provided by the National Bank of India (now the Kenya Commercial Bank). He and his wife decided to refurbish the Djinn Palace as their private residence, and they courted funding from the Commonwealth Development Corporation (CDC) to invest in irrigated vegetable production for the UK market. In his memoir, Zwager explains, "CDC, in those days, were looking for opportunities to invest . . . especially in the areas of agriculture and horticulture. We were a heaven sent opportunity." Zwager writes that "being a careful man when it comes to gambling, I didn't want to commit the whole of Oserian land to the project" (2005, 178). He formed a new company called Oserian Estate Limited and arranged for the new business to lease eight hundred acres of land from his original company. The CDC also provided a loan of just over a hundred thousand British pounds, which Zwager and his partners used to set up an elaborate irrigation system. After a rocky start, Zwager again bought out his partners, the CDC and a United Kingdom–based marketing company, and hired a new manager to solve persistent production, labor, and marketing problems. Oserian produced French beans, green peppers, and other vegetables for export for a little over a decade, but Zwager sensed that the venture was "not going too well" (179).

In 1982, at the suggestion of a Dutch business associate, Oserian began growing cut flowers for sale at Dutch auction houses during the European winter. Zwager explains, "We were given some seeds for purple and white statice, with basic instructions on how to plant them" (2005, 183). Although low in quality, the company's first consignment sold for a price Zwager considered reasonable, and he began growing additional flower varieties at Oserian. The business expanded rapidly, but Zwager became convinced that his Dutch associate, who served as the company's seed supplier and marketing agent in the Netherlands, was siphoning away profits. After a protracted legal battle, Zwager formally severed this business relationship. He then founded a separate company in the Netherlands (East African Flowers) so that he could sell produce directly and profitably to the Dutch auction houses. After getting out of "the whole mess" (186), Zwager writes, the business began to yield remarkable profits.

Roger, the former senior manager at Sulmac, confirmed that accessing the Dutch flower auctions became a major focus of his attention, too, in the 1980s. He explained, "The Dutch flower auction is a grower's cooperative, so at the time they didn't want to know about [Kenyan flowers]. They only accepted flowers for auction that were grown in Holland." Kenyan growers figured out how to "cheat" (as Roger described it) by relabeling flowers once they reached Holland, but this made it difficult for them to sell anything in significant quantities. When it became clear that flowers grown outside Europe were entering the market by other means, the Dutch auction houses slowly began to adjust their policies. Roger explains, "They realized that they were going to lose control of the market, which was becoming global, and they relented. Now [in 2008] 60 percent of the world's flower trade goes through Holland, and the largest supplier of flowers at auction is Kenya."

Two additional innovations allowed the Kenyan flower industry to grow at a rapidly accelerating pace in the late 1980s and early 1990s. Flower farms in the Naivasha area started growing roses, and supermarkets became a major player in the retail flower market in Europe. According to Roger, "Roses are tricky. They're much more capital-intensive, but if you get it right, they're much more profitable. In the early 1990s, the supermarkets in the United Kingdom—Tesco and, later, Sainsbury—and Albert Heijn in the Netherlands got very interested in selling fresh flowers, which they had never done before." These supermarkets helped expand the consumer base for cut flowers by marketing roses as an affordable, everyday luxury. Oserian and Sulmac had an early edge in rose production, but high profit margins inspired others to enter the industry. Roger explains, "With roses, the market is much more segregated, with more shapes, sizes and varieties. There were more niches

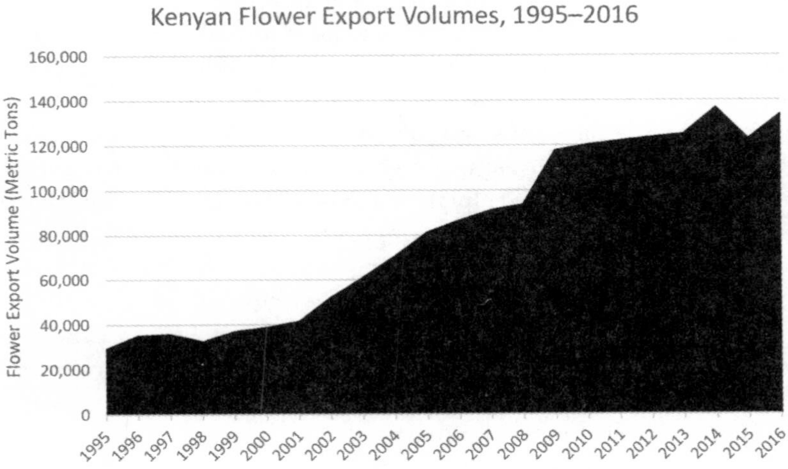

FIGURE 1.2 Kenya exports more than 120,000 metric tons (about 264,554,715 pounds) of flowers annually to markets in Europe and the United Kingdom. (Based on data from the Kenya Flower Council)

to be filled, and the market just went up and up. . . . People saw what we were doing and copied it. . . . Soon enough, everyone was in roses."

By the 1990s, floriculture had become the wunderkind of the Kenyan agricultural sector. As seen in figures 1.2 and 1.3, Kenyan production volumes continued to grow, as did the profits generated by the industry. Property values in Naivasha also began to rise, and the number of local flower farms expanded. In 1995, Zwager purchased the neighboring Kongoni estate to expand Oserian's flower production and fulfill a dream of developing a local game sanctuary and high-end tourist lodge. In the early 1990s, a group of Dutch investors purchased and leased land near Lake Naivasha, founding Sher Agencies, which would become one of Naivasha's three largest flower farms by 2007. In July 1998, as part of a corporate restructuring initiative, Unilever sold Sulmac to the Commonwealth Development Corporation. The CDC operated the farm until 2002 and then sold it to Homegrown Limited, a Kenyan horticulture company. At the time, the company envisioned the 256-hectare Sulmac farm as "a land bank for all of Homegrown's foreseeable expansions" (Wambalaba and K'Aol 2006, 2). In 2007, Homegrown owned and operated three separate farms in Naivasha, all of which were named after aquatic birds—Flamingo, Kingfisher (formerly Sulmac), and Hamerkop.

As the history of Sulmac and Oserian suggests, floriculture presents significant barriers to new entrants, especially smallholders. Growers must pay

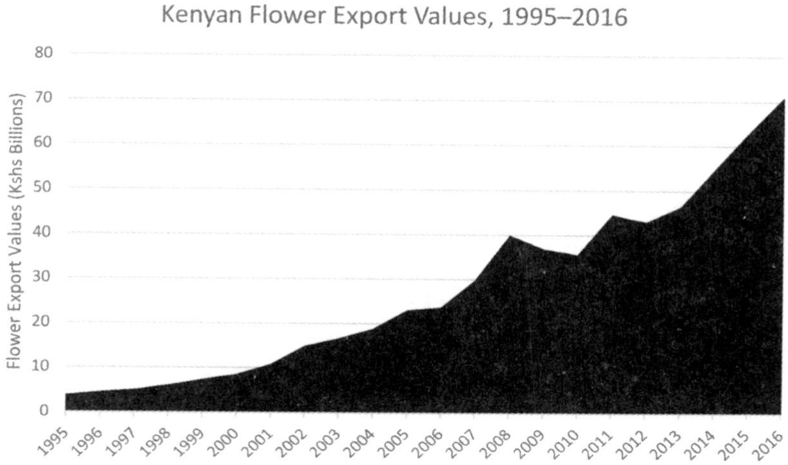

FIGURE 1.3 Cut flowers have steadily increased in profitability since the 1990s, and they represent a major source of foreign exchange. KShs = Kenyan shillings. (Based on data from the Kenya Flower Council)

large sums up front to license the rights to produce specific flower varieties, the infrastructure needed to grow flowers is expensive, and wholesalers and retailers prefer to work with well-established farms that can guarantee large quantities of high-quality produce. Although some smallholders successfully contract with larger firms to produce specialty flowers for bouquets, the industry has become increasingly consolidated under a few large producers. In 1975, a minimum of ten acres was needed to turn a profit in cut flower production. By 1989, the most profitable Kenyan flower farms controlled a minimum of five thousand acres and employed between three thousand and five thousand employees (Gibbon 1992, 71).

"Beauty and the Agony": Flower Production Comes under Fire

In the late 1990s, the meteoric rise of the cut flower industry inspired a politicized backlash centered on allegations of exploitative working conditions and ecologically destructive production practices. Throughout the late 1990s, and early in the following decade, articles documenting the "hidden costs" of floriculture circulated in the local and international media. These articles highlighted the sexual harassment and abuse of female farmworkers, illnesses caused by exposure to toxic farm chemicals and a lack of clean drinking water, low wages, long hours, overcrowded housing complexes, and insufficient environmental safeguards.[22] In 2002, the *East African*

Standard published a report titled "Beauty and the Agony," which summarized many of the sensational allegations against the industry.

The Kenya Human Rights Commission and a number of international NGOs demanded that farms act quickly to reform the industry and threatened to organize boycotts of Kenyan flowers in Europe. Facing mounting pressure from consumers, retailers began requiring Kenyan suppliers to subscribe to "codes of practice" that specify minimum standards for ethical and sustainable production. These codes are created by the supermarkets, retailers, and auction houses that purchase Kenyan flowers, as well as by trade organizations, like the Kenya Flower Council, that represent growers collectively. Independent firms routinely conduct farm audits to verify compliance; farms found in violation of these codes lose market access if they fail to correct problems quickly. The code-based system of regulation has introduced sweeping reforms within the industry, including zero-runoff irrigation systems, on-farm health and safety procedures, housing allowances to supplement low wages, access to basic health care, subsidized or free lunches, treated drinking water, and free transport to and from work.

However, this mode of regulation remains controversial. Noncompliant farms can still circumvent the system by selling produce to retailers or wholesalers that do not require such codes of practice. The costs associated with enacting these codes also privilege large farms at the expense of outgrowers and smallholders, furthering industry consolidation (Freidberg 2001). Anthropologist Catherine Dolan, who has researched Kenyan horticulture since the 1990s, and her colleague Michael Blowfield argue that the social and environmental stipulations within these codes are neoliberal technologies of governance that are unlikely to produce truly empowering or transformative results for Kenyan workers (Blowfield and Dolan 2008). Although living and working conditions in the industry have improved, code-based regulations will not result in enduring structural change.

These media and NGO campaigns have politicized floriculture and have helped place Lake Naivasha itself under an unprecedented level of international scrutiny. At the time of my research, most Naivasha flower farms were visited by four to five teams of auditors each year. They were also the subject of frequent media coverage, especially around the time of Mother's Day (in the United Kingdom) and Valentine's Day. In 2007, farm managers felt strongly that these codes helped them control labor and environmental conditions on-farm. However, they acknowledged that off-farm spaces remained beyond their regulatory reach. A number of studies have examined the relative efficacy of these code-based regulatory strategies, as well as cultural and moral affectations and neoliberal logics at work within corporate social responsibility strategies.[23] However, these codes often develop in tandem with place-based environmental and social governance initiatives. While these initiatives are shaped by neoliberal logics, they are also deeply entangled with local sociopolitical processes and environmentalities.

Environmental Politics in Naivasha during the Floricultural Era

In the mid-1990s, the meteoric expansion of floriculture triggered another reinvention of the LNROA. Andrew Cole, a lakeside landowner and a passionate environmentalist, took over as chairman and, under his direction, the organization's mandate changed dramatically. The organization removed the requirement that members be riparian land "Owners" and became the Lake Naivasha Riparian Association (LNRA); they opened membership to anyone with an interest in the area, and sought to bring together members of the Lake Naivasha community to discuss their shared interests in preserving and protecting the local environment. During one of my interviews, Michael, a longtime LNRA member, explained, "[Naivasha is] the most disparate community. . . . The only thing that really binds them together is the value of their land. And the value of their land—why is it different from the value of land anywhere else in the country? Because of the lake." The birth of the flower industry had caused local property values to skyrocket and had spurred rapid, uncontrolled development. LNRA members hoped that, if they could form a more inclusive, united community, they could assert more control over the lake's management.

The advent of multiparty politics in 1991 and 1992 also helped shake LNRA members out of a long period of fear and apathy. Michael explained, "There was a period starting in the midseventies through the nineties, when politics were overbearing. You couldn't say anything, you couldn't do anything, unless you had the right political connections, and so there was a degree of apathy. There was also total mismanagement by government. . . . All of the things that took so long to build, the infrastructure, fell apart." In the early 1990s, LNRA members felt that perhaps the time was right to reestablish a working relationship with local government and advocate change. "The democratic space expanded. The media could print things, and you could actually speak out. . . . We were able to come out more openly and work with the council, which we couldn't do before."

Despite renewed faith in the power of political action, LNRA members were still very concerned about corruption. Like past generations of lakeside landowners, they worried that skyrocketing land values in Naivasha would draw the attention of what they viewed as "land-grabbing" Kenyan officials. In the words of Richard, another longtime member, "We felt that Naivasha would be a target for grasping by corrupt government officials. So we recognized the importance of being seen nationally, and perhaps internationally, as an area of great importance. . . . We lobbied to become Kenya's second Ramsar site . . . to give it more international recognition and to make it harder to grasp." Concerned about rapid development and land-grabbing, LNRA members adopted a strategy of making Naivasha visible on an international stage. They invited scientists to study the lake's ecology and hydrology, developed partnerships with international environmental organizations, and promoted the ecological value of the lake in print and online forums. In 1995, they succeeded in having Lake Naivasha designated a Ramsar site, a wetland of international importance.[24]

By the late 1990s, however, LNRA members felt that they needed a more formal legal strategy for managing the lake. International attention and visibility were ultimately not enough to protect Naivasha and their interests. They could propose rules and regulations, but they remained powerless when it came to enforcement. Inspired by a community-based resource management approach, they worked closely with NGO partners, community members, and government representatives to draft a "community-based" strategy for managing Lake Naivasha. Because the LNRA's membership was still not representative of the local community, they formed a Lake Naivasha Management Committee consisting of representatives from fifteen important local stakeholders. These included:

1. the Lake Naivasha Riparian Association
2. the Lake Naivasha Growers Group
3. the Naivasha Tourism Group (a group created for the management plan process)
4. the Lake Naivasha Fisherman's Cooperative Society
5. the pastoralist community
6. the World Conservation Union
7. the National Environmental Management Authority
8. the Kenya Wildlife Service
9. the Kenya Electricity Generating Company
10. the Naivasha Municipal Council
11. the district commissioner's office
12. the Fisheries Department
13. the Water Resources Management Authority
14. the Department of Physical Planning
15. the ministry responsible for agriculture (which was in between official titles at the time)

Between 1998 and 2005, the LNRA leadership worked closely with representatives from these fifteen entities to draft a comprehensive and legally binding Lake Naivasha Management Plan. When I interviewed LNRA members in 2004, they were confident that this process would be successful. They argued that, while other attempts to establish local control over development and environmental regulation had faltered, this effort would not fail because they had worked so diligently to "involve the community" in the process.

The plan was officially gazetted into Kenyan law in early 2005; but before the LNRA could celebrate, a lawsuit blocked the plan's implementation. Initially, LNRA members were confident that they would prevail in court and win the right to implement the plan, but by late 2007 they had begun to suspect that they would never be allowed to appear in court. Multiple hearings had been canceled and rescheduled, only to be canceled again. Some LNRA members expressed frustration with the "corrupt" Kenyan legal system, insisting that the plan was legitimate; others viewed the plan as flawed and offered explanations for the proximate and ultimate causes of its demise. My interviews with actors involved in the management plan process, as well as those who felt harmed or excluded by it, reveal some of the key points of conflict that caused the LNRA-led process to unravel.

Flower growers involved in the process were adamant that the management plan should be based in scientific fact, specifically a comprehensive hydrological study of the lake that could be used to draft a water allocation budget. According to correspondence on file in the organization's records, the LNRA chairman feared this research would take too long to conduct, and that a narrow focus on water would distract from broader ecological issues. Although they continued to cooperate with the LNRA and take part in the management plan process, some growers questioned whether LNRA members should be leading the regulatory process and whether the management plan would be "reasonable" from an industry perspective.

Code-based regulations introduced starting in the late 1990s had also helped the industry improve its image. Naivasha flower farms worked diligently to cultivate a reputation as responsible, self-regulating enterprises with the influence, money, and technical know-how to clean up Naivasha. While the LNRA seemed like a more legitimate community-based organization in the 1990s, by early in the next decade the flower growers had succeeded in legitimizing their own claims to represent the best interests of the local community by engaging in demonstrative social and environmental projects in the area.

The LNRA also came into direct and personal conflict with the senior management of a prominent Dutch-owned flower farm in Naivasha. A survey conducted at the LNRA's request showed that some of the farm's greenhouses and a senior manager's private residence were built below the legal riparian line. The LNRA refused to grant an exemption for the house, and when the farm's owners refused to demolish it, the LNRA publicly criticized the farm for violating the terms of the 1931 Riparian Agreement. The farm's senior managers adopted the hardline stance that the LNRA was an elitist, colonial organization with no authority in the present and threatened to block the implementation of any plan that would give the LNRA control over the lake's development. This characterization of the LNRA as enduringly colonial appealed to many lake-area stakeholders, who began to view the management plan as an attempt by white Kenyan landowners to retain their power and authority at the expense of the public.

The LNRA leadership also struggled to recruit a committee member to represent pastoralists. The search for a single pastoralist representative ignored critical kinship and political subdivisions in the Maasai community, and those leading the process were reluctant to accommodate more than one representative. A LNRA member centrally involved in the management plan process explained to me, "Unless you have one of every family, one of every age, they'll never be happy, and we're not going to have six representatives."

The committee eventually recruited two representatives from the pastoralist community. However, their participation in the process did little to alter the prevailing perception that pastoralism was ecologically destructive and incompatible with modern agricultural development in the lake area. Committee members insisted that Maasai participation was necessary and welcome, but they also viewed Maasai demands as problematic and unreasonable. A LNRA member articulated this attitude in stark terms: "No matter which way the Maasai come they are trespassing over private lands, causing damage, cutting fences, eating landowners' carefully preserved dry weather grazing (and/or crops). . . . Sadly pastoralism and private land ownership do not mix." The member argued that, instead of granting pastoralists access to the lake, more should be done to improve conditions for grazing and watering cattle "nearer to their traditional grazing areas so that they don't have to trespass." This LNRA member did not consider Naivasha to be a traditional grazing area. While the official pastoralist community representatives voted in favor of the final plan, disagreements about access to the lake continued to simmer beneath the surface.

Civil servants and political officials participating in the development of the plan also remained uneasy about sharing power and authority with one another and with the community. At times, members of the Naivasha Municipal Council were particularly vocal about their objections to the management plan, which they viewed as a usurpation of the council's legal right to direct and control Naivasha's development. Although the final Lake Naivasha Management Committee included several government agencies, government restructuring and changes in Kenyan policy made the relative power and mandates of these agencies unclear. Government officials participated actively in the planning process; however, they remained uncomfortable with the idea of formerly surrendering regulatory authority to the committee.

In 2005, a prominent Maasai lawyer, who also worked as the human resources manager for the Dutch farm "named and shamed" by the LNRA, filed a lawsuit to block the implementation of the plan; an injunction was granted, pending further consideration of the case in court. The lawsuit named three plaintiffs, two Maasai community groups, and a local lakeside landowner. In 2007, a figure close to the case told me, "That plan is finished. We will never allow it to leave the courts." In October 2007, Andrew Cole resigned as LNRA chairman, giving the short speech that opens this chapter. His words echoed in many ways the sentiments expressed by those who had called for a coordinated management plan in the past. He hoped that new blood, fresh ideas, and a new approach would help the organization discard its elitist image and help the community "wake up."

In the wake of the management plan's demise, a new multistakeholder initiative for managing Lake Naivasha emerged, driven primarily by managers of Naivasha's major flower farms and made possible by significant changes to Kenyan water policy. This initiative may eventually "go pear-shaped" (as one LNRA member predicted), but in 2007 and 2008 it generated great enthusiasm among local stakeholders, especially those who felt alienated by the LNRA's approach. The Kenyan Water Act of 2002 created new opportunities for local governance of water resources. Ideally, stakeholders in each of Kenya's catchment basins would form a local Water Resource Users Association and work cooperatively to create a locally acceptable water management plan for each catchment area. In 2007, local stakeholders formed the Lake Naivasha Water Resource Users Association (LANAWRUA) to take advantage of this new space for public input and local control over water management.

This most recent attempt to create a central authority for controlling and monitoring activities in the lake area represented a significant shift in local power relations. Although the LANAWRUA also involves a multistakeholder approach, flower growers play a key role in running and setting the agenda for the group (a role similar to that played by the LNRA in the development of the Lake Naivasha Management Plan). In 2007, the chairman of LANAWRUA was the managing director of one of Naivasha's three largest flower companies, and although the executive board consists of representatives from the local tourism industry and the pastoralist community, the majority of active members come from the flower industry. Flower growers hoped to use this forum to place a strict moratorium on all new water permits in the area. They saw keeping newcomers out as central to protecting their fixed assets and investments and ensuring the availability of the water necessary for floriculture.

In 2007, most government officials and LANAWRUA participants told me that the LANAWRUA made a revival of the Lake Naivasha Management Plan unnecessary, and that the group would create a better, more inclusive scheme for managing the catchment basin. Other stakeholders, who by my observation seemed marginalized within the group, also expressed a remarkable confidence that a LANAWRUA-led process would be more open and participatory. When I asked them to explain why they thought this would be the case, many approved of the Kenyan state's direct and central involvement in the process and described this as a means of further "decolonizing" Naivasha.

For flower growers, the LANAWRUA process represented an opportunity to protect their vested interests in what they viewed as Naivasha's most precious resource—*water*. For other actors in the lake's catchment basin, LANAWRUA signaled an opportunity to replace informal regulations created and enforced by the LNRA, an organization they viewed as colonial (meaning dominated by white Kenyan actors and rooted in power relations and historical processes associated with the colonial era). Their enthusiasm for this neoliberal governance strategy had less to do with ambitions to rationalize water use and prioritize business interests over other social and environmental concerns, and more to do with a desire to *dis*empower white Kenyan actors and solidify *state* (and therefore black Kenyan) control over both this specific place and the direction of national development.

Postelection Violence in Naivasha (January 2008)

While the disagreements described above took place mainly in conference rooms, Naivasha can also be a "violent environment" (Peluso and Watts 2001), a place where conflicts over access to resources and political power, including the forms of wealth and influence generated by floriculture, can result in injury, displacement, and death. For four days in January 2008, Naivasha became a site of postelection violence. These events profoundly affected the results of my research and the Naivasha community more generally, and they highlighted many of the ways that floriculture has transformed the intersection of place, power, and possibility in Naivasha. These events reflect the darker side of aspiration in Naivasha—the vulnerability that accompanies interconnectivity and the inequality that accompanies prosperity. They also shed light on the ways that different actors view who "belongs" in Naivasha by virtue of their interpretation of the region's past, present, and multiple possible futures.

Although transnational corporations and elite actors technically own the lakeside land where flowers are grown for export, other groups and institutions also lay claim to this territory. As a nerve center, Naivasha also belongs to the Kenyan state, which can mobilize its security apparatus to protect its interests in the resources and global flows concentrated here. This place belongs to the Kenyan people, too, but in differential and complex ways. Farmworkers who migrate here for work see this as a temporary home, a space that they have a right to access as laborers but only rarely as owners (e.g., of land or businesses). Descendants of Kikuyu laborers who settled here before and immediately after the colonial era feel confident in their right to own land and businesses and to exercise power here (through their control of state institutions). However, they also recognize Maasai ancestral claims to this space. White and expatriate actors lay formal claim to land and resources in Naivasha, but in moments of crisis they are reminded that their land titles could be revoked by state actors who may view them as only temporary allies in the process of development. The short period of postelection violence that interrupted daily life in Naivasha for several days in January 2008 reveals the many ways that global commercial interconnections and neoliberal policies have not de-territorialized (Giddens 1990) this place. Naivasha remains deeply imbricated in Kenyan social and political processes and conflicts. This is a *Kenyan* (as well as a transnational) nerve center.

In the buildup to the December 2007 national election, political rallies in the villages surrounding South Lake Road were frequent occurrences. Candidates for national and local office asked farmworkers for their votes, promising to improve their labor and living conditions. Opposition-supporters proudly displayed photographs of presidential candidate Raila Odinga and told me excitedly that when Odinga prevailed in December, he would force Naivasha's landlords to lower house rents, require farm managers to raise wages, and help "Africanize" floriculture. My host family displayed a photograph of President Mwai Kibaki and told me that only Kibaki could continue Kenya's economic growth and protect the interests of "all Kenyans." In the months leading up to the election, tensions rose as political rhetoric became increasingly ethnicized and polarized.

On Election Day, December 27, I accompanied my host family to the polls, where they patiently stood in line for six hours waiting for their turn to vote. The mood in Naivasha Town was jubilant, with people flashing each other their inked pinkie fingers as proof that they had performed their civic duty. A *matatu* conductor jokingly refused to let me board a vehicle when he saw that my finger was not marked with ink. Cafes, restaurants, and bars in town were crowded with people who had gathered to watch the news. Election observers declared that the voting process had been "free and fair."

As the vote tallies began to come in the following day, Raila Odinga assumed an early lead. A friend invited me to watch the returns with his family in his small flat in Naivasha Town. Using a scorecard torn from the *Daily Nation*, we tracked the shifting balance of power in Parliament as Orange Democratic Movement candidates associated with Odinga unseated members of Parliament from Kibaki's Party of National Unity. With each victory, or predicted victory, my friend rose out of his chair, cheering and on the verge of tears. When I arrived home that afternoon, I continued watching the news coverage with my host family. We sat together in comparative silence, but over dinner, the mood lightened. "There's no question," my host father laughed. "Raila can't win. He can't. I'm not worried. Just you see. They have yet to count Central [Province]."

On December 29, there was still no official announcement about the results of the presidential election, and tensions began to build again. The television news reported that the Electoral Commission of Kenya officials had retracted some of the results announced the day before. Critics accused commission officials of tampering with ballot boxes and "cooking the results." Raila Odinga's lead began to shrink. A sense of impatience and helplessness hung over Naivasha. I asked a friend, a Kibaki supporter, whether she thought the results were being tampered with. She replied carefully, "You have heard what Raila has said. If they went forward with *majimbo* [a controversial and much demonized notion of the devolution of power to regional levels of government], all of the Kikuyus will have to somehow fit in Central. That place is squeezed. Kibaki is a good man. Why shouldn't he rig [fix the election result]? Moi did it for twenty-four years. Kibaki also needs time to continue his work. Besides, [the Orange Democratic Movement] can also rig." The friend with whom I watched the returns on the first day was distraught, already thinking about how he would protest an "unfair" result and what he might do to protect his family "if this thing came to bloodshed." Like many Orange Democratic Movement-supporters, he did not believe that the Odinga's evaporating lead was the result of legitimate vote-tallying in regions supporting the Party of National Unity.

In the evening of December 30, the Electoral Commission announced that Kibaki had won the election. Rather than holding a public rally and celebration, the government broadcast pretaped footage of Kibaki's swearing-in ceremony, which had taken place only hours before his first term in office was set to expire. Orange Democratic Movement-supporters insisted that the election results were not valid, and by the morning of December 31 there were reports that fighting had broken out in Kisumu and Kibera, Nairobi's largest slum. Not long after these reports first surfaced, the Kenyan government banned all live television broadcasts in an effort to stop the unrest from spreading. The media blackout cut Kenyans off from reliable sources of information; and in Naivasha, sensational rumors began to circulate by word of mouth and forwarded text messages. Few of these rumors were true, but they heightened the sense of confusion, disbelief, and anger gripping the South Lake community, where many farmworkers had supported Odinga's candidacy.

Over the next three weeks, tensions escalated and violence emerged in several locales. In the North Rift, long-standing conflicts over land ownership, tensions with deep and complex historical antecedents, reignited and took on new political meanings. Heated political debate dominated conversations in Naivasha. Both sides accused the other of rigging the election. Orange Democratic Movement-supporters in particular viewed the election result as a miscarriage of justice and a betrayal of democracy. "It's as if someone stole your phone," a farm manager explained to me, laughing. "Now, you go to see him to ask him to return your phone. You can see it there in his pocket, even it is ringing when you call the number. In his pocket. Just there. And he just tells you, 'I don't have your phone.' Now, Megan, how can you just continue talking to this man? He knows he is lying. You know he is lying. You can't." Supporters of the Party of National Unity insisted that the result was fair, or they insisted that election irregularities were rampant on both sides. They expressed fears that "Luos here in Naivasha will destroy this place like they did Kisumu."

On January 15, I left Naivasha for London, expecting to return when the situation had improved. A little over a week later, between January 26 and 30, violence erupted in Naivasha. When I returned to the field in March 2008, after a "power-sharing" agreement had been signed between President Mwai Kibaki and Raila Odinga, who was now Kenya's prime minister, I attempted to reconstruct what had happened during this critical four-day period. This was an extremely difficult task. Rumors made it hard to separate fact from fiction about what had happened during the worst of what people often called the "skirmishes." I focused on what people had actually seen and heard firsthand, but these memories were also in flux. Those who experienced the chaos in Naivasha had already begun to reinterpret what had happened as they struggled to justify their actions and make sense of how local events connected to postelection violence elsewhere. The truth about what happened was subjective, contested, and rapidly evolving.

The violence in Naivasha was most often characterized as a "revenge attack" by those seeking retribution for Kikuyus killed and displaced in the North Rift. Members of Naivasha's Kikuyu community insisted that what had happened here was a terrible necessity, a legitimate form of self-defense. In the words of one man, "If we hadn't shown our [Kikuyu ethnic] strength here, what would have happened in the North Rift?"

As early as December 31, young men reportedly began arriving "from elsewhere" to help "defend Kikuyus" living in Naivasha if and when it became necessary. Most people identified these men as either Mungiki members or youths employed by local politicians and businessmen.[25] They were reportedly hosted by local families and were armed mainly with *pangas* (machetes), although some also had guns. Some Naivasha residents also reported seeing *matatu*-loads of young men being dropped off on Friday, January 25. The idea that the violence was brought to Naivasha from outside was nearly universal. However, there were many signs that local people knew what was coming and had taken time to prepare. When the skirmishes began, all of the *matatus* had been cleared from depots in Naivasha Town, and most businesses were shuttered.

On the morning of Saturday, January 26, a group of men constructed a barricade of burning tires and rocks on the Naivasha-Nakuru highway. They allegedly stopped a Nairobi-bound *matatu* and a Nakuru-bound bus and killed three men identified as ethnic Luos, slashing them with *pangas* on the road in front of onlookers. These men then split into smaller groups and began seeking out Luo and Kalenjin households in Naivasha Town and the two nearest villages, Kihoto and Karagita. A friend who witnessed this process reported that a group of young men came to his plot and yelled loudly that "each should come stand in his door." They demanded that each resident identify his or her ethnicity and asked for verification of these identities from the neighbors. As word of the initial violence spread, residents from the targeted ethnic groups escaped their homes and took refuge at the Naivasha Prison and the Naivasha Police Station. If Luo- and Kalenjin-occupied plots were found empty, the men broke down the doors, removed any possessions, and burned them in the streets.

Although local people maintained that the violence was started by "outsiders," members of Naivasha's Kikuyu community were reportedly forced (or chose) to take part in the looting and burning.[26] The organizers brandished weapons and threatened people with death if they did not "come out to defend their people." A local pastor told me that he spent the next few days wandering the streets with a crude axe trying to look as if he was participating and warning people not to burn gas stoves. A man who lived in a rented plot in Naivasha Town explained that he was given a number and assigned to a larger group instructed to "patrol" his estate. He claimed that he avoided his "duty" by hiding during the day and returning to his room at night to sleep.

Many Naivasha residents reported seeing men in police and army uniforms participating in the violence and looting, rather than intervening to stop it. Organized groups also tried to disrupt the delivery of supplies and water to refugees at the police station and prison. By Monday, January 28, most of the Luo- and Kalenjin-occupied plots in Naivasha Town and Kihoto had been located, the contents burned or looted. A rumor that the Maasai had arrived "to slaughter every man, woman, and child" began to spread, generating additional tension and fear. A Kikuyu acquaintance described a confused woman in a torn dress, wearing only one shoe, stumbling down his street hysterical and in tears, crying out, "They're coming to kill us all!"

Some ethnic minority residents living in Karagita, the largest residential village along South Lake Road, fled to nearby farms to request protection. According to a white Kenyan farm manager who allowed refugees to hide at his farm, "They knew that we had people inside the farm. They'd gotten my number and were calling, texting threats. We didn't know whether they would go through with it or not." Farmworkers living in on-farm housing complexes near Karagita prepared for a possible attack by making crude weapons in farm workshops. One farmworker showed me his collection of makeshift knives and axes stored under his bed. Some farms helped their Kalenjin and Luo staff members leave Naivasha. They paid out salaries and final benefits and helped them organize transport out of town. Some farmworkers paid bus and *matatu* drivers exorbitant prices to transport their possessions and family members to their home areas elsewhere in Kenya.

Throughout this tense period, flowers continued being exported. Trucks loaded with roses were sent through to Nairobi with armed escorts. Many flower farm workers, especially those who lived within secure on-farm compounds, continued reporting to duty. Others left Naivasha and were replaced with casual laborers. White Kenyan and expatriate farm managers were shaken by these events, but they were also determined to proceed "normally." According to one white Kenyan resident, Naivasha's "European community" organized a caravan of vehicles to take women, children, and nonessential employees to Nairobi, where they hoped that affluent neighborhoods like Karen would remain free of the tensions erupting in Kibera and other shantytown settlements and slums.

On Tuesday, January 29, the Kenyan Army arrived in Naivasha with air support, using rubber bullets to disperse crowds in Naivasha Town and Karagita. This finally brought an end to fighting. Local residents, especially minority farmworkers, argued that this step was finally taken because the skirmishes were likely to spread down South Lake Road, and gangs were poised to burn flower farms. Flower farm managers reported that they lobbied the state (and in some cases, their foreign embassies) to intervene, but they also claimed that Maasai elders had met with the alleged Kikuyu coordinators of the attacks, reminding them that "this was not their place." Estimates of the final death toll varied from unofficial counts of "hundreds" to an official figure of twenty-three. The violence also displaced thousands of farmworkers.

These four days in January shaped the ways that nearly everyone living and working in Naivasha understood the intersection of power, place, and possibility in this nerve center. These events reminded farmworkers from western Kenya of their vulnerable status as "immigrants" in a territory "owned" by others, and it deepened their sense of political marginalization at a national level. Farmworkers who supported Odinga's candidacy had placed their hopes in a "new Kenya," in which their political benefactors would have the power to raise their wages, lower their rents, and create opportunities for Africans to move up in the industry. Although code-based schemes for regulating floriculture could do little to truly empower farmworkers, they imagined that political representation at the national level could produce structural change.

This short-lived political crisis also reshaped the rosy aspirations of farm directors and agents of the Kenyan state. This violence reminded farm owners of their dependence on the state's security apparatus. The Kenyan state had suffered a blow to its international image, and elected and appointed officials were eager to work with flower growers to restore the nation's reputation as secure, stable, and business-friendly. This postelection violence would help shape the evolving relationship between the flower industry and the Kenyan state.

Naivasha has never been a no-man's-land. Many communities lay claim to this place, and local, national, and international actors are deeply invested in trying to control the nature of its development. Neoliberal governance strategies in Naivasha have transformed—but not erased—power relations, agrarian aspirations, and social or political allegiances forged in earlier historical moments. Although the LNRA-led management plan process failed in its original intent, the association succeeded in making Naivasha visible on an international stage as a place of *environmental* (as well as economic) importance. The lake is a designated Ramsar site, and international consumers, scientists, and journalists recognize this place as ecologically significant and worthy of additional forms of scrutiny and protection. In many ways, these place-specific concerns have been incorporated in the neoliberal regulatory frameworks and governance strategies dominant in the contemporary moment. Naivasha flower farms adhere to codes of ethics that emphasize the need to protect the lake from chemical runoff, overabstraction, and the destruction of vegetation in the riparian zone. Although neoliberal technologies of governance often look generic and homogenizing from above, they appear more complex and socially embedded from below and in light of the past.

Viewing environmental and social governance in Naivasha in historical context also reminds us that power in this place is precarious and contested. Environmental conflicts in Naivasha are also struggles over access to territory, resources, and political power. While flower farmers participating in environmental governance in Naivasha may seek to protect the future of this industry in particular, other actors engage with these management processes with other aspirations in mind. They seek to protect Naivasha's potential to become something other than what it is now, a place over which they have greater control. Naivasha remains a place with both a contested past and multiple possible futures. Actors living and working in contemporary Naivasha reference historical events as they explain how and why they belong here, what kind of place this is, and who should have the power and authority to control and direct Naivasha's future.

CHAPTER TWO

Low-Wage Laborers

Sacrifice in a Slippery Context

EUNICE lives in Kamere, one of the villages that line South Lake Road. I know Eunice's family very well, and I have come to interview her about her experiences as a career flower farm worker. She meets me at the *matatu* stage and we walk together along the steep streets, which become raging gullies during heavy rain. Today is her day of rest, and she has spent the morning attending church and washing clothes. Eunice's house consists of a single room in a block of six that share a common toilet. The walls of her home are stone, and the landlord pays an attendant to clean the toilet weekly. Nearby homes with cheaper rents are made of wood or sheet metal (e.g., figure 2.1), and the tenants are responsible for cleaning the toilets themselves.

Her single room measures about six by ten feet. A sofa stands against one wall. Her bed, which she shares with her teenage daughter, stands against the other. She stores their clothes in a cardboard box at the foot of the bed. A blanket suspended from a rope separates the living space from the sleeping area. Her kitchen consists of a neat stack of cooking utensils and a small charcoal *jiko* (stove). The corner nearest the door is cluttered with plastic water jugs, which Eunice uses to collect rainwater from the roof for drinking. She occasionally buys lake water for bathing and washing clothes.

Like many farmworkers, Eunice has decorated the walls of her room with newspaper pages. Most are cut from the February 14, 1999, issue of the *Daily Nation*. I ask if these were articles that interested her, and she laughs. "These newspapers are just for decoration. It makes the place look nice and not so boring. I would put them on the ceiling if I could reach." There are also two pictures of Jesus, a testament to her devout faith, and several magazine photos that I remember seeing in the house of her son, Eddie, before he moved to Nairobi to look for work a few months ago. The glossy photos of

FIGURE 2.1 Flower farm workers and their children stand outside their homes in one of Naivasha's six villages. Each block of six one-room houses features a shared toilet. Permanent workers receive a housing allowance as part of their monthly wages.

European models, a coffeemaker, and an electric sandwich press seem out of place. Eunice laughs when I point them out, telling me, "I liked some of these things, and so I just put them here and there. They're nice to look at, and I don't miss him so much."

In separate conversations, her son, who has a serious physical disability, has told me that he will not be coming home from Nairobi until he has found a job that will allow him to support Eunice. "I would rather just die on the street here looking for work than die sitting around Naivasha waiting for a job that will never come. I pity her. She's too old to be working. I want to pay off the *shamba* [farm] so that she can take her retirement and go live there. I can't stay there and take money from her. I feel ashamed." On this day, Eunice tells me, "I pity him. I knew that he would have few other work opportunities [because of his disability], so we hustled to get him an education. I won't leave this job until I have seen the end of my son [until he is working and supporting himself]." She also supports her teenage daughter, who is in secondary school.

FIGURE 2.2 Female workers pack flowers quickly so that they can earn a piece-rate bonus on top of their regular pay. The pace is especially frenetic in the buildup to major holidays like Valentine's Day and Mother's Day.

Eunice has worked at the same flower farm on and off for nearly twenty years, through several changes in management. She is currently a full-time, permanent employee in the packhouse (e.g., figure 2.2), where she grades flowers. At close to fifty, she is older than most of her peers. I ask her to describe her typical work day, and she replies, "I report to the job at 9 a.m., sometimes 10 a.m. I look at the board the night before so that I know when to come. It varies depending on the work that needs to be done. I generally close the job at 6 p.m. or 7 p.m." I ask what her job as a grader involves. "We sort the stems by size and variety. We have a quota of 115 bundles of ten stems, and we are paid a few extra shillings for grading stems beyond this." She claims to average 280 to 300 bundles a day. I ask how this compares to the work of other packhouse workers. She answers, "Some of the young people defeat me, and I defeat some of them. It just depends on how you work. I don't chat much on the grading floor. It distracts you from your work."

She shows me her pay slip. Her base monthly salary is 5,480 Kenyan shillings (about $54.80), which is higher than the standard 3,300 that workers make at other farms. She also receives a housing allowance of 1,400. Her employer offers on-farm housing to long-term permanent employees, but Eunice chooses to live in Kamere so she can save some of her housing allowance and avoid having to register visitors with farm security. Landlords set rent prices at or very near the typical housing allowance, which makes it difficult to save this way. Eunice's current house rent is 1,200. Because she will be taking her two-week annual leave this month, she has also received a leave travel allowance of 1,600. She will use this to take her daughter to visit family in Molo.

The second portion of the pay slip shows a long list of deductions. Eunice has borrowed against her salary on several occasions. The slip shows an automatic Savings and Credit Cooperative Organization (SACCO) loan deduction of 1,635 shillings. A separate note also indicates that she took a midmonth advance, the amount of which is not recorded. Although her salary varies based on how many flowers she is able to grade, she brings home between 3,000 and 3,500 shillings each month after these deductions. I ask her if she is able to cover her everyday expenses comfortably, and she replies, "You see what we have here. It is very little. I don't even have a phone. But it is better to get a little money than none. Life is good. We're staying strong. We eat. You must love the life that you have or you will get sick. If you hate yourself and your life, you will get sick. Why hate your life when you're not sick, you're healthy, you're eating?" Like many women working on Naivasha flower farms, Eunice has chosen to sacrifice the present in the hopes of a more prosperous and secure future. By borrowing against her salary, she has been able to pay school fees, medical bills, and invest in a small piece of land.

Eunice was born in Machakos District, which lies southeast of Nairobi, but she was raised on a farm near Molo, a town about seventy miles northwest of Naivasha. She came to Naivasha in 1981 to look for work at the invitation of her father, who worked as a driver for a white Kenyan living in the lake area. In 1992, her family lost the farm in Molo following what she describes as "clashes." She shakes her head as she remembers this loss. "They can't just buy that land back even though they were the ones who sold it to us. They have to just grab it." Although her father has since bought another small plot with a house and leases land nearby for farming, Eunice is nostalgic about the sense of security the larger farm provided. "If something went wrong, we could just sell a cow. Now there's nothing. If something goes wrong, what do you do?"

She is in the process of buying a one-acre plot in another part of Molo that she describes as "less isolated, with better security." She has been buying the land slowly through a broker, starting with a SACCO loan of twenty-one thousand Kenyan shillings. She makes smaller payments when she can, using her leave time and travel allowance to make the journey to Molo. She still owes sixty-six thousand Kenyan shillings, which she is anxious to pay off as quickly as possible in case she loses her job. She explains, "If you have no *shamba* [farm], what do you do if you go in and they say there's no job and we'll pay your services [final benefits] and it's time for you to go?"

We share a meal of *ugali* (corn meal) and greens, and she asks me many questions about the farm where I stay with my host family. How much land do they have? How big is the house? Do they grow trees? What do they plant, and where do they get their vegetables and things? Do they have cows or other livestock? I answer her questions and she smiles, saying, "The land where I am buying this plot is fertile like the Kinangop [the area where I have been living]. God will provide me with the one [the plot] I have now [the plot she has been making payments on]."

After our meal, she asks to borrow my mobile phone to call the land brokers to make arrangements to meet them during her upcoming trip to Molo. She removes a plastic bag from the box at the foot of the bed; inside are her important documents and a few photographs. A stack of receipts indicates that she has made many small payments on a piece of land denoted by a lot number. She flips through a small notebook given to her by the flower farm where she works. The notebook contains information about company regulations and procedures, with blank pages for a worker to take notes. She uses the blank pages to record important phone numbers. She calls the two numbers that she has on file for the brokers in Molo. Neither works. She grows visibly agitated and calls another number on her list. A woman answers, but she is told that the man she is trying to reach is in Nairobi at the moment. The woman assures her that someone will be there to take her payment when she comes, and that it will be acceptable for her to pay nine hundred toward the plot instead of the two thousand requested.

She completes the call, and we continue talking about life in Naivasha. I hope these brokers are honest, that this stack of receipts will one day yield a one-acre plot, and that a one-acre plot near Molo can provide enough of an income for her to retire comfortably after a lifetime of work in Naivasha.

Workers like Eunice are the lowest-paid laborers on Naivasha flower farms. Many are employed as casual employees, who are hired on short-term contracts during peak points in the production season. Some hold permanent positions that offer a regular wage and some benefits. Many more are what I call "labor hopefuls," who come to Naivasha looking for work in floriculture but have not yet secured even a temporary position. Most migrate to Naivasha from elsewhere in Kenya seeking work in floriculture. Once they arrive, they find that life in Naivasha is challenging. Some leave after a short time, but many stay here for years. Workers like Eunice are often the subject of news articles, documentaries, and magazine features on floriculture in Kenya. Their lives are difficult, and many told me heartbreaking stories punctuated by hardship, loss, illness, and exploitation. However, their lives are also richer, deeper, and more complex than the standard journalistic narrative of a "typical" farmworker allows. The meanings that *they* ascribe to their work in floriculture and their lives in Naivasha deserve consideration.[1]

Like Eunice, an estimated 65 to 70 percent of flower farm workers in Naivasha are female (Dolan, Opondo, and Smith 2002, 11). The predominance of women in the labor force sets horticulture apart from all other Kenyan industries and agricultural sectors (Kenya Flower Council 2009; Dolan 2004). This is a result of both intentional recruitment practices and worker self-selection. As in other places, women's labor is undervalued in Kenya and women are largely nonunionized, both of which make women a more attractive labor force (Dolan, Opondo, and Smith 2002). Flower farm managers also expressed gendered understandings of women's special skills. In the words of a public relations agent working for a major Naivasha flower firm: "Women have smaller fingers, you know. They're more social and just better suited for this work. They can pick the flowers easily, and they enjoy life on the packhouse floor." Anthropologist Jane Collins argues that this "naturalization of skill" has been used by managers in numerous industries "to devalue women's work and reward it less" (2002, 921).

Workers likewise explained that certain farm tasks fit with traditional Kenyan gender roles. Women preferred to pick and pack flowers, while men preferred jobs in spraying, transport, or greenhouse construction and maintenance (figures 2.3 and 2.4). A few contemporary managers spoke of intentionally "mixing up" the gender balance within the labor force; but despite their attempt to sound enlightened when it came to hiring practices, their strategies were still rooted in problematic gender constructs. For example, a Dutch farm manager boasted, "The men don't want these jobs in the packhouse, but I think it's important to change things up. I like to staff the

FIGURE 2.3 New greenhouses under construction in Naivasha. Most employees who pick and pack flowers are women. Men generally perform jobs that involve construction, chemical application, and maintenance.

FIGURE 2.4

A greenhouse worker collects the flowers cut that morning. The roses will be packed, chilled, transported to Nairobi by truck, and then exported by plane. Within forty-eight hours of harvest, they will be available for purchase from florists and supermarkets in Europe and the United Kingdom.

packhouse floor with a fifty-fifty balance of men and women. I find that having the men there inspires competition between workers and speeds up the line."

Previous research suggests that, in Colombia, floriculture has been "a catalyst for positive social change" (Freidemann-Sánchez 2006, 178). Women working on Colombian flower farms use their wages to refashion gender relations at home and in the broader social sphere, in some cases facilitating "the breakdown of patriarchal marriage contracts and male domination of households" (176). Women live and work under very different circumstances on Naivasha flower farms. They are often single or widowed, and if they are married they often live apart from their husbands. Many Kenyan women come to Naivasha because they view themselves as even more vulnerable in their home communities, and they use their wages to support multiple dependents and make investments for the future. However, there is little evidence that their work in floriculture allows Kenyan women to catalyze structural change or challenge patriarchal relations in a profound way. They describe Naivasha as a "place of sacrifice."

Despite drastic improvements in on-farm living and working conditions since the late 1990s, the lowest-paid workers and labor hopefuls in Kenyan floriculture struggle to derive the benefits that they expect from their employment. Low-wage farm laborers have profound difficulties finding work, they struggle after falling into cycles of debt, and they experience the largest disconnect between their aspirations and their small earnings. Many of their stories reflect the consequences of uneven development within Kenya, employment insecurity, and gender discrimination. They describe floriculture as a risky or slippery form of employment, and they recognize that, in a structural sense, the deck is stacked against them. Many workers explain in no uncertain terms that this industry is meant to "exploit the labor of the African," and they recognize that a powerful Kenyan political class colludes with international actors to do so.

Despite these constraints, however, they still view migration to Naivasha as a necessary undertaking that might result in something worthwhile. They plan to work in floriculture just long enough to raise the capital necessary to invest in their own entrepreneurial enterprises, especially small farms and businesses in their home communities. Workers look for ways to make the most of the opportunities that floriculture affords, and they sometimes engage in political activities that might change the rules of the game in their favor. In order to succeed in even a small way, they must understand and strategically engage with the dynamic set of actors and institutions that holds power in Naivasha.

POWER: FINDING WORK IN FLORICULTURE

With only a few exceptions, most of the people we interviewed came to Naivasha because a family member or close friend had agreed to sponsor them and because they had heard that the prospects for finding work in floriculture were good. Many came alone but then arranged for their spouses or children to join them after several years. A married thirty-one-year-old man from Kakamega explained, "I came in 1995 to look for fortune. There were jobs here and my brother was here. He came in 1992. You didn't have to wait [for work] at that time. You could just come and sleep one night and work the next day. Since that time, five brothers and cousins have followed me and work just here [at the same farm]. My wife came to join me in 2003 and found work."

Some workers came to work in Naivasha when another family member retired or decided to return home. One young women explained, "My mother was working here, and when she retired she organized for me to come and take her place." An older woman from Kisumu explained that her husband came to work in Naivasha in the late 1980s. When he died from an AIDS-related illness in 1993, she sought out someone who knew him, and her contact helped her obtain a position so she could continue to support her children.

All of the workers we interviewed planned to invite additional family members to come to Naivasha in the near future. However, there was a sense that the rate of farm expansion had slowed and the availability of jobs for inexperienced or unskilled workers had started to decline. A woman who found work in Naivasha in 2000 explained, "There is something unusual about these farms. Even if you didn't go to school, you can find a job. All you need is an ID. Even if you can't write a capital A *[laughs]*, you can find a job. That's how it was then. Now you could really struggle to find a place." Many of the people we interviewed worked in the industry on short-term seasonal contracts (e.g., in the buildup to major holidays like Valentine's Day) and were unemployed for long periods in between.

Workers living in on-farm housing are required to register all visitors in advance and are not allowed to have overnight house guests for more than a few days at a time. Most of the labor hopefuls seeking work in the industry live with relatives in the villages that line South Lake Road. Some stay for only a few weeks, while others remain in Naivasha for years. One woman, who had yet to find work, described her living situation: "I came here two years ago to find work. This area has so many flower farms, so many opportunities for women as compared to other places. I have not yet found that work, but my brother works at KenGen [Kenya Electricity Generating Company, the parastatal company in charge of Naivasha's oldest geothermal power production facilities] and stays here at Kamere." Eight family members currently lived together in her brother's single-room house, including herself, her brother and his wife, and their five children. She had no immediate plans to give up her search for work. "I'll stay here for as long as God blesses me to stay. If I find work, I'll bring my children here. If it's too hard, I'll go home."

Workers argued that finding employment in floriculture requires kinship or patronage connections and, in the words of many local residents, "the grace of God." Workers who felt that they did not have these connections complained that, without them, you would "struggle in vain for work." A forty-seven-year-old man from Busia explained, "There are no other [ethnic] Tessos here, and I have no godfather [a well-connected patron, usually of the same ethno-regional background]. They ask for your name first. Who are you? Where are you from? If you don't have a godfather, you can have ten degrees, but you'll never get a job." Rumors of tribalism in the hiring process were common, but, especially in the wake of the December 2007 political crisis, direct discussion of these issues was difficult. Flower farms do not disclose any information about the geographic origin or ethnic identity of farmworkers, and farm managers were reluctant to discuss issues of ethnicity in the context of a formal interview.

Personal relations alone were rarely enough to secure a permanent job in floriculture. Workers also shared stories about the "contributions" they had made to a farm manager "who liked to eat" to help a family member secure a position. A man who "found" work for a female cousin in the late 1990s, laughed as he told his story. "Nothing was ever said directly. My cousin went out for a job. I saw the manager in a bar and we talked some. He knew my family. He mentioned that he was needing a new TV. I made some arrangements and had a TV just dropped at his place. She was hired some days after."

Only one woman that we interviewed spoke directly about her experiences of sexual harassment in the industry. However, some male farmworkers alleged that women were often abused by managers in exchange for employment or favorable job assignments. A thirty-three-year-old man who came to Naivasha from Ukambani in the early 1990s told us that, although his wife lives with him in Naivasha, he does not want her to work in floriculture. When we asked why, he explained, "You can't just get a job by asking or applying. . . . You have to go to the boss, get an appointment, and wait for a call. If you don't have someone you know, you won't get a job. I fear that my wife might be dehumanized by them. That she will be abused." He claimed that he saw this happen when he worked as a casual farm laborer. "I see so many managers walking around with these women that aren't even their wives."

In the late 1990s and early in the next decade, allegations of sexual abuse were frequent in media coverage of the industry (e.g., Wang'ombe 2002), and researchers working to "humanize the cut flower commodity chain" also reported that sexual harassment and abuse were central to women's experiences in floriculture (Dolan, Opondo, and Smith 2002; Hale and Opondo 2005). Many of the women we interviewed indicated that they were careful to avoid appearances of impropriety: they were careful not to drink in public, leave the house after dark, or engage in behaviors that would jeopardize their marriages or give people the impression that they were supplementing their wages through "inappropriate" relationships.

PLACE: LEAVING "HOME" TO BUILD A FOUNDATION

As Eunice's story suggests, many flower farm workers do not consider Naivasha home. They describe Naivasha as a place that belongs to others with a more legitimate ethnohistorical claim to this territory. In the wake of the violence that followed the December 2007 national election, migrant farmworkers were especially concerned about their personal security.[2]

Despite feeling acutely vulnerable in Naivasha, most described leaving a situation of even greater vulnerability in their home areas. Like Eunice, some had been displaced by clashes in earlier historical moments. Others left home because of strained family dynamics, dire poverty, and what they described as a "lack of opportunities." A woman who came to Naivasha from Eburru explained, "When people move to a new place, it's not because of good. It's because there is something that is lacking [at home]." She had separated from her husband, who had taken a second wife, and she was concerned that she would inherit only a small portion of her father's thirty-five-acre property. She had come to Naivasha two years before but had not yet found work. She explained, "I don't want to go home now. I need to solve my problems. I may inherit some land. It depends on my plans and an agreement with my parents and my brother. . . . I want to buy a *shamba* of my own so that my children can inherit. You know, my parents are old. I need to form other relationships, or how will our lives be?" Many workers expressed similar uncertainties about whether they would inherit enough land to support a viable, agricultural lifestyle. These concerns hinged on both gendered inheritance practices and the increasing subdivision of land in rural areas.

Women hold only 1 percent of registered land titles in Kenya, despite providing 70 percent of the agricultural labor (Ellis et al. 2007, 21, 30). Several recently passed laws, including the Kenyan Constitution enacted in 2010 and the Kenya Land Act of 2012, stress the importance of gender equity in land ownership and inheritance in Kenya. However, customary laws and practices remain fundamentally patriarchal; women are generally granted only secondary rights to land through their relationship with a male relative (Musangi 2017). Moreover, because land is often subdivided among siblings, farm size has decreased over time. Land subdivision poses challenges to agricultural productivity in many parts of Kenya (Museleku et al. 2018). Many workers in Naivasha indicated that, even if they inherited land, these plots would be too small to make subsistence or commercial farming viable.

Several of the workers we interviewed, especially young, single (or recently married) women, cited more personal conflicts with family members or spouses as a contributing factor in their decision to come to Naivasha. Although life in Naivasha had its distinct disadvantages, some women found freedom here from disputes and conflicts with cowives, spouses, parents, and in-laws. One woman compared her circumstances in Naivasha to her home near Amagoro, close to the Ugandan boarder in the Busia District: "My husband is here. I am just comfortable here. I have freedom. Things are bad at home. My father-in-law has two wives, and there is so much fighting between them. I prefer to stay away." When I asked her to explain what makes her feel freer in Naivasha, she explained, "There's no witch hunting here. If you just pass here, people don't say you've done this, done that. No one is watching everything you do like at home. When I am at home . . . everybody wants to find fault in you." For this woman, Naivasha offered freedom from the social censure and ostracism that she faced after leaving her own family to live in her husband's home area after marriage. Patrilocal residence seems to have been a particularly important push factor, especially for young women whose husbands had also migrated to find work, leaving them alone with their in-laws.

Other women indicated that they came to Naivasha when they lost their husbands to separation/divorce, alcoholism, or death. Many suggested that, in their cases, additional circumstances made it more difficult to remain at home after being widowed. A few explicitly volunteered that their husbands had died from AIDS-related illnesses or suggested that they had left an abusive domestic situation. A female farmworker from Kisumu described her circumstances: "My husband died, and I came here to try to support myself. I found another husband here, but he was a drunkard and it didn't work." She laughs and says, "Men are a headache! Those of us who were employed here in the early days [in her case, around 2000] are widows, maybe some 50 percent. More recently, there are more young women just out of school." Her estimation of the percentage of widows working in floriculture is difficult to substantiate, but the death of a spouse was an oft-cited push factor within our sample. Despite conflicts with family members, many of these women still maintained ties to their home regions, sent money home to family members or children, and in some cases planned to return home after "closing the job." For these women, floriculture provided a potential route to self-sufficiency and a way to support dependent children and relatives.

Most workers saw rural networks of social security and support as key benefits of home versus Naivasha. However, for those with entrepreneurial ambitions, rural social obligations presented barriers to personal profit. A woman who operated a small shop in one of the villages described Naivasha as a place where she could conduct business transactions with strangers. She had lived in Naivasha since the 1970s, when her husband found work on a chicken farm owned by a white Kenyan. When farmworkers began streaming to Naivasha in the 1990s, she opened her shop and met with a level of success that exceeded her expectations. She explained, "Home is good, but here you can find money and operate businesses. Home becomes a problem when you want to invest or find money to put up a business. . . . People want credit; and when you won't give it, they go and tell people you have *maringo* [arrogance or pride]. They say you despise others. And if you give credit, they never pay back. Here, you can lend someone money and they will pay, because they know they'll need your assistance again. And you can refuse someone credit." The more impersonal nature of commercial transactions and the ready supply of cash made Naivasha a place where small business owners could accumulate wealth with fewer obligations to redistribute their earnings. Prices rose and fell according to the timing of salary payments, and traders hustled to sell as many of their wares as possible at "end-month," when farmworkers had cash on hand.

The major pull factor motivating labor migration to Naivasha was the opportunity to raise capital through a combination of wages and loans and to buy land, establish a small business, and/or pay school fees for dependent children. Although all workers indicated that they eventually planned to invest in property and/or a small business, many female farmworkers indicated that they would first use their wages to pay school fees, with property and other investments coming later. A young woman who had recently secured employment on one of Naivasha's largest farms explained her long-term ambitions: "My first priority is to educate the children. My second is to buy a *shamba* in our place. The purpose of life here is to get our daily needs, but you can't stay with the whole family here and do some small farming. We can all fit there [at our home place]. When I retire, I'll start a business there at home, maybe a *posho* mill [for grinding grain]." Others planned to operate salons, buy and sell clothes, sell foodstuffs, or open small shops. Most also intended to grow crops for personal consumption and/or regional markets.

These jobs were a means to an ends, a way that they could support family members at home and secure money for a number of personal goals, with land ownership foremost among them. Most workers intended to invest in property in their home areas and viewed Naivasha mainly as a place of work. In the words of one woman: "Life is how you make it. Here is a workplace. Kisumu is home, but if you go there, you go hungry. This is not home, but it is a place where you can find work." Another young male worker, from the Mumias District, contrasted life in Naivasha with life at home: "Here is a matter of sacrifice. Life here is full of challenges, economically and physically. But at home, there's no capital, no steady flow of income to help you keep up your objectives. You have to come here to have a foundation." Like most flower farm laborers in Naivasha, this young man had aspirations that were decidedly future-oriented; sacrifices and discomfort in the present might allow him to build a foundation in the near or distant future.

Although workers and other village residents complained of joblessness in their places of origin, most argued that, given enough capital, they could establish comfortable lives in their home areas. They described their home regions alternatively as spaces of want or pastures of plenty. In the words of one worker: "Life here is good. We have water, we have electric. Home is nice, but there is no money. If you want work or do business, it's not there. But life is good if you can put up a business there."

The impetus for eventually investing at home versus the Naivasha area (or elsewhere in Kenya) is multifaceted. Most workers described home as a place of relative social and financial security. There was a desire to be closer to relatives who needed their care and who could care for them as they aged. Nearly all local residents also explained that, "in Naivasha, *kila kitu ni pesa* [everything is money]." In their home communities, they could barter and trade with neighbors and family members and derive a significant portion of their diets from small-scale agriculture or fishing. In Naivasha, they were solely dependent on their wages.

Most workers, especially women, spoke of wanting their children to inherit property. Investments at home ensured that future generations of their family members would remain tied to these places. In the words of one female farmworker, "I have a plan to buy a *shamba,* but only in our place. Our property there belongs to the father. I need to get money to buy something for the children to inherit." Another farmworker, a young Luo man, also desired to leave his children with a secure inheritance and take part in developing what he called the "motherland." He argued, "You must develop and invest in your own motherland. There is a need to be close to the family. When you die here, you must be buried at home." He laughs. "It cuts down on the funeral expenses if you die at home. And your family members can inherit."

Some workers said they might invest in a small plot in one of Naivasha's villages to build rental flats, but they dismissed the idea of trying to build a house or farm in the lake area. This idea was seen as preposterous for two reasons. First, Naivasha was often described as "a kind of desert" unsuitable for small-scale agriculture. Second, village residents from western Kenya repeatedly emphasized that "this place is not ours." In January 2008, they had been violently reminded of Kikuyu and Maasai claims to this space. There was also a broader sense that land in Naivasha was too expensive, and that the best plots were already in white or elite Kenyan ownership.

A thirty-two-year-old female farmworker who had just resigned after ten years of employment explained, "Migori is a good place. It's very fertile. Naivasha is not good, not fertile, and it's cold all the time. You will farm what? At home, we grow groundnuts, cassava, finger millet, potatoes. Here, I don't know. It's too dry for these things." She paused and began to laugh and shake her head. "Naivasha is a Kikuyu place. We've learned a big lesson." She laughed again. "Even before the chaos, I could not think of living here. I was planning to resign, but the skirmishes hastened this. I have a family at home to support, and I had to take my children home to safety. . . . I was only living here for a short while." Her older son and her mother were waiting for her in Migori. Her father had passed away recently; and in the wake of the postelection violence, she had decided that Naivasha was no longer a space of security and possibility. Only at home could she find the security needed for a comfortable retirement.

Another worker, a thirty-one-year-old Maasai man from Narok, expressed a similar sentiment: "*Zamani* [in the old days], this was Maasai land. Now, they say it is *wazungu* [European], but it's ours. The *wazungu* are just here because they're working, and then they are supposed to go back." I asked him if he would use his wages or a loan to invest in land here, since he viewed it as a Maasai place. He laughed nervously. "I won't buy land or invest here, no. We're not sure that it will turn out to be Maasai land. . . . The Maasais working here are few, maybe 5 percent from all the groups. It is better to invest at home in Narok. Home is the place where you were brought up; you're tied to that place. . . . At home, you don't have to buy things—milk, *mboga,* meat. Here you buy everything. There's no one whose home this [Naivasha] is."

A Meru woman who lived in worker housing on one of Naivasha's largest farms, and who had not been directly affected by the violence of January 2008, also argued that she would never consider investing in Naivasha. She shook her head emphatically. "I cannot buy or build here, because of what I have seen. I cannot even think of keeping something here." She gestures to the empty room where we are sitting. "I had to take away all of my clothes [during the chaos], and I lost them all." She sighed. "At home, no one cares whether you're Luo or Kikuyu. If I had the money, I would go home and start a business. Life at home is cheaper. You don't have to buy everything. . . . The climate here is not good. It's not fertile. Home is fertile. You can have a good harvest." She planned to buy a small farm in Meru. She wanted her children to inherit this land and hoped they would avoid the kinds of violence she saw in Naivasha.

As these statements reflect, most flower farm workers were emphatic about the lack of investment possibilities in Naivasha. However, many of the landlords and small business owners who owned plots in the villages along South Lake Road were former flower-farm workers who had invested their wages locally and now made a relatively secure living providing services to the growing community of contemporary farmworkers. In most cases, local business owners identified as ethnically Kikuyu, and patronage or kinship relations had played a role in structuring their investment opportunities. Some had been among the first generations of farmworkers who secured jobs at DCK and Sulmac. When major landholdings in the South Lake area were first subdivided, they were among those offered the first chance to buy plots.

A prominent landlord and bar owner in one of the South Lake villages explained how he eventually made the shift away from wage labor. "I worked for twenty-six years for Sulmac and took many SACCO [Savings and Credit Cooperative Organization] loans. My first was in the 1970s to try to start a small business selling clothes. I was still selling clothes and made the money to repay those loans. . . . I saved up and up and started another shop selling foodstuffs." After buying land locally, he resigned from his job at Sulmac. "It was too many hours and very little money, and by then I had established myself in business." He paused and gestured at our surroundings, "I was the first person to buy this plot here. [The owner of the land that the village was built on] came to me and told me he was subdividing and gave me the opportunity to buy. He was also from Murang'a." By reinvesting his wages in local businesses and establishing personal and professional relationships with influential figures from the same home area, he was able to segue into a new life as a successful local landlord and bar owner.

For Kikuyu farmworkers with deeper connections within the local business and political community, investments in contemporary Naivasha remained a very real and very lucrative possibility. A thirty-two-year-old woman living in one of the most recently constructed villages along South Lake Road described how she became a landlord: "We came here from Kiambu in 2001. My husband works at [one of the largest farms], in the carpentry department. His parents live in KenGen, so he knows this area well. Each year, he takes a SACCO loan of one hundred thousand to buy and build here. He built these twenty-two houses in 2003, and I also run a kerosene pump." In this case, a well-connected farmworker with access to credit and guarantors (in the form of his parents) was able to invest locally and build several businesses, for which his wife and other family members provide the labor. Over time, he may be able to repay his loans, a task made easier by the fact that he works in a skilled job category with slightly higher pay.

Naivasha's villages are also home to many Kikuyu business owners who make a living providing services to farmworkers. Although some maintain close ties to their home areas in central Kenya, some of these entrepreneurs see their investments in Naivasha as permanent and do not plan to return home. A fifty-one-year-old man operating a shoe repair business explained his ambivalent relationship with his home region: "Nyeri is Canaan. Everything is there. Here is a desert. But when you're born in a place, you want to go explore other areas and seek greener pastures. That place is your father's, and you want your own things. Land there is too expensive. I can only go there to visit and not to live. There are more opportunities for me here." He arrived in Naivasha in 1996, and has six children, none of whom have worked in floriculture. He "would rather they have their own business," and he cited poor working conditions and low pay as serious drawbacks of working in this industry. He sees these jobs as a last resort that he would prefer his own children avoid.

An older woman from Nyeri, who had invested in a small plot and ran a business in one of the villages along South Lake Road, expressed a similar sentiment: "It's comfortable here. I have my own place. I can't go back to Nyeri, and I'm married to my husband. I can't go back to his place because it's too small. I bought my property here with my own means." She raised the capital by working in the floriculture industry and sold small foodstuffs along the roadside. "At my husband's place in Murang'a, they grow bananas. Here I am able to grow corn to eat. . . . In Nyeri, you have to grow tea and coffee and sell it to someone else. There's no subsistence. Here we can grow corn, potatoes, and have food in three months." Nyeri and Murang'a offered opportunities for cash crop production, but on her small farm here, she could grow food for subsistence and for sale on the local market in Naivasha.

A few migrants did have tentative plans to settle in the lake area. A man from Ukambani, who made a living bouncing between short-term farm contracts and operating a local butchery owned by his brother, described his hopes for the future: "I have a plan to buy land and start a business, either in Naivasha or Mombasa. I've lived in both of those places and people know me. At home, not many people know me. I can't even get a lift!" In his case, his father, too, left Ukambani to work in Naivasha and never returned. His family's connections in Ukambani were now so diminished that returning home made little sense. Another worker, from Machakos, had used multiple SACCO loans to purchase a quarter acre in the Kinangop, which he described as "green and fertile." He planned to continue working in floriculture for many years while his wife farmed this small plot.

While most workers from fertile regions saw Naivasha as a "desert," a worker from Isiolo, a northern town located on the edge of a highland desert, described the lake area in very different terms:

> At our place, it is *jua kali* [meaning both "the sun is hot" and "work is hard"]. The rain is not reliable. It is a place of drought. There are no trees. Here there are many trees, rain, hills and mountains. The air here is always fresh. If God gave me a place, a place to settle, I could stay here. With land, I could stay here. Every person here comes from faraway. Other people here come from places where the cultivation is easy, and they prefer home. I would prefer to be here because I can't cultivate at home. If God opens a door, I will follow.

A woman from Kajaido District, who jokingly described herself as "half-caste" (her mother was Kikuyu, her father Maasai, and her husband Meru), had settled in Karagita after working for many years at one of Naivasha's largest flower farms. In her case, a fortunate turn of events put local land ownership within her reach. She explained, "I came here in 1980 and worked for [a prominent hotelier] before I found a place on [the flower farm]. I sold *changaa* [a popular home-brewed alcohol] while I was working there, and in 1995 I stopped to start a business in Karagita. I was so oppressed by those *wazungu*. The money was too low. I just walked out one day and did not even go to take my last pay." She was renting a house in Karagita when the European owner of the adjacent horticulture farm decided to sell out and leave Kenya. She explains, "He called a meeting of all the people who were renting here and promised to sell us our plots for small payments. I raised the money and bought a quarter acre here and built a house and a *duka* [shop]." She also supplemented her income by preaching for small donations. Although this type of arrangement to subdivide and sell land to workers was a rare event, it allowed a small group of former renters from minority ethnicities to realize their dreams of land ownership locally.

POSSIBILITY: ACHIEVING ASPIRATIONS THROUGH FLORICULTURE?

To what extent are these farmworkers able to achieve their personal and professional aspirations through floriculture? The answer to this question is complex, and responses were varied. Some farmworkers succeeded, but many indicated that they had fallen into cycles of debt and disappointment. A twenty-five-year-old man from Bongoma District put it eloquently: "Life here is very slippery. If you cannot manage to reduce that slippage, you cannot meet with success. Life here is full of challenges. At the end of the day, you feel worn and torn physically. Economically, whatever little cash you can get doesn't go far, because life is very expensive and you have to buy everything. Life is hard, but if you can reduce the slippage, if you can save some money, you can build a life."

He followed his older brother to Naivasha in 2004 and found work as a sprayer on the same flower farm. Unlike many workers, he expected to inherit some land at home. He had taken out a forty-thousand-shilling SACCO loan to build a small house on his father's property and buy some cattle, and he had managed to repay this initial loan amount. His efforts to repay the loan and establish some savings had been hampered by his daily expenses in Naivasha and the remittances that he sent home monthly to care for his wife and child. Since his elder brother was also employed in Naivasha, they shared the financial burden of caring for his aging parents in Bungoma. He complained about his daily expenses in Naivasha but remained hopeful about his future and his plans to return home once he had achieved his goals.

Farmworkers enumerated similar demands on their salaries, and nearly all had taken out some form of loan through an on-farm SACCO, the local branch of Equity Bank, and/or a self-help group to finance their ambitions. A typical worker used her salary to pay for (1) local living expenses, which were viewed as appreciably higher than in rural areas and always on the rise; (2) school fees for her own children or, in some cases, for siblings (generally male) or other close relatives; (3) remittances of varying amounts sent to family members living in rural areas; and (4) loan repayments. One older man, who had already purchased or inherited land and started construction on a house, also indicated that he had used his wages and a loan to pay bridewealth to his wife's father nearly twenty years after his marriage. This was likely the case for other male farmworkers, although it seems that this type of family debt was repaid only after workers had made investments that they felt would secure their financial futures. Although many workers spoke of furthering their own education, most indicated that they had invested instead in schooling for their children.

Although all workers claimed to send money home whenever possible, they reported sending widely varying amounts per month. Some claimed to send a few hundred shillings, and others over one thousand (nearly a third of the typical worker's monthly salary), each pay period. This money was used to support dependent children left in the care of family members, aging parents, and unemployed siblings and other family members. Few workers were able to send consistent payments home; they sent what they could spare when they could spare it.

All workers viewed access to credit as the key benefit to working in floriculture; they saw loans against their salaries as a way of "building a foundation" for the future. Wages were nearly universally described as "too little," but workers and labor hopefuls made elaborate plans for both the money that they expected to borrow during the course of their employment and for their retirement benefits. Between 2000 and 2005, most Naivasha-area flower farms began paying workers' wages directly into bank accounts established in their names. This prevents workers from carrying large sums of cash and helps reduce the rate of violent crimes at end-month, when they are paid. This arrangement also connects permanent (or longer-term) workers to formal banking institutions and forms of credit that are not accessible to most rural Kenyans. By one estimate, only 15 percent of rural Kenyan households have bank accounts (Dupas et al. 2012, 2), and national surveys conducted in 2006 and 2009 suggest that more than 60 percent of Kenyans are totally excluded from the formal credit market (Mwangi 2011, 206). Farmworkers may be the only members of their extended families connected to credit opportunities in this way, and they often feel obligated to borrow on behalf of others.

Unfortunately, many workers indicated that they had taken on too much debt. Some used emergency loans to pay for unexpected expenses, such as medical treatment for themselves or family members, and some had fallen prey to scams. Some had invested in pyramid schemes and fraudulent enterprises or paid "land brokers" for plots that did not exist. Some workers spoke of "inheriting" a loan that a family member had not finished repaying when they left Naivasha. Some had, in the words of one farm manager, "mortgaged their salaries" so severely that they took home very little pay after their loan payments were automatically deducted. Debt was a key element of what made life in Naivasha "slippery."

Although farm managers expressed disgust at the ways that some workers became trapped in these cycles of debt, they admitted that these loans helped stop turnover in the industry. One of DCK's former managers explained, "In the early days, you would train them, put in that time and effort, and then they would just leave." Setting up cooperatives that could offer credit helped solve this problem. "People are holding their jobs now, and they don't just push off like they used to. They have taken loans from the cooperative and they have an incentive to stay and pay those loans so that they can borrow again."

Workers viewed their prospects within the industry in a hopeful light, but they also described the future as fundamentally beyond their control. They described floriculture as extremely physically taxing, and they worried about their long-term health. One women explained, "The chemicals affect you very much. You feel dizzy, stomach problems. . . . When you resign, they check you for contamination before paying you your final benefits. If you are positive, they give you compensation and treatment, but, you know, these things become so dangerous over time." All expressed anxiety about job security in the industry; they explained that "even small things could cost you the job"—a change in management, a dip in the market, a prolonged illness, an accusation of misconduct. Many believed that God would ultimately determine whether they succeeded. In the words of one worker, "How should I know if I will succeed? These things are only for God to know. I just pray for God to make a way for me."

TONY AND PRISCILLA: "SOMEDAY I WANT TO HAVE ALL THIS"

Tony works as an assistant production manager at a newer, midsize flower farm in Naivasha. His wife, Priscilla, works as a quality control supervisor at a neighboring farm. Tony and Priscilla met in their home region, in Nyanza Province, shortly after completing secondary school. They came together to Naivasha in the early 1990s at the invitation of family members working in floriculture. Tony initially found a job with another firm and moved into his present position two years ago. Priscilla found work at the neighboring farm about five years ago. They have four children, three of whom attend primary school in Naivasha. Their firstborn attends secondary school in Nyanza.

The family lives in a two-room house in the labor camp associated with Priscilla's farm. The camp features running water, electricity, and shared toilets and showers cleaned regularly by an attendant. The first room of their house serves as the main living and entertaining space; it is cluttered with a sofa, a love seat, a coffee table, and a long cabinet that holds Tony's prized possessions: a television and DVD/VCD player. When the family is home, the television is always on, tuned to a local news station or playing one of Tony's music video DVDs. A portrait of Raila Odinga hangs on the wall above the television. At night, the three children sleep on the sofa and love-seat cushions, which are pulled onto the floor to make mattresses. The rear room serves as both Tony and Priscilla's bedroom and the family kitchen. A chest of drawers holds the family's clothes, and Priscilla cooks on a small gas *jiko.*

When I visit the family on Sundays, the children are usually playing in the camp's common area. Tony's friends drop by to trade DVDs or talk politics. Instead of greens and *ugali* alone, we eat tilapia, which Tony buys from local poachers. By virtue of their dual income, life in Naivasha is slightly less slippery for Tony and Priscilla. Tony often boasts that his income pays for all of the household's living expenses, but in separate conversations both he and Priscilla confirm that her wages pay for most of their everyday expenses. Priscilla uses loans against her salary to pay school fees and expenses for their children. Tony has taken out SACCO loans to buy land and build a house at home, and he recently completed his bridewealth payments to Priscilla's father. Both also send small amounts home to their aging parents.

Although Tony is proud of his home and his family, he still yearns for *maisha bora* (the good life). I ask him one day what he means by *maisha bora,* and he takes me to visit his "uncle" (who is actually an extended-family member) who works at KenGen. The uncle and his wife live in a free-standing cinder block home with a sitting room, a kitchen, two bedrooms, and a private bath. The yard is carefully landscaped with a close-cropped lawn and flowering bushes, and the family's car, a beat-up secondhand sedan, sits in a circular drive. We eat fish together and watch multiple episodes of the South African version of *Big Brother* via satellite television. When we leave, Tony says, "Someday I want to have all this. Why should I just suffer working in that heat for very little pay, when I could be working here and having a car? I keep begging for a job at KenGen, but I cannot find that opportunity. I think the way forward is in politics."

Tony also uses his wages to enhance his social status and cultivate relationships with powerful local actors who might become his patrons. He goes for beers at the flower-farm manager's club, the KenGen bar, and the Railways Club in Naivasha Town, spaces popular among local residents with disposable income. He helps organize local political rallies for opposition-party candidates, and he tells me that a friend working for Raila Odinga's presidential campaign has promised to facilitate his appointment to the civil service as a fisheries officer if Odinga is elected. "I want to work for the fisheries," he says, "because it will allow me to live at home in Nyanza. You just wait; when Raila is elected, our fortunes will change."

Shortly before the end of my time in Naivasha, Tony's contract is not renewed. He is not given an explanation, but the farm's general manager assures Tony that he will give him a positive reference. His dismissal could be due to job performance, his political activities around the time of the December 2007 election, his reputation among his colleagues as boastful, or something much more arbitrary. Without an explanation, he becomes paranoid about who or what might have caused his termination. His severance pay covers the amount of his most recent SACCO loan, but there is little left after he clears his debts.

Although Priscilla's salary is still enough to provide the family with basic necessities, Tony becomes despondent as his search for another managerial position proves fruitless. He is offered a supervisory position at another farm, but he is offended by the salary, which would be less than his wife makes. He is offered a management role at a farm in Limuru but does not want to leave his family alone in Naivasha, especially following the harrowing events of January 2008. He is embarrassed because his wife is now supporting him and he can no longer afford to go out on the town. He tells me, "A man needs to be the breadwinner. I would rather go home [to Nyanza] and live in my house there, than just stay here without working and the wife supporting me." Priscilla goes on working; her salary covers their everyday needs, but the specter of their son's school fees looms on the horizon. Tony may find another position, but until then life will go back to being slippery.

Naivasha is a place where many people come to seek fortune and raise the capital necessary to "build a foundation" in their home communities. Some manage to secure permanent positions in floriculture or establish successful businesses that cater to the people working or seeking work in this industry. Others survive on short-term contracts, odd jobs, and the goodwill of the family members who host them. Although most meet with significant frustrations in their attempts to profit by floriculture, stories of those for whom "God found a way" fuel the labor imaginaries that motivate migration to Naivasha.

Laborers like Eunice, who work at the bottom of this global commodity chain, viewed their employment as relatively precarious or insecure. They hoped to remain employed until it was time to retire and return home. None expected to be promoted to management, but they did hope to be made permanent or eventually earn higher wages. They used loans against their salaries to educate their children and invest in their futures, but they described life in Naivasha as difficult. Although they were acutely aware of the many ways that their aspirations could meet with failure, they viewed Naivasha as one of a few places in Kenya where they could "build a foundation." They viewed their home areas as comparatively disconnected from the forms of economic development and political and social activity concentrated in this nerve center.

They understood that success in Naivasha could be "slippery"—grasped loosely for days, weeks, or even years and then quickly lost owing to termination, illness, or other circumstances they viewed as beyond their control. In order to gain some traction in this slippery context, they worked to carefully cultivate their relationships with more powerful actors, the middle-class professional patrons who might be able to help them secure employment or advocate for better working and living conditions. They also used their wages (and loans against them) to invest in their home communities, their children, and their kinship networks. By hosting other labor hopefuls, they sought to connect their relatives and their home communities more securely to floriculture and to Naivasha. We often concluded our interviews with a final question about Naivasha's future: "If you could have any form of industrial or agricultural development here in Naivasha, what would you like to see?" Workers struggled with this question, in part because their long-term ambitions generally lay elsewhere. In the end, they all answered in a similar way. In the words of one farmworker, "Flowers are OK. The work is OK. We want to be treated humanely and to have the opportunity to continue working."

Supervisors and low-level managers like Tony and Priscilla imagined themselves as upwardly mobile professionals. They could afford some small luxuries, including televisions and DVD players, and they used SACCO loans to successfully invest in similar aspirations. As Tony's story suggests, however, they were still vulnerable to layoffs, illness, and political insecurity. Like Tony, many hoped to use their jobs in floriculture to leverage employment in other industries. They carefully cultivated relationships with local patrons, used their positions to secure favors for others, and supported political candidates who promised to give them real access to the wealth generated by floriculture. Many saw the manicured KenGen estates as emblems of the middle-class lives they aspired to lead. Floriculture provided them with their "daily bread," but they hoped that, with luck, "the grace of God," and political savvy, they would eventually lead *maisha bora* (the good life). Although life in this Kenyan nerve center can be slippery, they viewed Naivasha as one of a few places in Kenya where they could access the credit, connections, and employment opportunities necessary to achieve their aspirations.

The rosy aspirations of these actors matter, even when they are denied or delayed, because they provide a window on what people working at the bottom of this commodity chain really seek to cultivate through the work in Naivasha floriculture. They understand very well that life here is precarious, but they sacrifice the present so that they can connect with one another and with the forms of future possibility seemingly concentrated in Naivasha. They view their work in floriculture as a temporary means to much more desirable ends—prosperous lives in business or agriculture in their home regions, intergenerational economic security (e.g., the ability of their children to inherit their land and educate their own children), and a national Kenyan economy rooted in industries that were not designed to "exploit the labor of the African" (e.g., parastatals like KenGen, where employees seemed—at least superficially—to have more equitable access to the good life).

CHAPTER THREE

Black Kenyan Professionals

Seeking Exposure

DENNIS, the production manager I present in the introduction, whose "dreams of flowers" inspired me to investigate more closely the rosy aspirations of people living and working in Naivasha, is one of many middle-class black Kenyan professionals who work in floriculture. These professionals include labor advocates (e.g., human resource managers, welfare officers, and NGO employees), who promote social welfare on Naivasha flower farms, and technical experts, who specialize in irrigation or fertilization, manage quality standards, and enforce labor and environmental regulations specified by Kenyan law and codes of ethics.

Middle-class professionals working in Naivasha are better politically and socially connected than low-wage farm laborers. Many have attended university, and some hold advanced degrees in law, agriculture, economics, business, and other disciplines. Some use their influence and connections to secure jobs for spouses and family members on Naivasha farms. Many have traveled abroad to trade shows, and they regularly attend workshops at luxury hotels in Naivasha and Nairobi. These experiences fuel a desire for continued upward social and economic mobility. They have higher expectations of their labor in floriculture, and their disappointment is often more acute when these expectations are violated. Like low-wage farmworkers, middle-class professionals plan to use floriculture as a springboard to landownership and business ownership. However, many also see floriculture as a stepping-stone on a path to a more desirable career in politics or the international NGO sector.

As a transnational nerve center, Naivasha is particularly attractive to these professionals. They describe their work in floriculture as providing them with what one farm manager called "the right kind of exposure" to advance their coconstitutive goals for personal, regional, and national development. While low-level workers view themselves as relatively powerless, middle-class professionals working in floriculture see themselves as uniquely responsible for holding this industry more accountable to Kenya. Many of the actors who speak in this chapter describe themselves as moral economic intermediaries working to prevent "foreign investors" or "corrupt" members of Kenya's elite from exploiting local workers and environments. As patrons, they also seek to redistribute the wealth, resources, and opportunities associated with floriculture through their social networks. In a variety of ways, these actors utilize their careers in floriculture to exercise different forms of power and influence. Their viewpoints provide a window on what it means to be middle class in contemporary Kenya and why black Kenyan professionals view Naivasha as a critical space for innervating change.

While other elite actors living and working in Naivasha (e.g., expatriate farm managers) viewed my presence as potentially threatening, these professionals saw my gaze as one of the many positive forms of exposure that living and working in Naivasha afforded them. I interviewed fewer middle-class professionals than I did low-level farmworkers, but my interactions with them afforded many more opportunities for participant observation. They invited me to accompany them to meetings and seminars in Naivasha and Nairobi and allowed me to join them while they performed their everyday duties on the job. Although Kenyan flower farms and nonprofit organizations have made efforts to combat gender discrimination in floriculture, patriarchal conditions within the industry (and in Kenya more generally) make this process difficult. For this reason, most of the actors profiled in this chapter are men.

PROFESSIONAL LABOR ADVOCATES

The perspectives presented below are those of four individuals who represent four different types of actors working as professional labor advocates in Naivasha in 2007: Kasaya (a welfare officer), Isaiah (a senior human resources manager), Tom (the founder of a community-based organization focused on issues of gender equality), and Kariuki (the Naivasha district labor officer, a civil servant). In one way or another, all of these men were tasked with promoting the welfare of flower farm workers. Their experiences and viewpoints demonstrate the ways that black Kenyan professionals living and working in Naivasha view their work in floriculture as a means to many complex ends. All four desired to use their exposure to the resources and opportunities concentrated in this nerve center to bring about forms of both personal and structural change. Their rosy aspirations involved radically reshaping Kenyan law and politics. Naivasha floriculture provided a lucrative, interconnected venue for their work, but they intended for their efforts to have deeper and wider effects.

They were confident in their relative abilities to generate some positive change, but like low-level farmworkers they worried that their power and influence could easily slip away. Many of the improvements in living and working conditions that they had negotiated depended on the strength of their personal relationships with particular farm owners and elected officials. They worked to formalize these agreements (e.g., through Kenyan law) and to strengthen the channels they had opened between this nerve center and the many different communities they saw themselves as representing.

Kasaya: "You See, I Know These People"

The Zawadi Farm Welfare Office lies nestled among the company-owned worker flats, blocks of one- and two-room houses with shared latrines at the end of each orderly row. Children dart in and out between the clothes hung to dry on the communal lines. Zawadi is one of only a few farms in Naivasha that allows workers to unionize, but this has not diminished the critical importance of the welfare officer, Mr. Kasaya. He reports directly to farm management and advocates on behalf of the labor force. His position is a precarious one. His local reputation depends on his ability to move the company toward desired reforms; his job depends on his ability to keep the workforce in order and push for changes that improve efficiency without harming the company's bottom line. Zawadi's welfare officer has a reputation among workers and NGO campaigners as a "good man" who is not afraid to "be a bit political," and thus far he is also regarded professionally as a reasonable man who can be trusted to act in the company's interests. Kasaya has worked for Zawadi for only four years. Before that, he spent nearly two decades in the civil service, working in social services at the municipal level and then for the Ministry of Local Government.

Kasaya ushers us into his office enthusiastically. He has granted us two days in Zawadi's labor camp to conduct interviews with farmworkers, but first he is eager to tell his own story. He examines our proposed list of interview questions and, as a means of demonstrating his intimate knowledge of the labor force, he explains at length how he thinks the workers will answer. "For most workers," explains Kasaya, "this will never be home. They come here to work so that they can earn the capital to develop plots in their home places. Some seek to educate their children, and they use SACCO loans to do this. Some are successful; others mortgage their salaries until they make only five hundred shillings a month and struggle to survive." Kasaya's bold assertion of his intimate knowledge of Zawadi's workers is not far off the mark. His guesses at how workers might answer our questions fit well with the patterns that later emerged during our interviews at Zawadi and in the six villages surrounding Naivasha.

"You see," Kasaya says, "I know these people. I was hired here four years ago [in 2003] to change everything. It was like hell before that. People were dying like hell. From AIDS, from cholera in the camp, from the chemicals. When I came here, I found three to four families living together in a ten-by-ten room. After six months on the job, they had housing allowances, buses, and the farm was building new houses." Kasaya denies that these reforms, which took place on many Naivasha flower farms around the same time period, were due mainly to outside pressures from consumers and NGOs. "The internal pressure really outweighed the NGO pressure. You can't access the farm without the goodwill of management. You need this partnership to effect change. We really lobbied for these things from the inside, provided them with solutions." He also pays extended tribute to the role played in generating these reforms by Zawadi's human resources manager, a close colleague who, like many who have built a loyal following among farmworkers, aspires to national political office.

Kasaya speaks with increasing candor: "I feel strongly that the farms should reciprocate to the worker. The wage structures now are meant for maize farming *zamani* [in the old days]. Horticulture makes much higher profits, and yet they leave people to lead miserable lives." He explains that the farm has recently been sold to new non-European owners, and he fears that they will remove him from his post or begin to ignore some of the changes he has overseen. He expresses little faith in the codes that theoretically ensure ethical practices in floriculture, especially if the new owners can identify new markets overseas that are not subject to these controls. He also fears political collusion between farm management and corrupt state officials. He explains, "The investors enlist political heavyweights as farm directors. They look for a godfather to protect them, and the people suffer. Even before God, that's not fair. I get frustrated from agitating. I think of leaving, but I stay. People should not take advantage of the scarcity of employment to exploit people who are of prime, productive age." In Kasaya's assessment, this collusion has nearly stalled the union's negotiations for a new collective bargaining agreement that will raise wages to modern levels.

He sees the long-term solution to these issues in increasing the capacity and will of the state to regulate floriculture. If Zawadi's human resources manager runs successfully for elected office, if Kenyan law can be changed to adjust salaries to a level proportionate to profits, and if the union can do more than be "just there," the fruits of his own labor, the reforms and policies that he has worked to implement, might be more permanent. At the moment, his own future at the company depends on his personal and political connections to specific personnel, whom he fears may be replaced by the new owners. In his mind, future positive changes for workers depend not on regulations in place at the international level but on personal relationships between a professional class of labor advocates like himself and trusted farm owners who agree with these reforms at a philosophical level. He sighs. "The previous owner really valued workers and came up with the idea for the hospital, the primary school; but the new owners don't have that human heart toward their workers. They are behaving like thieves who are looting, behaving just like they just want to make money and then run."

In his capacity as a welfare officer, Kasaya considers more than just the codes that stipulate specific on-farm labor practices. He evaluates his job performance according to his ability to satisfy workers' understandings of the *potential* value of their labor; his understanding of how workers should be treated is grounded in his own understanding of Kenyan social and political relations. By meeting these expectations, he builds a network of social and political support that might help satisfy his own political ambitions and his vision of floriculture's potential contributions to Kenyan national development. However, recent changes in the farm's management threaten the stability of his connections, and he views the process of building trust and finding common ground with the new owners with caution and weariness. European retailers view codes of ethics as part of an exhausting process of "cleaning up down South," an extension of the colonial "hygienic mission" of teaching Africans to engage in proper agricultural practices (Freidberg 2003). "Down South" labor advocates like Kasaya view their own work as part of an exhausting process of training upper-level farm managers and retailers not to blatantly exploit their labor force.

It is unlikely that Kasaya and his human-resources colleagues at Zawadi can be given all of the credit for generating significant changes in on-farm labor practices in 2003 and 2004. Around this time, Zawadi was subject to a media blitz focused on accusations about a string of deaths from waterborne disease in its labor camp. The farm also became subject to new codes and auditing procedures imposed by supermarkets and auction houses. These changes came about through a combination of external and internal pressures (to borrow Kasaya's phrasing). The backlash against Kenyan floriculture has allowed for the emergence of a professional class of labor advocates in the form of union officials, welfare officers, and NGO activists who now play an important, if limited, role in farm affairs. Many of these professional advocates begin their careers in the union, are then recruited by flower companies to serve as welfare officers, and hope to one day use their influence among workers to launch political careers. As Kasaya's comments suggest, these advocates have keen insights into the ways that floriculture is tied to the state and the Kenyan political class, which many hope to join. They also serve as intermediaries between the workforce and upper-level farm managers and owners, who turn to them for insights into the needs and desires of the workforce.

Like lower-level farm laborers, black Kenyan managers and labor advocates also described their participation in floriculture as a way to earn their "daily bread" and obtain the capital necessary to buy land, build houses, and invest in businesses in their home areas. Many had migrated from rural areas or left less lucrative jobs in business or the civil service to take positions on Naivasha flower farms. Some owned luxury items, such as DVD/VCD players, digital cameras, maybe even vehicles. Black Kenyan professionals were generally influential patrons with large networks of family members, political and social allies, and other clients to represent.

However, members of this professional class expressed additional aspirations that set them apart from lower-level workers. These ambitions were often founded on their understandings of themselves as members of an upwardly mobile cosmopolitan elite with a responsibility to advocate for *Kenyan* interests in this global industry. They conceptualized the interests of the nation and the worker in ways coincident with their varied backgrounds and political affiliations. Advocating for Kenyan interests meant protecting flower farm workers from exploitation by non-African interests. In advocating for workers, they made it more difficult for non-African "investors" to essentially de-territorialize Naivasha by extracting labor and natural resources for global markets at the expense of the local and national economy.

When I first started working in Naivasha in 2004, professionals like Kasaya described the most troublesome "non-African" investors in floriculture as *wazungu* (white Europeans), a term that included both white Kenyan and expatriate European investors. In Kasaya's eyes, he and his colleagues had worked diligently with their international counterparts to identify ways to force farm directors to institute reforms by waging war on both their moral sensitivities and their pocket books. When Zawadi Farm was bought by a multinational corporation based in India, Kasaya feared major setbacks in his struggle to protect workers. He viewed the rising influence of South Asian investors in Kenyan floriculture with racialized trepidation, arguing that "the new owners don't have that human heart for their workers." When I asked him to explain this in more detail, he based his conclusion on his observations of the ways that South Asian Kenyans treated their African staff and on his understanding of labor conditions in India. "With the Dutch, the other *wazungu*, we could argue that they should extend benefits to workers like you see in Europe. Do farmworkers in India have such things?"

South Asia, of course, has a rich history of labor activism, and South Asians in East Africa have helped advance Kenyan labor struggles. In this moment, however, Kasaya felt exhausted by the prospect of negotiating new cultural and moral territories. Bangalore was not the metropole, and he viewed "South Asian" social norms as troublesome unknowns. Black Kenyan professionals expressed similar ambivalence about Chinese investment in Kenya in 2007. A Chinese firm had been awarded the contract to repair several major roads in the vicinity of Naivasha, and inexpensive goods from China were ever-present in the local market. These goods allowed people to dress smartly on low wages. Chinese investment was not cast as predatory, a trope common in the international press, but there was a sense of nervousness about whether these new connections could be controlled. New markets and new trade partners meant establishing new moral economies.

While middle-class professionals working in floriculture shared a commitment to national development and human rights, their aspirations regarding floriculture were also profoundly ethnicized. In Kenya, ethnicity is not a primordial category of identity referring to membership in bounded communities but rather a malleable social construct that plays a critical role in local, regional, and national politics. The "godfathers" whom Kasaya saw as colluding with farm directors to exploit the workers were members of a ruling elite that he viewed as hostile to development and political empowerment in western Kenya. His job as a self-identified ethnic Luhya working in floriculture was also to protect migrant farmworkers from the ill effects of tribalism. The farm labor camp was a venue where labor advocates aspired to democratize Kenyan politics by empowering workers from their own (and closely allied) ethnic communities. Kasaya's aspirations for personal gain, national development, and regional empowerment were coconstituted, and floriculture provided a fertile political and social space for actualizing these desires.

Isaiah: "When You Come to Kenya Next, I Will Be an MP"

Isaiah was hired in 2002 at what he describes as "the peak of concern for human rights issues on these farms." An influential member of the Maasai community and a practicing lawyer specializing in industrial relations, Isaiah was recruited by one of Naivasha's largest flower farms as part of a deliberate plan to improve an image sullied by allegations of terrible on-farm working and living conditions. In the wake of the backlash against the industry that began in the late 1990s, the makeup of farm management became an especially politicized issue. Although black Kenyans had held managerial and supervisory positions before this time, further "Africanizing" key management positions became an important part of the ways that Naivasha flower farms responded to criticisms from national and international civil society.

Isaiah explains, "I didn't apply for the job. I was on my way to Nakuru, and I was called and told that [the farm directors] wanted to see me. I knew who they were. The farm had been in the press, and they were drowning in charges of unfair labor practices, sexual harassment, bribery, environmental issues." He initially refused to take the position but then reconsidered when farm managers seemed genuinely open to change. He explains, "I asked for a free hand, and I transformed the company into an internationally known positive company in only a few years. First, I convinced them that the business needs a human face. Then we went to middle management and told them that a change has come. The job at [the farm] gave me great exposure, locally and internationally."

Like Kasaya, Isaiah takes singular credit for reforms brought about through the cumulative efforts of members of Kenyan and international civil society. In doing so, he creates an image of himself as a great man, a patron and reformer who took seriously the challenge put to him by the farm directors. He was essentially invited by foreign investors to serve as an intermediary between management and the labor force. By performing this critical role, he strategically positioned himself as a champion of workers in Naivasha, which gave him a politically valuable reputation.

Beyond Isaiah's bravado and political posturing, he adopted an interesting approach to reforming working conditions and altering labor relations in Naivasha. When Isaiah took over as human resources manager, he insisted that workers be organized under the Kenyan Plantation and Agricultural Workers Union. He explains his rationale: "I insisted that we allow the union because that way these things would be based on Kenyan law; there would be a real, legal basis for our demands." In this way, floriculture, with its unprecedented number of wage laborers, could be used, at least in appearance, to strengthen the Kenyan labor movement and the influence of this particular union. He hoped that, through the institution of the union, his efforts at reform might eventually be translated into more permanent changes in Kenyan labor law, rather than remain alterations in farm policy that might be reversed with a change in management, weakened political pressure at the consumer end of the commodity chain, or the identification of new markets that would allow a farm to circumvent code-based regulations.

This commitment to strengthening the role of Kenyan institutions and law also helped Isaiah ingratiate himself with members of a Kenyan political elite made uncomfortable by trends toward self-regulation in the industry. Should the need to please farm managers arise, however, Isaiah could also use weaknesses in the Kenyan system to stall further efforts at labor reform in a politically legitimate manner. Unionization gave the farm an additional air of political and social legitimacy in the face of growing consumer concerns. Black Kenyan professionals in Naivasha frequently expressed nationalist sentiments and a desire to make floriculture work for Kenya. "Nationalist" sentiments, however, were shaped by the shifting terrain of ethnic politics in Kenya, which reflected an ongoing struggle for democratic outcomes in terms of ethno-regional political representation and access to development.

Isaiah's employment at this farm brought him exposure at two distinct levels. First, he took part in publicizing and correcting human rights violations taking place within floriculture. Working in this high-profile global industry helped generate exposure for these issues, about which he was genuinely concerned. Second, and perhaps more importantly, his labor in floriculture provided him with the positive political exposure that allowed him to build a base of supporters among flower farm workers and those in his home district who saw his transformative role in the company as a marker of power and prestige.

In 2007, he took an extended leave of absence to run for a seat in Parliament in his home district on the ticket of a political party with a name meaning "let us milk" in Maa. One of his most enthusiastic supporters explained to me that this meant that he would "work to squeeze the resources [needed for regional development] from government in the same way that he had squeezed better pay and benefits [from the floriculture industry]." He lost the race to an incumbent who was able to secure a direct nomination on the Orange Democratic Movement ticket. However, this was a preliminary run for office, a way of growing his exposure ahead of a future election after the aging incumbent died or stepped down. At the close of our interview, Isaiah told me brashly, "When you come to Kenya next, I will be an MP."

When I spoke with others living and working in the Naivasha area, it was clear that Isaiah's strategy had brought him the exposure he desired, but to controversial and polarizing ends. For some, he was a friend of the people, a well-positioned political figure likely to seize the reins of power and deliver on his promises to his constituents. Others viewed him as someone whose political fortunes could rise or fall. The challenge that Isaiah posed to the sitting member of Parliament made seeking out his patronage a risky prospect in an increasingly unpredictable political climate. The multiparty system made it possible for virtually anyone to run for office if they could raise the fees necessary to register a new party. Those who voiced support for Isaiah in 2007 might withdraw this in 2012 as they pursued their own political ambitions or invested in other candidates.

Unsubstantiated rumors also accused Isaiah of several types of corruption—embezzling workers' pensions payouts, colluding with farm management to grab land along the lakeshore, and (within the Maasai community) using his power and connections mainly to advance members of his own section over others. His desire to protect Maasai rights to access Lake Naivasha also intersected suspiciously with the farm directors' desire to access the lake's riparian area for expanded flower production.

Despite these rumors, however, Isaiah's exposure was mainly of the helpful and positive variety. He was regarded as influential, regardless of whether or not he might occasionally abuse this influence, and he was given substantial credit for improving working and living conditions at Zawadi. He had successfully embedded himself deeply in the politics of floriculture, positioning himself both as a reformer who would advocate for the rights of all workers and as a champion for very specific Maasai interests in the Lake Naivasha area. Controversial and polarizing though he may have been, his political and professional talents and his nascent political power were readily apparent.

Flower farm workers in Naivasha often expressed frustration about tribalism, nepotism, and corruption. Workers, especially women, also criticized managers who used their positions to meet selfish desires for money or demand sexual favors. They used interviews with researchers or journalists as an opportunity to "name and shame" these individuals and make instances of corruption or abuse public. However, farmworkers described Kasaya and Isaiah as "good men." As brokers and intermediaries, they had secured tangible benefits for workers, and farm laborers had faith that they might also deliver on their larger promises.

Tom: "To Make Radical Changes and Get Access to Central Funds and Resources"

Notions of exposure were echoed in my interviews with others among the class of professional labor advocates in Naivasha, even those who were critical of politically ambitious managers like Isaiah. Even if their labor brought only "frustration" (as Kasaya explained), at least they had dedicated themselves to "making noise" and setting in motion processes that exposed problematic working conditions and allowed them to advocate for the rights of Kenyan laborers on a global stage. In the process of advocating on behalf of workers, they also cultivated relationships with international activists and scholars, achieving membership in transnational civil society.

Tom, who was the founder and director of a small NGO focused on gender equality in Kenya, also spoke of his involvement in floriculture in terms of exposure. Tom moved to Naivasha in 2001 after finishing a college degree in motor vehicle maintenance and community development. He found employment as an assistant on a research project sponsored by the Peace Corps and Amref Health Africa examining the factors affecting condom use. This experience left him well-positioned to assist with the wave of NGO-led activism and research that followed the backlash against floriculture. He formed his own NGO with some colleagues and identified gender as a topic that would allow him to pursue his many interests and get access to lucrative grants from national and international organizations. Between 2003 and 2006, he bid for and was awarded many small contracts to facilitate discussions of gender sensitivity on flower farms and conduct research on issues critical to the maintenance and improvement of worker welfare.

Like Isaiah, Tom had been able to further his own career by becoming a professional labor advocate. He was also able to harness some of the international attention and money invested in reforming floriculture to advance his broader agenda as an activist—exposing the links between gender inequality and poverty, poor health, and violence in Kenya. When I asked him about his future ambitions, he explained, "My ambition is to see me as Tom making a change for the people I work for. To grow [my organization] to make radical changes and get access to central funds and resources. I am also interested in research work—how can change be brought about? Many things are at the idea level."

Following the backlash against floriculture that came in the late 1990s and early in the following decade, many educated professionals like Tom found employment with the international NGOs that came to Naivasha to investigate working conditions in the industry and advocate for critical reforms. My own research assistant had gotten his start conducting interviews with village residents on household water use for a study funded by the German government. During my time in Naivasha, I tracked the activities of more than a dozen small community-based organizations that competed, and sometimes cooperated, with one another for grants from international agencies and institutions. These organizations helped conduct research on problems related to floriculture, assess farmworker's needs, and design and implement programs related to these concerns. Like flower farm workers, those who made a living from their community work and activism in floriculture also saw themselves as hustling for opportunities that were scarce but potentially lucrative and transformative.

Albeit indirectly, Tom's livelihood heavily depended on floriculture and the opportunities for research, training, and aid work generated by the industry's notoriety. When he encountered someone like me, a researcher interested in floriculture's effects in Naivasha, Tom delighted in the opportunity to collaborate professionally and voice his frustrations about the factors that limited his ability to take "radical" action on behalf of flower farm workers. Tom eloquently explains the structural barriers that often kept him from realizing his ambitions in this line of work: "The funding comes from Europe. If you use too much force, you get called and told to make the campaign less forceful." In one case, Tom was reminded that his mandate covered gender, human rights, and labor laws only. He was instructed not to delve into environmental issues. Tom continues: "Smaller organizations have to go to larger ones for money and, in the process, interests get shifted. They often identify the wrong partners for the right program. They focus only on sustaining their own staff and organization, rather than addressing the issues or forming real partnerships with local civil society." He could make a living working in the NGO sector, but his autonomy was still severely limited. Like many of his counterparts in Naivasha, Tom spent a great deal of time trying to convince larger organizations that he was the right partner, the most authentic representative of local civil society.

Tom also conceptualized his work in the NGO sector and his desires for "radical" change in the context of Luo ethnohistory. He explained, "When [Jomo] Kenyatta [Kenya's first president] betrayed Raila's father [Oginga Odinga] and [activist and intellectual] Tom Mboya was assassinated [in 1969], we realized that politics was somehow so dangerous, and so we really prioritized education. That's why, you see, so many of the white-collar professionals are Luos. This was somehow a way forward when other roads were blocked." Tom saw his work as a professional labor advocate as a way of bypassing tribal politics that limited the political futures of "Kenya's Otienos" (a common Luo surname). Membership in an increasingly transnational civil society allowed him to potentially bypass structural constraints and create positive political pressure to effect change. In this sense, he saw himself as carrying on a Luo ethnohistorical tradition of radicalism and educated dissent embodied by figures like Tom Mboya. For Tom and his colleagues, the results of the 2007 presidential election and the violence that followed in Naivasha were further evidence that multiparty politics and "democratic reform" had not created the opportunities for political empowerment that they desired. They would remain forcibly marginalized and would continue to follow a strategy of extraversion (Bayart and Ellis 2000), cultivating transnational relationships to help ensure their own personal fortunes and to improve the lives of those from their home communities.

While Tom competed with other NGO directors for funding and sought more autonomous control of these monies, his goals remained deeply embedded in key forms of relational dependency, especially patron-client networks and ethno-regional politics. He viewed his participation in the NGO sector as part of his responsibility to his own ethno-regional community, as well as to the "modern" Kenyan nation. To some extent, his transnational colleagues became his patrons, and his own employees or local research collaborators became his clients as they sought to make the agendas and monetary investments garnered from NGO work relevant to their own livelihood needs and their specific visions for the future of Kenyan development.

Kariuki: "When You Don't Know Where Your Next Bread Is Coming From, You Cannot Be So Effective"

One last actor is relevant to this discussion of professional labor advocates in Naivasha floriculture—the district labor officer, a civil servant assigned to enforce Kenyan labor law in this area. I first met Kariuki at a gathering of local businessmen organized by a member of my extended host family, an uncle in fictive kinship terms. My uncle and Kariuki were members of the same investment club. Each member of the group set aside a small amount of money monthly; when the group had collected a substantial amount, they invested it together in various business opportunities. On this particular occasion, they had gathered to drink honey beer and enjoy a meal while they discussed their plans and profits. The faces in the crowd were familiar: all owned small businesses in town and the surrounding estates, and some held salaried positions in the civil service or municipal government. Many also owned small agricultural plots on the Kinangop Plateau. My uncle introduced us, and Kariuki invited me to his office the following day to discuss his work as a staff member in the district labor office.

The next morning, I found Kariuki sitting at his desk. A quiet, thoughtful man with graying temples and wire-framed glasses, he was wearing a suit with faded stripes and lightly frayed cuffs. A government-issued anticorruption calendar hung on the wall behind him, reminding Kenyans not to tolerate requests for bribes or favors. Christmas cards from three local flower farms stood in a neat row across the front of the desk. Written in each was a short message of thanks and a holiday greeting from the farm's general manager. In 2007, discourses of corruption and anticorruption animated political thought and professional performance in both the private and the public sectors. The calendar reminded me that Kariuki and his colleagues among Naivasha's black Kenyan professional class grappled constantly with the concept of corruption as they discussed their work and aspirations. Some used the language of "openness" to dispel suspicions of corruption, and others explained in detailed terms why "some corruption" is a virtual necessity.

Kariuki greeted me warmly and we discussed at length the controversies surrounding labor conditions in Naivasha. Like Kasaya, Kariuki objected to the use of colonial-era wage scales in floriculture. He showed me a weathered copy of the legal minimum-wage scales for agricultural laborers according to Kenyan law. "This is very unfair," he said, "because [the flower farms] are not growing maize. They are large commercial firms and they make much more money from flowers." He leaned forward, resting his forearms on the desk, his hands folded, "I have lobbied Nairobi to improve the law to make workers more comfortable, but they [the flower farm owners] came here for cheap labor. . . . Immediately after the election [in 2002] most workers felt that the new government belonged to them. There were many strikes on the farms, but the growers said that they were within the law. I arbitrated to determine what is a living wage in Naivasha." He praised flower farm owners for voluntarily signing the Agricultural Employers Agreement, which guarantees slightly higher wages in floriculture.

He still viewed wages as too low, and as an interim solution he had joined what he repeatedly referred to as "our government" in insisting that Naivasha farms provide housing, health care, and basic social services to farmworkers as part of a "living wage." He saw himself as an "arbiter" in this process, working to promote "industrial harmony" in this sector. However, while Kasaya, Isaiah, and Tom boasted of the changes that they had already instituted (or would in the near future), Kariuki was much more reticent, even apologetic about his powers to effect change. When I asked him toward the end of our conversation about his aspirations for the future, he chuckled softly and gestured at his spartan office. The door hung open, with "Labor" written across the green paneling in black marker. He explained, "This is a very difficult job, much like being a magistrate in court. The pay is very low. When you don't know where your next bread is coming from, you cannot be so effective." He wiped his brow with a small handkerchief and continued: "I have no vehicle. I have a staff of seven including myself. We are really overwhelmed. We are free and transparent, and we want to be partners in progress. The nation is still growing. . . . [W]e have a lot of problems and we need a lot of assistance."

His perspective revealed a sense that his career in the civil service was a strategic dead end in matters of personal, professional, and national development. Despite this sense of stagnation, Kariuki had chosen as his "partners in progress" the three largest Naivasha flower farms, which he argued were in a position economically to provide for their workers. He argued, "If you cannot provide a better wage, stop growing flowers and let the bigger farms provide better wages and conditions. Smaller farms have a tendency of paying less. The workers do not benefit." He praised these farms for their commitments to worker welfare and their responsiveness to the demands of the Kenyan state.

Kariuki also critiqued the leadership of Kenya's unions, warning me to be wary of at least one local union official, whom he branded "a very controversial person." He also doubted that floriculture would ever be a heavily unionized sector, because of a weakness inherent in the industry's workforce. "Being in a union," he argued, "is like being in politics. Usually you don't find so many women active in the union. They just say, 'Let the men decide for us.' We need to sensitize women on their rights and let them join the union." In a more telling critique, he concluded: "When you are heading a union, you are a big man in this country and you have a lot of influence over the workers. You could paralyze the production capacity of the country. The weakness of the union is because the heads stay in power for too long. We need youthful people in the branches and national offices. They [the old leadership] had the habit of doing the same thing over and over again."

Although he did not explicitly link these conclusions to ethno-regional politics, his mention of specific figures within union leadership suggested that the old "habits" that crippled the union involved corruption and a commitment to politics that ran afoul of "our government," threatening the economic stability of the country. He viewed Kibaki's government as his own in a way that ethnic minority labor advocates no longer did; and from his perspective, the best way to "grow the nation" was not to antagonize the industry but to form lucrative partnerships and arbitrate disputes in a measured manner in deference to floriculture's critical role in Kenya's political economy.

In a sense, Kariuki had been exposed to the transformative power of floriculture, but he did not share the sense that his contributions as labor officer would induce radical change at a personal or societal level. His work in floriculture was difficult labor for which he was underpaid. As a civil servant, he felt excluded from the forms of enterprise and opportunity on which the others pinned their hopes and aspirations. He would work to maintain industrial harmony and help forge the partnerships that would enrich others, while his own fortunes would remain frustratingly stagnant. Kariuki may or may not have respected the directive issued by the "anticorruption" calendar that hung above his desk. Although I heard rumors about the corrupt activities of other local officials or civil servants, I was never privy to any such stories about Kariuki. For those working in the increasingly impoverished public sector, however, the temptation to fulfill personal aspirations by taking *kitu kidogo* (a small thing) for performance (or nonperformance) of their services was ever-present.

Kariuki's story illustrates the aspirations of black Kenyan professionals working at the juncture between Kenyan floriculture and the civil service, especially branches of the state apparatus focused on agriculture and labor. As I discuss in the following chapter, younger civil servants in other sectors, particularly those working in natural resource management, did not share Kariuki's disaffection and sense of alienation from the promises of floriculture. These civil servants worked in sectors transformed by major changes in Kenyan law (e.g., the passage of the National Environmental Management and Coordination Act of 1999 and the Water Act of 2002), and as a result their regulatory relationship with floriculture was categorically different. However, the differences in their perspectives also involved a generational element. Born around 1950, Kariuki was a young teenager when Kenya gained independence, and his career in the civil service began under very different political and economic circumstances in the late 1970s. He had seen the fortunes of Kenyan industries rise and fall and had presided over the transference of the duties of the state to the private sector. While younger civil servants in other sectors spoke of the possibilities for public-private partnerships with great excitement and perceived themselves as agents of positive structural change, Kariuki's viewed these changes with less enthusiasm and spoke of Kenya as a nation in need of outside assistance.

TECHNICAL PROFESSIONALS

While professional labor advocates worked to highlight (and correct) aspects of floriculture they deemed blatantly exploitative and establish careers in politics or international civil society, technical professionals worked to take advantage of the positive externalities (Gallagher and Zarsky 2007) created by this industry. Working in floriculture could provide exposure to foreign cultures and international business partners, lucrative business opportunities, and a chance to take part in the development of state-of-the-art agronomic techniques and technologies. The technical professionals that I met in Naivasha rarely expressed overt political ambitions. Instead, they spoke at length about the potential, or lack thereof, for upward mobility within the agricultural sector and a desire for greater recognition of their training and skills. They avoided the controversial strategies of professional labor advocates and focused instead on engaging very seriously in technical and entrepreneurial endeavors that would enhance their professional reputations and secure their financial futures. Despite their aversion to politics, they also aspired to make floriculture work for Kenya. As technocrats, they viewed their professional performances as a means of demonstrating a greater Kenyan capacity for development and self-governance.

The Kenyan flower industry has matured considerably over the last decade, and an increasing number of Kenyan universities and colleges now offer certificate and degree programs in horticulture. Many of the midlevel managers and supervisors that I encountered in Naivasha had specifically trained to work in the horticulture industry. These managers and supervisors expressed greater excitement over the nature of their work in floriculture and took advantage of every opportunity to enhance their professional development. Among the larger Naivasha flower farms, those that offered training opportunities for employees were considered the best companies in terms of working conditions. Training sessions ranged from seminars on procedures for testing water quality, to the types of gender sensitivity workshops that Tom organized, to seminars on the Lake Naivasha ecosystem. Even general laborers who had completed these training sessions often showed me the official notes or certificates they received for attendance as evidence of their specialized training and education on the job. Any additional skills and training received might also enhance the possibility of retaining their jobs in the face of persistent employment insecurity, and they took pride in their ability to seize whatever opportunities arose for self-development and professionalization.

These desires for technical training, self-professionalization, and international visibility were on display in November 2007 as I accompanied a team of black Kenyan farm managers while they completed a self-audit mandated by the National Environmental Management Authority (NEMA). In Kenya, auditing is pervasive in a growing number of sectors, including the civil service and on farms that supply fresh produce to global markets. Codes of ethics developed by retailers and auction houses in Europe have become the primary means by which Naivasha flower farms are held to specific labor and ecological standards. Depending on their markets, Naivasha flower farms may be audited four to five times a year by each supermarket that they supply, organizations that oversee special labeling initiatives such as fair trade, and national organizations like the Kenya Flower Council.

Scholars studying the advent and proliferation of "audit culture" argue that these codes of ethics are an extension of neoliberal political processes originating in the global North (Blowfield and Dolan 2008; Hughes 2004). Auditing arose in the world of finance as a way of demonstrating accountability and transparency; and over time, a checklist approach to systematically assessing performance using predetermined measures and indicators has become pervasive in global business, agriculture, education, and *governance* more generally. A rich body of research in anthropology and sociology examines the pervasiveness of audit culture in contemporary life (e.g., Power 1997; Shore and Wright 1999; Strathern 1997, 2000). Auditing is a disciplinary technology designed to change the ways that people behave in the workplace. The goal is to transform employees into managers who essentially govern themselves without supervision. Scholars question whether audit culture enhances performance and productivity or whether it creates an elaborate illusion of control and compliance, undermining and silencing productive forms of critique and reducing expertise and professional relations to "crude quantifiable and inspectable templates" (Shore 2008, 291). As audit technologies spread beyond the nation-state, they create new spaces, subjects, and forms of power (Shore and Wright 2015).

In 2007, the Kenyan state was adopting the form and spirit of the audit as a means of extending its regulatory authority in floriculture and in Naivasha. The white farm manager who granted me permission to attend this audit saw it as a relatively minor bureaucratic matter, a symbolic demonstration of compliance with Kenyan policy. He was confident that his efforts to comply with stringent codes of ethics imposed by European supermarkets would mean that the farm would easily meet the demands of the NEMA. For the black Kenyan professionals to whom this self-audit had been delegated, however, this was a much more meaningful task.

They took the *self* in this audit extremely seriously. By performing the audit, they were engaging in both self-regulation (in industrial terms) and self-governance (in personal terms). Behaving, in a sense, as co-opted agents of the state (Pigg 1992; Springer 2000), they were enforcing Kenya's laws and ensuring the safety of Kenyan workers and the local environment. In doing so, they assumed that their performance was being observed by both their peers and an *international* audience of retailers, consumer, and industry professionals. In proving their own technical prowess, these professionals saw themselves as demonstrating a Kenyan capacity for self-governance and their ability as a generation to hold both floriculture and Kenyan institutions accountable to international standards.

The NEMA self-audit provides a glimpse into how black Kenyan professionals exercise agency within (and become subjects of) both "audit culture" and "good governance" discourses that challenge members of an emergent African middle class to "act as the democratizers of their societies" (Abrahamsen 2000, 63). Although the team was given a general inspection checklist, they did not see this process as undermining the value of their labor, nor did they view it as a problematic extension of European regulatory power into Kenyan lives and spaces. They viewed the audit as a way for them to (re)establish *Kenyan* control over the direction of development in this nerve center and to (re)center the state as the locus of regulatory authority in this place.

The Art of the Self-Audit: Closing Loopholes

I report to Kiboko Farm in the early morning. The guard at the front gate contacts the general manager on a handheld radio to verify my permission to enter, and a second guard escorts me to the managerial offices at the rear of the farm. We walk between the neat rows of greenhouses, each door marked with a set of regulations and a board indicating when the last round of pesticides was applied. Workers walk quietly in and out of greenhouses and bend to pick roses behind translucent plastic walls.

My escort leaves me with Henry, the farm's environment and health supervisor, who is uncharacteristically nervous and distracted. He pulls off his red cap, a gift from a chemical salesman that advertises a brand name fungicide, and scratches the top of his head. "They've just called from the road. They're running late. We won't get started as early as I would have liked." The other two members of the audit team have been delayed by car troubles en route from Nairobi. Paul, a manager at one of the company's other flower farming locations, and Alice, a supervisor at the company's airport packhouse facility, might not arrive for another hour yet. "I'm concerned about time," says Henry. "I really want to have time afterward to discuss the observations with the auditors. Otherwise, they just rush through, and you don't learn from the process."

Henry, thirty-one, has worked for Kiboko's parent company for three years. Born in the Kajaido District, he holds a university degree in agriculture from a prestigious public Kenyan institution. In separate conversations, he has told me that he enjoys working for the company, which he views as one of the best in Kenya, but he "would leave in a minute for a position with higher pay." He would like to retrain in an environmental field so that he can be more competitive on the job market. He sees the training opportunities in floriculture as unique among Kenyan industries. He explains, "You know, in Kenya, they don't care if you've trained. Anyone can compete for the job. But that is one thing that is really exceptional about [this company]. They are known for valuing training. We have the best training programs for workers." He acknowledges that "[the farm directors] mainly do this [the training] for auditing purposes, but it's one of the reasons that this farm is known for being so good compared to the others."

Despite his desire for higher pay and his recognition that the on-farm training sessions are "mainly organized for auditing purposes," Henry clearly takes great pride in his work on Kiboko Farm. Today's review will be an assessment of his performance as much as it will be an audit of the farm, and he is excited for the opportunity to learn from the process. A few months ago, he participated in the same self-audit at one of the company's other locations, an experience that he describes with great enthusiasm. He explains, "It was just brilliant! They really performed well. It was so impressive. Absolutely brilliant." He firmly believes that code-based regulations have led to important improvements, and he sees himself as helping improve them further. He explains, "These codes, they really improve conditions for workers and force the farms to respect the environment. . . . But even in the codes, there are loopholes. We need better government regulation and oversight by the Kenya Flower Council to fix these. The NEMA audit is not perfect, but it gives us a chance to close some of these kinds of loopholes."

Henry and his colleagues have been trained as auditors by several international agencies, including Checkmate International, Bureau Veritas Quality International, and Societe Generale de Surveillance. They have also completed a course for internal auditors organized by the Fresh Produce Exporters Association of Kenya. Henry proudly displays framed certificates from these and myriad other training programs on the wall above his desk. Ultimately, however, he thinks that these procedures should be the responsibility of the Kenyan state in partnership with the Kenya Flower Council. Performing the NEMA self-audit with serious attention to detail and a commitment to compliance will help demonstrate the increased capacity of Kenyan institutions to carry out these functions.

While we wait for the rest of the auditing team to arrive, Henry and I attend a training session for select managers and health and safety supervisors. The farm has recently switched to a new company that will be testing its water samples. Henry explains that the former contractor "became unreliable," which in this case serves as a euphemism for "corrupt." He explains, "You know, after a while, we realized that their reports could not be verified. They just say, 'Oh, it's from [Kiboko Farm], it's usually like this.' They were just sending us reports and not testing the new samples." Today, two representatives from the water-testing company, both black Kenyan professionals with higher degrees in chemistry, have come to train farm employees to take test samples properly. The training session offers Henry and his colleagues a chance to both enhance their technical knowledge and help expunge corruption from the testing process.

Following their presentation, members of the audience pepper the testing company's technicians with an impressive number of questions that reveal their frustration with inaccuracies and inconsistencies in the sampling process. A woman asks, "With the former company, we were told to collect different volumes of water each time. How much do you need to get an accurate result? We really need to standardize these procedures." Another woman asks, "We received these results that tell us what is in the water, but we receive no assistance in interpreting them. Will you advise us on how to proceed if you detect something? How do I correct the problem?" This is greeted with a chorus of "ayes" from the audience. A young man raises his hand and asks, "How do weather changes affect the sample? It seems that we should be aware of rain and temperature to ensure that the sample is accurate. How do we make these adjustments?" A commissary supervisor chimes in from the back of the room, "We take weekly samples of drinking water, but it takes too long to get the results. If these samples do not meet standards, how can we detect this more quickly so that we find a solution? We have been having so many problems with this." A man in a lab coat at the back of the room adds, "Shouldn't our sample bottles be opaque so that the light doesn't affect them? You've given us only clear bottles, which will only work if we place them in cool boxes. Can we have some of these?" An older woman shakes her head in conclusion: "We have not been following proper procedures for sampling. There is an extremely high potential for errors. We must correct this." The company representatives promise a further training session to address these concerns.

Henry shakes his head. "This training was really fabulous. These are the problems NEMA will help us correct. The audits require water samples to be taken, but there is no verification of the accuracy of the results. We discovered this problem with the documentation from the lab in the last self-audit. We've been so frustrated by this issue. Now we can develop strict procedures for sampling, and we can be sure that the lab will be inspected."

During this and other on-farm training seminars and sessions that I attended, both educators and attendees spoke frankly about the need for improvement in industrial practices. Provocative issues arose frequently, especially during question-and-answer sessions. Dialogue often focused on “taking responsibility” for their actions on and off the farm and working diligently to make the industry more responsive to Kenyan needs. Upper-level management may have created these training sessions mainly to comply with code-based standards, but they have become an important arena in which black Kenyan professionals work to ensure that rules are actually enforced. Henry and his colleagues are also driven by a desire to be taken seriously as technical professionals with the capacity and skills necessary to make these farms compliant with both international and Kenyan law.

Henry’s mobile phone rings. The rest of the audit team has arrived at the farm gate. The colleagues greet each other with handshakes and hellos. Paul, the lead auditor, laughs when we are introduced. “We’re really going to put this guy to the task!” he exclaims, gesturing in Henry’s direction. “But seriously, I’m really eager to see what kinds of procedures they have in place here. He really gave us hell last month, and now it’s our turn.” Henry smiles shyly and ushers us into his office to review the documents relevant to the audit.

The process focuses mainly on the recommendations and “mitigation measures” resulting from the farm’s 2006 audit. Has the farm made these adjustments, or do they have a time frame in place for doing so? After discussing these matters, we complete a systematic tour of the various sections of the farm—the packhouse, the areas where chemicals and fertilizers are stored, the farm’s wetland and other waste-disposal sites, the chemical spray-off areas, and the workshop where farm equipment is fabricated (figure 3.1). In each of these locations, the auditors work from a checklist. They verify that facilities are clean, exits are marked, signage explaining hazards and emergency procedures is present, equipment is in working condition, and workers are wearing proper protective equipment and are aware of farm safety protocols. Throughout the audit, they ask exacting questions of Henry, who gamely provides answers or promises to provide the necessary information shortly.

The team focuses most closely on the labeling of dangers and the measures in place to reduce on-farm energy consumption. The farm receives negative strikes for using energy-intensive incandescent bulbs to speed the drying of personal protective equipment in the sprayers’ changing room, for the improper separation of waste in the packhouse (some plastic was found in the “Combustibles” bin), and for failing to accurately post the decibel level in the engine room. Moreover, the grease separator installed in the pipe leading from the commissary may not be functioning properly. “Aye, man, KFC [the Kenya Flower Council] will really get you for that one,” warns Paul in a serious tone. Henry calls a *fundi* (carpenter or handyman) to repair the problem. Overall, the team seems impressed by the orderly nature of the

FIGURE 3.1 The audit team inspects the farm's outdoor facilities. An employee explains how the farm disposes of cuttings, the waste stems left over after the harvest and packing process.

farm, especially the facility's well-maintained chemical storage areas and its artificial wetland, which is used to filter wastewater discharged to the lake. Henry's explanation of these technologies produces a chorus of "wows" and praise for the farmworkers who maintain these facilities.

The latter portion of the audit checklist deals almost exclusively with "adequate documentation." After touring the farm, the team retires to Henry's office to review paperwork—procedure manuals, operating permits, certificates on file from independent auditing bodies, lists of the training programs provided for workers, the farm's energy audit, the results of chemical analyses conducted on the farm's effluent, a contractor-waste-collection log detailing the pounds of plastic sold to a subsidiary company, and so on. The farm maintains a log for nearly everything that can be tracked and quantified, every energetic input (whether human or natural), and every waste output. These materials take the team hours to review.

Having spent time among professional labor advocates who speak constantly of "big picture" issues, such as wages, off-farm living conditions for farmworkers, and health care concerns, I am struck by the auditors' extremely serious attention to technical minutiae. However, this is their professional domain, and to some extent the farm has become so hypercompliant with Kenyan and international standards (at least in form, if not in substance) that, within the framework of the audit, only minutiae remain to be corrected. As Henry has said, this is an exercise in closing loopholes, and the auditing team approaches this task with a bureaucratic seriousness of purpose. This does not mean, however, that technical professionals are lulled into believing that this kind of audit is enough to make floriculture fair in a broader sense.

Over lunch at the farm commissary, the auditors and I discuss labor politics in floriculture. The packhouse technical manager, who has just joined us, entertains us with a story of an incident that he observed in 2003. "You know, this farm has a reputation among the *wazungu* as being the worst [to manage] because of the freedom that [the farm's owner] gave to workers." He continues: "When they were having all these strikes and there was so much unrest, [the owner] came from the UK to speak to the workforce. He really thrashed them, [saying] that they were going to make him shut down the farm. This I will never forget." He shakes his head, beginning to laugh. "They had a kind of microphone there for workers who wanted to make speeches or maybe ask questions. One old woman came to the microphone." He mimics her hunched back and warbling voice. "She just said, 'You shut it down, [calling the farm owner by his first name]. You're running around with your mineral water, and we're here working. You just shut it down.'" The auditing team laughs uproariously, and he continues: "The workers just started cheering, and then [the owner] began screaming, 'I'm out here looking for markets for you and giving you jobs, and this is how you treat me?' I can never forget it." The auditing team is now in stitches, laughing and wiping away tears.

Paul shakes his head and says, "Aye, they can say things even we [as managers] can't." The rest of the team agrees. Henry argues that workers at this farm prefer their welfare associations to the union, which "does nothing and just takes their dues." At least on this farm, it is the responsibility of workers to advocate for their rights, and it is "for the government" to make necessary changes in law that will improve wages and address these issues that are beyond the audit team's authority and expertise. In the meantime, these particular technical professionals have dedicated themselves to regulating the on-farm working environment and maximizing the power and authority given to them by the self-audit procedure. I leave the team poring over documentation at the end of a long day. Henry takes a short break to walk me to the buses waiting to carry workers back to town. He apologizes for the need to rush back to the team: "I have so many questions to ask them before they leave, so that I can discover how to implement these changes. And I will need to report to [the farm's general manager] tomorrow." While I wait in line for transport, I see him run back down the path toward his office and his chosen means of making floriculture work for Kenya (and for himself) by closing loopholes and, in the absence of a satisfying wage, taking advantage of every available opportunity to increase his knowledge and demonstrate his expertise.

These technical professionals were certainly aware of the structural conditions that make cut flower farming in Kenya profitable, but they also hoped that the future of the industry would not depend on inexpensive labor and the equatorial sun alone. To a certain extent, the future of Kenyan floriculture is also contingent on compliance with international law, greater efficiency in the use of natural resources and energy, and the development of a skilled labor force better qualified to enact these changes and devise better operating procedures and technologies. Growing flowers might remain more cost-effective in Kenya, as opposed to, say, Ethiopia, if a professional class continues to discipline the industry by improving its technical efficiency and helping devise low-cost ways of meeting the basic needs of the workforce (if not their demands for higher wages).

While their colleagues with political ambitions used their labor in floriculture to increase their wealth in people (Guyer 1995), many technical professionals relished the opportunity to practice their particular craft. They desired wages and job opportunities requisite with their level of education and expertise, and they worked to establish a meritocracy that would be at least partially antithetical to the patron-client system that their colleagues with political ambitions used to enhance their power and influence. For Henry, closing loopholes meant holding the flower industry accountable to exacting standards that would prevent the base exploitation of Kenyan workers and environments. However, it also meant extending the power and regulatory oversight of an educated Kenyan middle class to additional spaces and institutions, including subsidiary businesses like the laboratories that contracted with farms to test water samples. Henry and his colleagues would ensure that these businesses would also be held to international standards for reliability and accuracy.

Each of the black Kenyan professionals profiled here is acutely aware of the privileges and the pitfalls presented by the exposure that floriculture offers. In a positive sense, *exposure* means the opportunity to accumulate personal wealth, cultivate lucrative relationships, and (ideally) generate enough power and influence to enact structural change. However, this exposure also makes them vulnerable in the sense that they become subject to both "audit culture" and development discourses that hold them responsible as a class for democratizing and governing Kenya. Their job performance is closely scrutinized by an international audience looking for signs of corruption, by employers looking for signs of efficiency and accountability, and by a general Kenyan populace looking for signs that they are fairly redistributing the wealth concentrated in this industry. However, middle -class actors also map their own agendas onto the process of governing social and environmental relations on these farms. Their management practices remain deeply imbricated in Kenyan forms of relational dependency and sociopolitical practice, and they work diligently to close the loopholes inherent in industrial self-regulation by advocating stronger Kenyan laws and institutions.

Professional labor advocates view floriculture as a venue for exposing inequalities and inducing social change. However, they also see their work as a launching point for careers in politics or the NGO sector. They describe themselves as moral economic intermediaries fighting to make floriculture more responsive to Kenyan needs and desires. Technical professionals embrace the opportunity to become experts and to further their training and education. This expertise could give them power over their politically influential peers in an imagined future, glimpsed through the institution of the audit, when scientific techniques and data collection could become more central to Kenyan social and environmental policy. Despite their focus on perfecting the technical aspects of their professional performance, they share a commitment to protecting Kenyan workers and resources from exploitation.

Like Dennis, these middle-class black professionals view Naivasha as a nerve center, a place where they can strategically agitate for structural change and innervate their aspirations for personal, regional, and national development. As they do so, they often work closely with the civil servants whose perspectives and experiences I turn to next.

CHAPTER FOUR

Floriculture and the State

Building and Branding Kenya

In 1992, future Nobel laureate Wangari Maathai clung to the stump of a freshly cut indigenous tree in a dramatic attempt to halt the clearing of eighty acres of land near Nairobi for the construction of a rose farm. At Maathai's side were a number of other demonstrators who had gathered to protest this radical change in the local landscape. Their act of resistance ended abruptly when army personnel arrived to forcibly remove them from the premises. In justifying this use of military intervention, Philip Leakey, who was then the Kenyan minister for environment and natural resources, announced, "The rose[s] will be better for the country than the few shrubs that were on the farm" (Cege 1993).

Floriculture has always enjoyed a close relationship with the Kenyan state. Since the 1990s, export horticulture has been one of Kenya's top four sources of foreign exchange. The top three earners fluctuate, and they include, variously, tea, tourism, horticulture, and remittances from Kenyans living abroad. The lion's share of the foreign exchange generated by Kenyan horticulture comes from the sale of cut flowers. Despite persistent accusations that flower growers "may be shifting profits to other jurisdictions to dodge Kenyan tax" (Lawrence 2011), the state derives significant revenues from taxes and fees paid by Kenya's top flower-producing companies. Many prominent members of the Kenyan political class are also farm investors or owners, and the state has long promoted the industry as a cornerstone of Kenyan development. As Wangari Maathai discovered in 1992, the government views protecting the interests of the floriculture sector as a matter of national security.

Despite this close relationship, however, development economists and growers often cite the *lack* of formal government intervention and oversight in floriculture as a key element in the sector's success. Operating a successful flower farm in Kenya means cultivating the right relationships with powerful figures in politics while simultaneously bypassing what historian Frederick Cooper (2002) calls the Kenyan "gatekeeper state." To a large extent, the post-colonial Kenyan state derives its power and influence from controlling the "gate" that stands between Kenya and the global economy—through tariffs, agricultural marketing boards, and other mechanisms that allow it to keep a tight hold on the most lucrative flows of goods and capital in and out of the country. While Kenya's other major cash crops—tea, coffee, pyrethrum, and cereals—are subject to laws that assign the state a significant role in pricing and distribution, export horticultural products are not subject to similar state controls. In Kenya, an era of agricultural parastatals and cooperatives (Bates 1989) has partially given way to one of vertically integrated, self-regulating corporate enterprises—at least in the case of floriculture.

When I first began working in Naivasha in 2004, flower growers expressed a lack of confidence in the state's ability to channel monies collected as taxes and fees into the maintenance of local infrastructure, let alone national development. In the words of one farm manager in the Lake Naivasha area, "We'd love to cooperate with the Kenyan government, but the level of corruption is such that it never works. We do pay taxes—because we have to or it doesn't look good with consumers—but we never see any returns on those investments. Any money invested in Kenya that way just disappears." In the Naivasha area, growers collectively funded repairs to the road that carries their products to the Nairobi airport, partnered with NGOs to provide limited social services to farmworkers, and stockpiled fuel and generators so that they could continue to operate if and when the central power grid failed.

When I returned to Naivasha again in 2007, I found that a shift had occurred in the way that both flower growers and Kenyan officials viewed the potential relationship between this industry and the state. Frustrated talk of government corruption and complaints that growers hide profits to avoid taxation had given way to enthusiastic discussions of strategic public-private partnerships for building the capacity of both the industry and the Kenyan state. The managing director for one of Naivasha's largest farms provided a pithy summary of this new and very different attitude among growers: "We've realized that we can't take on all of the responsibilities of developing Kenya, providing services to workers, building infrastructure. The consumers have asked us to take on all of these things, but these things have to be the responsibility of the government. We have to focus on growing flowers. That's our business. But we can work on these other things in partnership with the government."

In 2007, flower growers were willing to sacrifice some of their carefully cultivated sectoral self-sufficiency if the state would agree to perform some critical functions on the industry's behalf. Kenya was transitioning from a "rollback" phase of neoliberalism focused on the strategic dismantling of the state, to a "creative," or "rollout," phase focused on the strategic reconstruction of the state (Peck and Tickell 2002). During the rollback phase of neoliberalism, elaborate corporate social (and environmental) responsibility (CSR) programs took the place of state-run social and environmental welfare services. Initially, this suited flower growers because it allowed them to *self*-regulate, giving them the flexibility to develop programs that met ethical standards that would not significantly compromise their profits.[1]

By 2007, however, many of the owners of Kenya's largest flower farms had grown dissatisfied with self-regulation for three reasons. First, large farms were expected to engage in significant and demonstrable CSR programs; but, they complained, many small and midsize farms were not expected to do so. According to Kenya's most influential flower companies, these smaller, noncompliant farms created a bad image of the industry that essentially tainted consumer perceptions and undermined the companies' CSR efforts. Second, the proliferation of audit culture meant that CSR programs were not really that flexible for growers; they were increasingly required to provide services and upgrade farm infrastructure in a manner that compromised their economic viability. Third, CSR programs did little to help them protect the natural resources on which their now-considerable investments depended; they were especially concerned about the availability and quality of water. As more flower farms "blossomed" in the Naivasha area, lake levels fell, and growers had no real mechanism for protecting their rights to a continued supply of freshwater. These concerns about the industry's image, the rising costs of self-regulation, and declining water levels caused flower growers to seriously rethink their opposition to state-led regulation. By 2007, flower growers were keenly interested in transferring the responsibility for worker and environmental welfare back to the Kenyan state. In order for this to be possible, however, public-sector institutions and functions that had been rolled back during structural adjustment would need to be rolled out again, in ways that made sense within a neoliberal framework. In this context, major growers became increasingly open to the (re)construction of state authority in Naivasha, provided they could exercise significant control over the process by which new regulations were developed and implemented.

The perspectives of elected officials, civil servants, and flower growers involved in three collaborative initiatives under way in Kenya in 2007 and

2008 demonstrate the complex and evolving relationship between floriculture and the Kenyan state. These three initiatives entailed the development of a cohesive "Brand Kenya" marketing strategy that would appeal to foreign investors, the creation of the "Grown under the Sun" campaign designed to market Kenyan flowers as less carbon-intensive than those grown in Europe, and the emergence of a new a public-private partnership for regulating water resources in Naivasha. Each provides insight into how the creative phase of neoliberalism (Peck and Tickell 2002) works as a process, *who* takes part in this process, and the meanings and significance that they assign to the collaborative project of (re)constructing state power in contemporary Kenya.

Anthropologists understand the "state" not as a fixed entity or structure but as something that is always in flux, always in the making (e.g., Gupta 1995; Sivaramakrishnan 1999). Statemaking involves many agents who engage in everyday practices that are, in effect, an exercise of state power. These agents include civil servants and elected officials, but other actors (e.g., flower farm owners involved in public-private partnerships) may also act in this capacity. These agents do not merely exercise the will of the state. As they engage in the work of governing, they interpret, negotiate, make, and remake the state in collaboration with those whom they seek to govern (Pigg 1992; Donham 1999; Springer 2000). Through their participation in these initiatives, the actors who are the subject of this chapter played important roles in (re)making the contemporary Kenyan state and strategically crafting an appealing national image meant to be embraced by both Kenyans and international investors.

Kenyan flower growers felt certain that, by playing an active role in the (re)construction of some forms of state power, they could help curb its tendencies toward corruption and (re)build institutions that would help them address ethical concerns while preserving a business-friendly operating environment. State officials viewed the opportunity to reestablish regulatory authority in Naivasha with great enthusiasm, because this would help them "brand" Kenya as a well-governed and lucrative site for investment. In doing so, however, they ultimately hoped to attract forms of investment that would move Kenya *beyond* its dependence on floriculture. Although state agents and flower growers draw on neoliberal logics and tools of governance to actualize their aspirations, they also see their actions as part of an ongoing postcolonial project of nation building in Kenya. Contemporary statemaking in Naivasha is motivated by both neoliberal logics and enduring postcolonial desires for self-governance, global importance, and greater gatekeeping over profits generated on Kenyan soil. As a nerve center, Naivasha has become central to these experiments in (re)constructing the relationship between state and corporate power in Kenya.

BRANDING KENYA

In May 2008, I visit the Nairobi offices of the Kenya Flower Council (KFC) to interview Naomi, one of the organization's senior employees. Founded in 1996, the council is a member-based organization that represents the interests of about 70 percent of Kenyan flower farms. The council lobbies on behalf of growers at home and abroad and administers a certification scheme that allows growers to qualify as KFC silver-level producers or KFC gold-level producers by complying with a lengthy set of operating standards. Naomi invites me to sit in the chair across from her desk, which is covered in neat stacks of files and papers. She sets aside her mobile phone and offers me a warm smile. "I was eager to meet with you," she begins. "This is a critical time in the history of Kenya. We're breaking out of a difficult period of governance—[she hesitates] at least economically. We're dealing with the [December 2007] election and its aftermath, the negotiation of the Economic Partnership Agreement, the climate change debate, and the development of a national environmental policy. All of these things are happening at once."

In one sentence, Naomi highlights several critical events and processes that made Kenyan flower growers increasingly aware of the limits of self-regulation and self-sufficiency in this historical moment. When postelection violence spread to Naivasha in January 2008, as discussed in chapter 1, thousands of ethnic minority farmworkers were displaced, more than twenty-three local residents were killed, and property worth millions of shillings was destroyed. The Kenyan military intervened after three days of fighting, and growers managed to avoid a major production crisis immediately before Valentine's Day. However, this period of intense tension and violence reminded growers of their dependence on Kenya's political stability and of the limits of their self-sufficiency when it came to security issues. The political crisis also tarnished Kenya's national image abroad.

In an attempt to reassure investors and remind the world of Kenya's potential, the government announced plans to relaunch a Brand Kenya campaign that began with much fanfare in early 2007 but then languished as officials focused on the national election. A reconstituted Brand Kenya Board overseen by the Ministry of Information and Communication declared via its website the visionary goal of ensuring that "Kenya, 'the cradle of man,' would become a distinctly visible player in all global aspects."

The practice of nation branding evolved in part from early studies of the "country of origin effect" on consumer preferences. These studies suggested that consumers were more likely to buy goods manufactured in industrialized nations because of their positive perceptions of these countries and the tendency to equate development with quality and reliability (e.g., Wang and Lamb 1983). Early examples of nation-branding campaigns include the Café de Colombia (Colombian coffee) label launched in 1981, which sought to reposition Colombia as a producer of fine coffee, and Scotland the Brand, a joint venture between government and industry launched in 1994 to promote Scottish trade and tourism (Jaffee and Nebenzahl 2001). In launching Brand Kenya, the nation joined a long list of postcolonial, postsocialist, and postindustrial states that were experimenting with nation branding, including South Africa, India, Estonia, Poland, Spain, and Finland.[2]

In 2008, the Brand Kenya Board's website described Kenya as the home of phenomenal wildlife, elite runners, and several successful export crops, including tea, coffee, and horticulture. A stunning image of the Nairobi skyline slowly transitioned into a photo of the Kenyan national soccer team embracing after a successful goal. Additional pages described Kenya's "crown jewels" in greater detail, and web links directed visitors to the separate websites of some of Kenya's most lucrative brand names, including Kenyan Airways, Kenyan Coffee, and East African Breweries. Since then, the website has become more sophisticated. The 2017 version of the homepage declares that Kenya is "bursting with generosity, rewarding beyond imagination." A short video, titled *Think Future, Think Kenya,* features a female narrator who speaks as the voice of the nation. Over triumphant music, she declares, "I am one of the fastest-growing economies in Africa. My natural resources are some of the most sought after in the world. My people are talented and entrepreneurial. I am home to some of Africa's most attractive trade and investment opportunities. . . . I am Kenya." A web page offering specific tips on "where to invest in Kenya" describes government-led projects in transport, energy, agriculture, real estate, tourism, water supply, health, education, manufacturing, and finance.

Although greater internal cohesion is a stated goal of Kenya's nation-branding initiative, the main objective is to cultivate positive perceptions of Kenya in international circles. Ishita Sinha Roy argues that "nation branding is a strategic act to secure ideological terrain in the global/national cultural imaginary" (2007, 572). This campaign allows Kenya to court the attention of wealthy *individuals*—high-end tourists or, more importantly, entrepreneurs looking for investment opportunities in Africa. In terms of geopolitical agency, this is a significant departure from a development strategy that requires Kenya to lobby Western nation-states for access to traditional forms of aid. These funds also come without the patronizing stipulations placed on aid money and development loans (e.g., family planning initiatives, good governance audits, and so on), and they allow the Kenyan political class to cultivate lucrative business relationships that directly enrich their patronage networks.

Nation branding also holds discursive appeal for the postcolonial state because of what branders call its "aspirational element," which moves Kenya away from narratives of instability and corruption that are pervasive in popular depictions of Africa. Following a critical discursive analysis of the Brand Estonia campaign, Sue Curry Jansen argues, "Nation branding does not just selectively distill and valorize what is. It is a dynamic process that incorporates a vision of a new reality. . . . As part of the branding process, government and corporate sponsors are expected to commit public and private resources to creating this new reality, which is designed to further amplify the nation's marketable qualities" (2008, 122). Naomi hopes that her public relations activities on behalf of the KFC will help create a positive new national image, for which the state can then be held accountable. In a sense, Brand Kenya presumes that the commercial imagination will eventually stoke the political imagination.

While Brand Kenya promoted a vision of the nation as commercially successful and wealthy in terms of its human and natural resources, state officials also struggled to preserve Kenya's status as a relatively poor nation in need of special trade concessions. Under the terms of the Lomé Convention, which expired in January 2008, Kenya was listed as a "least-developed country," and its exports were not subject to tariffs in Europe. In June 2000, the Lomé Convention was replaced with the Cotonou Agreement, which attempted to reconcile trade relations between the European Union (EU) and the African, Caribbean, and Pacific Group of States with the free trade stipulations encouraged by the World Trade Organization. Under the Cotonou Agreement, signatory nations are required to negotiate reciprocal economic partnership agreements with EU member states.[3] If Kenya wanted to maintain its duty-free exports, it would have to eliminate all duties on imports from EU countries. Countries designated least-developed countries by the United Nations would retain the ability to export to the EU duty-free and quota-free. However, Kenya no longer appeared on this list. If some agreement was not reached soon, flower growers would face an 8.5 percent import tariff, and green beans would be subject to a 10.1 percent duty (Mugambi 2007a, 2007b). Growers had been anxious about these negotiations for years in advance of the Lomé Convention expiration date.[4]

Amid fears that tariffs would significantly reduce their profits, growers were also concerned that new forms of regulation would considerably increase their operating costs. In 2006, Kenya's Ministry of Environment and Mineral Resources initiated the process of drafting, through a "participatory and consultative process," a new National Environmental Policy Act (Republic of Kenya 2013).[5] This would replace the 1999 Environmental Management and Coordination Act, Kenya's first attempt at a national-level environmental legal framework. In 2008, flower growers were hopeful that a new environmental policy would help them gain better control over water use in Naivasha and potentially penalize growers who did not comply the with "best practices" required by retailers. However, they were also concerned about the cost of compliance with new environmental regulations. They planned to play a central role in the "participatory and consultative process" that would inform the new policy. Although they preferred industrial self-regulation, they realized that they could neither monitor resource use nor make best practices universal without the help of the state.

Although Naomi did not mention this, Kenyan growers were also preoccupied by the emergence of the Ethiopian flower industry, which had the full support of the Ethiopian state and had begun to attract considerable foreign investment. Growers feared that Ethiopian suppliers might be able to, at least temporarily, undercut their prices, especially if new environmental policies placed an additional financial burden on Kenyan producers. They needed a strong environmental policy to keep new entrants from establishing farms in the Naivasha area and tapping already scarce resources, but they also needed limits on the regulatory burden these policies would impose on existing farms.

Naomi and I continue to speak about the importance of the KFC and her day-to-day activities. Her answers to my questions are frank but carefully phrased and organized around prepared talking points. Midway through our time together, the phone rings and she excuses herself to answer it. After a brief conversation, she lays down the receiver. "That was the minister of foreign affairs. It looks as if I'm going to Japan next week," she says, rubbing her temples and paging quickly through her diary. "Frankly, the Japanese markets will probably never be a major source of sales for us; they have their own suppliers and we don't grow the desired varieties. . . . But the minister is being very insistent." She calls her assistant to make the necessary travel arrangements and then continues: "With this new Brand Kenya initiative, the government insists that we represent the nation in all of these global venues. I tried to explain that these aren't our markets and we'd prefer not to go to the expense, but he insists that Kenya must be present." She pages through her diary again and returns to our conversation. "We're really one of the few successful Kenyan enterprises, and the burden placed on us is a bit unfair. And expensive. I make six trips a year to Europe, and it's exhausting. The government should promote Kenya itself. But when the minister of foreign affairs calls, how can you say no?"

She closes her diary and reconsiders her initial response to the minister's request.

> I'm actually happy to do this. These are positive developments. With the Brand Kenya discussion, the government is accepting responsibility for fostering national trade, and I'm happy to play a role in protecting the image of the nation's industry. In return, the government is helping us to protect our interests. We'll never have 100 percent membership [of growers in the KFC], but right now our members control 70 percent of exports. We're within our rights as the largest stakeholder to make sure that others don't tarnish and jeopardize that reputation. We want membership in the KFC and compliance with our code of conduct to remain voluntary. It's critical that it not be seen as a trade barrier. This is why the government is key. We cannot make the regulations, but we play a key role in implementing them.

Without the state, Kenyan flower growers could not negotiate favorable terms of trade brokered on an enduring notion of national underdevelopment. They would also have difficulty building the image of a strong national brand that would help them compete with Ethiopian flower producers, who might undercut their prices. Without state assistance, KFC members could incentivize, but not really enforce, compliance with specific social and ecological standards. Anything they could do to help make these standards less voluntary would help KFC member farms protect their fragile reputation in the global market and reduce competition for valuable natural resources, especially water. The state could help growers market Kenyan flowers as the most environmentally and ethically viable option on the global market. In Naomi's words, growers realized that they needed the state, as a legitimate regulatory authority, to set policy and *make* regulations. However, they intended to strategically *implement* these policies in ways that would serve their own interests.

From the point of view of the minister of foreign affairs, the Brand Kenya campaign helps the state remain at the center of Kenyan economic development and regain some of its gatekeeping power. As the manager of Kenya as a corporate brand (Anholt 2002), which includes several successful "sub-brands" (e.g., the Kenya Flower Council and Kenyan Airways), the state can exert influence over industries that depend on a positive national image for their success. Brand Kenya is a marketing campaign, but it is also one facet of an ongoing nation-building project centered on collective aspirations for Kenya to become a regional and global economic leader. The success of these sub-brands allows the state to take credit, whether or not it is due, for fostering the most successful forms of enterprise on Kenyan soil. As the manager of a "corporate brand," the Kenyan state can also delegate some of its diplomatic functions to the floriculture industry. If the minister of foreign affairs asks, how can Naomi say no?

GROWN UNDER THE SUN

As Naomi noted, the climate change debate in Europe and the United Kingdom also posed a threat to the Kenyan horticulture industry in 2007. This issue dominated many of my conversations with Kenyan growers. Having finally managed to convince consumers that buying Kenyan roses can be an ethical practice, they were now faced with the growing concern that the industry contributes recklessly to global warming. The success of one extremely successful Brand Kenya subcampaign—a strategic coproduction of the Kenya Flower Council and the Kenyan state, designed to combat the threat to the industry posed by growing concerns about climate change—reveals the value of branding campaigns to both the industry and the state.

On July 2, 2007, at the Royal Agricultural Show in London, the Kenyan High Commission unveiled a new campaign for marketing the country's fresh horticultural products in the United Kingdom. Under this campaign, Kenyan exports would be marked with a prominent yellow label reading "Grown under the Sun." This new label referenced much more than the equatorial Kenyan sunshine. This was an explicit attempt to shift the grounds of the debate in the United Kingdom about "food miles," a measure of the distance that food travels from farm to market. Tim Lang, a professor of food policy at London's City University, coined the term *food miles* in 1992 as a way "to say to ordinary people—wherever you are in the world—'think where your food comes from'" (Lang quoted in an interview with Adams 2008). Amid growing consumer concerns about global climate change, Tesco, the largest UK supermarket chain, announced plans in early 2007 to begin labeling all air-freighted produce with a small airplane logo. This would theoretically allow consumers to make informed product choices and exercise some control over their personal contribution to global warming.

Tesco also expressed a desire to source more products locally over time, especially if the airplane logo led to declining sales in air-freighted produce. The airplane logo would serve as a first step toward developing a more complicated labeling system using "food miles" to flag products with larger "carbon footprints."

Just before my arrival in Kenya, a representative from Tesco had given a presentation on the new food-miles-labeling scheme to Kenya Flower Council members. While Kenyan growers were supportive of labels that highlighted their compliance with voluntary regulatory schemes and the positive development impacts of the industry, they viewed Tesco's airplane label as a thinly veiled nontariff trade barrier designed to protect European producers at the expense of African growers. Kenyan flower growers and the Kenyan state immediately initiated a coordinated effort to stop this newest label, pointing out that food miles alone were a misleading and problematic index of a product's true carbon footprint.

The largest Kenyan flower firm commissioned a study comparing the carbon footprints of two hypothetical roses, one grown "under the sun" in a Kenyan greenhouse and one grown in an artificially heated and lighted greenhouse in the Netherlands. The study was conducted by Adrian Williams, a research scientist affiliated with Cranfield University in the United Kingdom, who specializes in environmental lifecycle analysis, a method used to "quantify all the resources used and emissions to the environment that occur in the production of a commodity" (2007, 1). Using this approach, Williams compared the carbon dioxide emissions associated with the production and delivery of twelve thousand cut roses grown on a Naivasha flower farm with roses grown on a farm in southern Holland. According to his calculations, carbon dioxide emissions associated with the Dutch farm were 5.8 times larger than those associated with the Kenyan farm. After including other greenhouse gases, notably methane and nitrous oxide, Williams estimated that the Dutch farm's emissions where six times larger in terms of their global warming potential. He attributed these differences to the use of natural gas and electricity to artificially heat Dutch greenhouses. In his final report, which was not subject to peer review, Williams cautioned that, owing to "uncertainties" inherent in the analysis, his calculations were accurate to within a +/–30 percent margin of error. Even with this considerable margin of error, the study made the point that food miles alone constitute an oversimplistic measure of a product's overall carbon footprint.

Williams's conclusion that the Dutch rose has a carbon footprint six times that of a Kenyan rose formed the central message of the Grown under the Sun campaign. However, Kenyan growers also insisted that carbon emissions should be measured against the livelihood benefits of horticulture. As a Kenyan High Commission press release put it, "Isn't there a case anyway for justifying the import of fresh produce from Africa because it provides a sustainable income for at least one million workers on the continent?" At the Royal Agricultural Show, the Kenyan minister of agriculture asked participants to consider a central question that he deemed a matter of Kenyan national security: "Are food miles fair miles?"

Although agents of the Kenyan state took center stage during the unveiling of the Grown under the Sun campaign at the Royal Agricultural Show, the influence of the flower industry in developing and circulating this strategic intervention in the food miles discourse was clear during my conversations with KFC members. An interview with a senior-level manager from one of Kenya's largest horticulture firms highlights the role played by the industry in devising the content of this marketing campaign.

In early December 2007, I take the City Hopper bus from Nairobi City Center to the business offices of one of Kenya's largest flower and vegetable producers. The offices lie on the outskirts of Nairobi in an upscale industrial park. Since I am early, I order a cup of tea at a nearby café that borders the Kenya Police Dog Training Facility. My fellow patrons and I sip our tea nervously as a wall of flame erupts on the opposite side of the fence. Someone yells, "Fire, fire, fire!" and the dogs bark loudly and incessantly. The uneasy juxtaposition of the café and the police facility reminds me of the contradictions inherent in neoliberal Kenyan governance. In contemporary Kenya, the state establishes legitimacy and authority by stimulating economic growth. Elected and appointed officials work diligently to attract foreign investment, foster tourism, and help Kenyan producers access international markets under favorable terms of trade. Initiatives like Brand Kenya are attractive to both investors and the general Kenyan public because they are rooted in the aspirational vision of Kenya as a peaceful, democratic exception to Africa's "failed" or authoritarian states, a place where middle-class Kenyans sip tea in cafés before heading in to the office. However, the state's ability to deploy dogs (or soldiers) against its own populace also underlies its legitimacy and authority. By strategically deploying violence, the state upholds its promise to provide a "stable and secure" operating environment for investors.

At the appointed time, I am ushered into the office of Mr. Stone, the man in charge of "all aspects of the overall business" for this particular company. His duties include overseeing production, maintaining shareholder interests, and ensuring the sustainable operation of the company. Stone first came to Kenya from the United Kingdom in 1978 out of what he calls a "fear of the unknown." Trained as a civil engineer, he worked on a major water supply project and was recruited, in 1982, by a colleague and friend who founded the company that currently employs Stone. He felt that there were "synergies between engineering and horticulture" because of the demand for irrigation systems and technologies, and he was excited to be a part of this new and potentially extremely lucrative Kenyan industry. Soon after I take my seat in his office, Stone announces that he can give me only thirty minutes of his time. Like many farm managers, he is wary of speaking with researchers, given the negative press that the industry has garnered, but he notes that these interviews are a critical opportunity to change the way the industry is viewed abroad. Following a few biographical questions, he begins to steer the direction of our conversation toward the topics that he finds most critical.

Stone reaches for an item leaning against the base of his desk lamp and hands it to me. "Look at this picture and tell me what you see," he says. I take the photograph, which has been printed from the internet and mounted on a piece of poster board. It is a satellite image of the earth taken from space. Instead of the usual brown and blue masses of land and sea, the image depicts a composite view of the earth at night. Europe and North America glitter with countless points of light, while most of the Southern Hemisphere is swathed in darkness. Breaking into a knowing half-smile, Mr. Stone leans back in his leather office chair and awaits my response. I study the baseball-card-sized image for a second and say, "Ah, I see. Africa is dark, while Europe is glowing."

He leans forward and takes the picture from my hand, "Yes, Europe is glowing, it's developed, it's massively carbon-intensive, and Africa is still dark. This is the point that we're trying to make. There are some flat-earthers out there who refuse to believe it, but man is obviously having an impact on the global climate. People are becoming aware of this at the moment, and the supermarkets are responding to this; but most of what is happening now is an underinformed, knee-jerk reaction." He runs his hand through his graying hair. "The debate about carbon is still an immature one. We don't know how many kilos of carbon really go into making a product. So you can't put this on a label just yet. And there should also be complementary studies on the developmental benefits of the industry. Europe benefited from its enormous carbon emissions; why limit development here?"

He opens his desk drawer and stows the photo in its proper place, ready to be handed to the next researcher or journalist to pass through his office. The most remarkable aspect of Mr. Stone's speech is its word-for-word similarity to conversations that I have had with several other Kenyan farm managers. Before meeting with Mr. Stone in Nairobi, I had seen reproductions of this photograph (or heard verbal descriptions of it—"If you look at the earth from space at night . . .") in numerous farm offices in Naivasha. I suspect that Mr. Stone may be the original author of these talking points, the first person to suggest that this photograph might serve as a useful prop. What I am witnessing is a remarkably coordinated response on the part of Kenyan flower growers to the emerging debate about food miles and carbon-footprint labeling in the United Kingdom. As I leave his office, Stone suggests that I investigate the Grown under the Sun campaign's new website.

At an e-café in Nairobi, I settle in to explore the campaign's web page. The banner at the top of the home page is dominated by an image of two smiling Kenyan workers. A woman dressed in an orange smock cradles an armful of freshly cut stems. A man wearing a bright red jumpsuit and white leather gloves stands with a hoe resting on his left shoulder. Behind them stretches a field of blooms waiting to be cut. A logo superimposed over the left half of the image reads, "Grown under the Sun."

The elements of this image are, of course, carefully chosen. Both workers are wearing uniforms, signaling their status as professional employees of a larger company. The man wears the protective clothing required by the various codes of ethics that farms must follow in order to market their produce in Europe. The woman wears a gold band on her left hand. She is not a young, single woman but a provider who supports a family on her wages. The workers are also performing what might be viewed as gender appropriate jobs. The woman picks and packs the blooms, and the man prepares the soil for cultivation. Both workers are performing their tasks by hand, without the aid of machinery. No greenhouses or permanent structures grace the landscape behind them. The image has been expertly scrubbed of any evidence of fossil fuel use, the many complex technologies that play a central role in flower cultivation and harvesting, and the forms of rapid, unplanned urban development that generally accompany floriculture. This idyllic rural image does not look much like Naivasha, with its high-tech facilities, supermarkets, and shantytown settlements.

The associated text reads, "High-quality fresh produce is grown under the sun on farms and smallholdings all over Kenya. Farmers and farm laborers work hard to grow and export flowers, fruit and vegetables so that consumers in Europe can enjoy the produce while helping farming communities in Africa to earn a fair living." Explicitly citing the results of the Cranfield University study, the website proclaims that the food miles concept is "flawed" and urges consumers to "go on, buy Kenyan and support farming communities in Africa."

Although nation branding allows postcolonial states to communicate directly with consumers and potential investors, these campaigns must still mobilize "fetishized sites/sights of underdevelopment" (Roy 2007, 574) to underscore the need for assistance and the moral, ethical, and financial imperative to "buy Kenyan." Instead of migrant laborers who live and work in peri-urban landscapes and struggle to invest small portions of their wages in distant home communities, flower farm workers are depicted as smallholders or wage laborers who work in idealized rural landscapes and confidently invest their wages in communities that can be seen from the farm gate. The elimination of greenhouses and the focus on the manual aspects of flower farm labor make sense given the central message of this campaign. These sleights of hand accentuate the carbon *extensive* nature of Kenyan floriculture. However, they also downplay the aspects of this industry that are state-of-the-art, obscuring the elements of floriculture that many Kenyans, especially black Kenyan professionals, find most compelling and attractive as they imagine their own futures within this industry. Simon Anholt, who is often recognized as the originator of the nation-branding concept, recognizes this as "the conundrum of harmonizing the typically low-tech, old fashioned, and often rural imagery favored by tourist boards with the typically high-tech, modern, urban images favored by inward investment boards" (2002, 231). The architects of this campaign assumed that European consumers would also prefer the "rural imagery favored by tourist boards."

The simplified image of Kenyan horticulture presented on the Grown under the Sun website and the results of the Cranfield University study resonated with European journalists. The question "Are food miles fair miles?" formed the basis of a BBC radio program shortly after the campaign was launched. By late 2007, the Kenyan case study had emerged as a key trope in mainstream media articles criticizing the moral and economic utility of the food miles concept. A November 9, 2007, article in *Time* magazine pitted "Kenyan farmers" against "Euro Environmentalists" and criticized a carbon-footprint approach that considers only airfreight (Crilly 2007). A *New Yorker* article dated February 25, 2008, adopted the results of the Kenyan rose–Dutch rose comparison to illustrate the argument that "in measuring carbon emissions, it's easy to confuse morality and science" (Specter 2008). A *Guardian* article printed on March 13, 2008, drew on a description of a "typical" green bean farmer in Kenya to explain "how the myth of food miles hurts the planet" (McKie 2008), and on March 27, a frequent contributor to the United Kingdom–based online magazine *Spiked* wrote, "At last, people are questioning the eco-parochialism of the local-food lobby. . . . Even the dreaded green bean from Kenya, which has become the *bête noire* of foodies, cannot be so neatly cast as a villain" (Lyons 2008). Three months after its launch, the campaign had managed to place Kenyan produce at the symbolic heart of an emergent backlash against the local-foods movement.

In April 2008, the Kenyan High Commission announced that the Grown under the Sun label had yet to be implemented because of a lack of funding. Although the label never materialized, the campaign had an important discursive impact. Tesco implemented its plan to label air-freighted produce and found that sales of these products were not negatively affected. Africa-practice, a United Kingdom–based firm hired by the Kenyan government "to advocate for their interests abroad and to manage perceptions of Kenya in the UK," argued that "Grown under the Sun" could still be deemed a success. In a post published on its website in 2008, the firm concluded, "Extensive press coverage of the issues has ensured that the 'food miles' concept is challenged and Kenya's concerns are well publicized. British retailers have been reminded of their commitments to fair trade and many have reported no loss in sales of Kenyan fresh imports since the commencement of the campaign." A well-designed website and a press release had taken care of the issue, and a larger labeling initiative was no longer necessary.

During a follow-up conversation in May 2008, Mr. Stone laughed as he told me about how the food miles crisis had developed since we last spoke. "I've just heard from one of our retailers that the research suggests that consumers are actually encouraged to buy produce labeled with the airplane logo because they associate it with speedy delivery and greater freshness." He chuckled to himself and then continued on a more serious note. "We [still] have to be very careful with these things, because these labels may convey the wrong information and unravel everything we do here." Kenyan growers viewed themselves as permanently engaged in an unpredictable struggle to control the industry's image abroad. The state served as a critical partner in helping them convey the right information to keep everything from "unraveling."

For several more years, Tesco remained true to its 2007 promise to revolutionize green consumerism and become a leader in addressing climate change (Finch and Vidal 2007). Working with the Carbon Trust, a "not for dividend" private company based in the United Kingdom, Tesco developed a more complex carbon footprint label for its products using a full life-cycle-analysis approach. The label format was based on input from consumer surveys. In 2008, Tesco began printing these carbon footprint labels on twenty products, including laundry detergent, orange juice, potatoes, and light bulbs, sold under the Tesco brand name. On October 23, 2010, the *Guardian* reported that, at the current rate of about 125 products per year, it would take Tesco centuries to label all of its more than 70,000 products (Smithers 2010). In January 2012, the company announced plans to abandon carbon labeling entirely, citing the "minimum of several month's work" necessary to accurately calculate the carbon emissions associated with a single product (Vaughan 2012). Since other retailers had not adopted this practice, carbon labeling had also proved impractical from a business standpoint. Tesco could no longer bear the costs associated with the program if neither consumers nor its competitors saw value in the project.

Although Kenyan actors did not cause the death of Tesco's carbon labels alone, the Grown under the Sun campaign helped render the carbon footprint initiative both impractical and morally circumspect. By asking if food miles were "fair miles," they reminded consumers of their earlier commitments to ethical trade in a global system; and by questioning simplistic methods for calculating carbon footprints, they forced retailers to base their labels on more complex (and costly) forms of life-cycle analysis. The Grown under the Sun campaign allowed both the state and Kenyan flower growers to strategically reframe public discussions of corporate and consumer responsibility in relation to climate change. As co-opted agents of the state, Kenya Flower Council employees and upper-level flower farm managers represented the interests of the Kenyan government at trade shows and as members of the formal Kenyan delegation tasked with negotiating the Economic Partnership Agreement with European trade partners. In exchange, elected and appointed officials praised horticulture as a cornerstone of Kenyan development and directed state resources (more symbolic than financial) to the marketing and promotion of the sector. Each worked to protect the financial interests and the image of the other.

Although they denied contributing in a significant way to the *causes* of climate change, Kenyan flower growers and agents of the Kenyan state remained very concerned about the possible *effects* of climate change, especially in the Naivasha area. If climate change caused surface and groundwater resources to shrink, floriculture would still "unravel." To address these concerns, growers partnered with the state to roll out new strategies for monitoring and enforcing regulations on water use in the Lake Naivasha basin. While state officials and farm directors spoke of the critical importance of the branding initiative in protecting Kenya's markets abroad, civil servants working in Naivasha focused on the state's potentially important role in protecting the natural resources necessary for flower production.

While the Grown under the Sun campaign required the state to depict Kenyan spaces as relatively underdeveloped, more localized efforts to strengthen the state's role in water management gave civil servants and elected officials the opportunity to demonstrate their technical proficiency and professional skills. The Lake Naivasha basin would be the first Kenyan watershed for which a successful, data-driven, and cooperative strategy for managing water resources would be devised. This articulated with civil servants' desires to harness the power and influence of floriculture to strengthen Kenyan policies and institutions. The viewpoints of the growers and state agents who served as the architects of these new public-private partnerships for resource management reveal the enthusiasm that these professionals brought to this process.

PUBLIC-PRIVATE PARTNERSHIPS FOR WATER MANAGEMENT IN NAIVASHA

The food miles debate was not the only issue that preoccupied Mr. Stone during our December 2007 interview. His other major concern was water, and he was one of a number of flower farm managers and owners who had become centrally involved in the management of water resources in the Lake Naivasha area, principally through the Lake Naivasha Water Resource Users Association (LANAWRUA). The origins of the organization reveal key shifts in Kenyan natural resource and development policy over the previous decade.

In 1997, the Nakuru District, which included Naivasha at the time, undertook a water resources assessment and planning project funded by the Dutch government. The goal of this project was to collect five years' worth of hydrological data so that the extent of water resources in the district could be accurately assessed. Future water policy would then be based on these data.

A Kenyan civil servant who worked closely with Dutch consultants during the early stages of this project initially viewed the Dutch government's involvement with suspicion. He explains, "At first, I thought the Dutch government just wanted to support their people. A lot of the investors here in flowers come from Holland. But after some time, I came to understand that they wanted just to make sure they have a basis of planning and a way of ensuring that whatever they're doing is not detrimental to the environment." By 2007, he had become an avid proponent of a data-based approach to water use planning. "Initially people used to do planning without assessing. . . . Kenyan policy used to be focused always on development and water provisioning, but you're developing something you don't know. This now would allow us to know the resource."

Consultants involved with the initial assessment project installed monitoring equipment, including river-gauging stations, lake-level stations, groundwater stations, and rain gauges, and began collecting data in earnest. In 1998, the majority of this equipment was destroyed by El Niño–related rains and flooding. These setbacks made it difficult to "know the resource," but the idea that planning should be based on scientific assessments of ground- and surface-water availability had taken root.

In 1999, the Kenyan Ministry of Water introduced a new National Policy on Water Resource Management and Development, and in Sessional Paper no. 1 of the same year, Parliament called for the repeal of the existing water act in favor of one that would radically restructure Kenyan water management. In 1999, the attempted overhaul of Kenyan water policy suffered a major setback when the Dutch government withdrew funding for the assessment project. A project participant explains, "That was still the end of the Moi era [Daniel arap Moi's long-running presidency, 1979–2002], and there was a lot of misappropriation of funds. Every international government was really talking strictly on utilization of funds. The government seemed to be doing nothing, and there was a kind of mistrust. So they canceled the project." With the funding revoked and the equipment for monitoring destroyed, the situation seemed dire, but a Dutch hydrologist who had worked as a consultant on the government-funded project continued monitoring efforts in Naivasha by bringing his masters of science candidates to Kenya to conduct research. He also began to work with members of the Lake Naivasha Growers Group, convincing them to provide some of the funding and political pressure necessary to continue the policy process set in motion in 1999.

These efforts eventually led to the passage of the Water Act of 2002, which created a new Ministry of Water and Irrigation to coordinate governance in the water sector. Issues of water provisioning, water resources assessment and management, and water policy were separated and assigned to separate subagencies within the new ministry. A new Water Resources Management Authority (WRMA) would be principally responsible for developing and implementing policies related to water planning, permitting, and provisioning.

In addition to creating a new institutional framework, the act also declared that key elements of water management would be partially privatized, and that water development projects would be funded through fees collected from water users. Ideally, private and public stakeholders in each of Kenya's catchment areas, defined as the geographic areas from which rainwater flows into specific watercourses, would form local Water Resource

Users Associations (WRUAs) and work cooperatively to establish and implement a management policy for their catchment area.[6] Members of these WRUAs would have the power to review and approve new water permits within their jurisdiction and would decide how to spend a portion of the fees collected from water users in the area. These fees would be collected by civil servants working for the new Water Resources Management Authority and held in the Water Services Trust Fund until a grant application from a WRUA for a specific project was approved and funded.

Thanks largely to leadership and funding provided by the flower industry, the Lake Naivasha Water Resource Users Association was the second to successfully form in Kenya and the first to draft a Catchment Area Management Plan. In 2007, those involved in this initiative spoke enthusiastically about the potential for the LANAWRUA to "serve as an example for the rest of Kenya" in how water resource management could be radically improved through public-private partnerships in environmental governance.

The LANAWRUA initiative arose in the wake of the demise of the controversial Lake Naivasha Management Plan, a multistakeholder effort for community-based management in the lake area spearheaded by the Lake Naivasha Riparian Association (LNRA). At a local level, these two efforts were intimately linked, and the potential success of the LANAWRUA model was often framed in opposition to the shortcomings of the previous management plan. I first met Mr. Stone at a LANAWRUA planning meeting, and despite his hesitance to speak with researchers and journalists, he agreed to discuss with me his perspective on issues related to water management in Naivasha. His viewpoints echoed those expressed by other (white) upper-level farm managers and owners in Naivasha.

According to Stone, Naivasha flower growers lost confidence in the LNRA-led management plan process when it became clear (from their perspective) that the policies and decision-making processes that it outlined "were not based in reliable hydrological data." The plan placed restrictions on future agricultural and industrial development in the Naivasha area under the assumption that the lake's carrying capacity had already been reached or exceeded. Growers in the lake area insisted that decisions regarding use of resources be based in hydrological science, specifically modeling exercises that used the "best available data" to predict how, when, and from where water could be extracted without further degrading specific markers of water quality and ecosystem health. Members of the Lake Naivasha Growers Group (LNGG) commissioned a consulting firm called Rural Focus to conduct research on the lake and develop what Stone and others often referred to as "a more sensible plan" for managing the lake.

Stone explained the series of events that led to his own involvement in the LANAWRUA: "We [the growers] tried to convince the LNRA to accept the recommendations of Rural Focus, but relations between the two groups were uneasy. The LNGG eventually supported the management plan, but then it ground to a halt. After the Water Act was passed in 2002, growers saw this as an opportunity to develop a community-based water abstraction plan." When I asked about whether the LNGG or the KFC was directly involved in the drafting of the new water policy, Stone described their influence as indirect. He replied, "Rural Focus was certainly involved, and they had a finger on the pulse of what was going on and what we wanted. Since the LNGG had already gone a ways toward this [developing a water use policy in the area], we felt we should continue to be proactive in this process."

Rather than drafting the policy themselves, the LNGG worked through Rural Focus to ensure that the new regulations reflected the interests of growers in Naivasha. Stone explains, "We contacted Rural Focus and asked them to work with the Water Resources Management Authority [to change Kenyan water policy]." According to Stone, Naivasha's two largest horticulture enterprises also paid Rural Focus to help the WRMA establish WRUAs in the lake's upper catchment basin. In response to research conducted by David Harper, a limnologist based at Leicester University in the United Kingdom, growers were concerned about sediment pollution entering the lake through its feeder rivers. Establishing these WRUAs might give the LNGG greater influence over farming practices in the lake's upper catchment.

Because of what Stone describes as "friction" in the Lake Naivasha area, the LANAWRUA took longer to establish than growers had expected. Local actors who had been most active in the LNRA-led process remained focused on their efforts to "revive" this management plan, but growers active in the LNGG agreed with Stone that the LNRA plan should be replaced by something "more realistic." They viewed the LANAWRUA process as critical to protecting their interests, and they were anxious to establish some form of "control" over water use. Despite the very recent demise of the LNRA plan, they remained convinced that this latest effort would be successful in establishing order and in cementing their authority in the new regulatory process. Stone's own viewpoint reflected this complex mix of anxiety over a declining resource base, entitlement to resources based on a doctrine of prior appropriation, and confidence in this new governance strategy.

> There is a growing recognition in the grower's group that we needed a management plan for water. We can't just sit

> back and wait. We need to conserve the lake, and it needs to be self-regulating. There is a huge amount of investment locked in the lake. It's a finite resource, and it should be managed on a first-come, first-serve basis. We need a moratorium on further abstraction, and permits need to be based on the models developed from the data we have. Maybe we can adjust abstraction levels later, but only after further data collection. We're really just getting started.

In Stone's view, a greater reliance on science would limit the pernicious grip of "politics" in community-based management and create greater incentives for the "rational and sustainable" use of local resources. Under this system, flower growers, who viewed themselves as using state-of-the-art technologies for the efficient use of resources, especially water, would have an edge over smallholder agriculturalists, pastoralists, and vegetable growers in the North Lake area using center-pivot irrigation (an open-air irrigation method using sprinklers that rotate around a central pivot point). Claims to land and resources in the Lake Naivasha area, they argued, should be based on efficiency and the rate of economic return, rather than ancestry, length of time in the area, or other "political and cultural" elements that they viewed as essentially excusing unsustainable and economically irresponsible land-use practices. This logic played a central role in the early development of both the LANAWRUA and the changes in the Kenyan Water Act of 2002 that enabled its existence.

At first glance, the LANAWRUA seems to be primarily the product of the flower industry's strategic intervention in the Kenyan policy process. Growers in Lake Naivasha paid Rural Focus to conduct hydrological research and lobby the state to engineer a policy overhaul that would allow private enterprises to participate in water management at a local level. The LANAWRUA would theoretically have the authority to review and approve all new water permits in the area, and flower industry executives on the board planned to expand the standards of water-use efficiency in place on Naivasha's largest flower farms to all entities seeking (or renewing) water use permits in the lake's catchment basin. In 2007, flower growers played a key role in running and setting the agenda for the association. The chairman of the LANAWRUA was the managing director of one of Naivasha's three largest flower companies. Although the executive board consisted of representatives from the local tourism industry and the pastoralist community, the majority of active members came from the flower industry.

As Stone indicated, flower growers planned to use this forum to place a strict moratorium on all new water permits in the area. They saw keeping newcomers out as central to protecting their fixed assets and investments. The industry would still be self-regulated, but the central involvement of the state would provide more commercially powerful growers with a way to restrict access to water resources. The state's central involvement would also make this governance strategy appear more legitimate from the viewpoint of both Kenyans and European consumers.

To my surprise, however, civil servants working in the Naivasha area, as well as other local residents participating in the development of the LANAWRUA, resisted the characterization of this as a problematic takeover of resource management by big business. They viewed it as a legitimate private-public *partnership*. In these early stages of the process, they expressed excitement about the opportunities that the LANAWRUA presented to the Kenyan state—which they viewed as having the ultimate authority over resource management—and about the impact that it might have on their own professional and personal lives. The Water Act of 2002 provided mechanisms for reconstructing Kenyan institutions and devolving governance to local or regional levels. Members of Kenyan civil society had long advocated for policies that would achieve these broader goals. Working for a new institution that had not yet been mired in accusations of corruption offered a new generation of civil servants a chance to demonstrate a capacity for self-governance, further decolonize political and economic relations by working with international actors (e.g., consultants) more likely to view them as peers, and play the role of expert in a manner befitting their training.

Although flower growers were confident that they would always be the private sector "partner" most actively involved in the LANAWRUA, state agents knew better. The "public" might be far more permanent than the "private." Agents of the Kenyan state living and working in Naivasha saw the LANAWRUA as an opportunity to demonstrate a regulatory power and capacity that might help them attract even better partners in the quest for Kenyan development.

Kariuki, the district labor officer introduced in chapter 3 as an example of an older civil servant whose livelihood was tied to Naivasha floriculture, expressed frustration with his inability to generate change within the industry, given what he described as the "poverty" and "problems" that Kenya still needed "help" to overcome. Not all civil servants in Naivasha expressed a similar form of disaffection and frustration. Younger civil servants working in government agencies like the WRMA that were new (or radically restructured) expressed greater enthusiasm and confidence in the capacity of the state to regulate resources human and natural. The perspective of Harrison, a WRMA employee, illustrates this (at least momentary) enthusiasm about the transformative potential of the Water Act of 2002.

Harrison: "They're Saying, 'It's Not Working!' And We're Saying, 'Now, It's Working'"

In November 2007, I attend a stakeholders meeting on urban waste management at the Kenya Forest Service office in Naivasha. The meeting has been organized by Beatrice, the project officer for the Naivasha Watershed Conservation and Management Project (NAWACOMP), a three-year collaborative project funded by the European Union through its Community Environment Facility funds. The stakeholders who have gathered here today include more elected officials and civil servants than representatives of the four community-based organizations awarded the grant. These "strategic partners" include the area chief, the provincial administrative chief, and representatives from the Ministry of Water and Irrigation, Kenya Wildlife Service, the Water Resources Management Authority, the Kenya Forest Service, and the Naivasha Municipal Council.

Like most meetings that I attend in Kenya, especially those organized by NGO employees, the forum unfolds according to a standardized format. Beatrice stands at the front of the room with a set of colored markers and easels bearing large flip-style pads of presentation paper. She opens the meeting with a prayer, noting that the purpose of conservation is "to preserve God's creation." Then she reviews the origin and goals of NAWACOMP and solicits a set of expectations from the stakeholders in the audience. A few attendees express a desire to promote "community awareness" of waste management issues. The district officer hopes "to discover how to achieve waste disposal" in Naivasha. Drawing on Kenya's most popular environmental discourse (thanks to the Green Belt Movement), a representative from a local self-help group hopes to get funds to plant trees in his community. A representative from the notoriously cash-strapped Naivasha Municipal Council reminds the group of the council's authority in these matters. She expects "to learn how NAWACOMP can help the council" develop its waste disposal programs.

After some discussion of these expectations, the forum's objectives, and its proposed interventions (e.g., sensitization of the local community, tree planting, and strategies for further fund-raising and "mobilizing more resources"), the most important portion of the program begins. Each stakeholder is given a chance to describe his or her agency's contributions to waste management and answer questions from the audience. For the elected officials and civil servants present, this is a chance to publicly define their mandates and convince those gathered of their professional capacities to generate change. Representatives from the municipal council, the district office, and the Ministry of Water and Irrigation explain their current waste disposal programs but focus mainly on the "challenges" that they face in trying to implement these policies—a lack of manpower, problems with transportation, a lack of facilities for waste storage and disposal, inadequate or confusing policies that do not inspire public confidence, and "noncooperative members of the public" who refuse to pay taxes and fees and ignore recommended procedures for waste disposal. Members of the audience ask probing questions about technical aspects of their programs, and the conversations that follow clearly delineate the profound structural challenges that frustrate local waste management strategies.

The tone of the event begins to shift, however, when Harrison, an employee of the newly created Water Resources Management Authority, rises to explain his agency's potential contributions to urban waste management. Like his other black Kenyan professional counterparts, Harrison is well educated. After completing O-level exams in his home district, he attended the University of Nairobi for a short time before deciding to train for a career in the civil service. He received a diploma from the Kenya Water Institute, and then waited for three years to receive his appointment to the public sector. He recalls the exact date in 1996 that he received his letter of appointment to the Ministry of Water Resources, which informed him that he had been assigned to the Nakuru District as an assistant hydrologist.

Harrison is in his midthirties, and in his own words, "he likes to take care of his body." He lifts weights at a small gym owned by a friend in Naivasha Town, a gym that is nearly always deserted, the exercise machine covered in a thick patina of Naivasha's famous dust. The result of his efforts is a small but muscular frame that attracts some good-natured teasing from his age-mates in resource management, who also give him guff about the *piki piki* (motorbike) that he rides while conducting borehole and well surveys. Among his peers, however, he is also known as an articulate and "inspirational guy" because of the passion he expresses for his profession and the relationships that he cultivates with international researchers. In a separate conversation, he has shared his thoughts on leadership with me: "You need to influence people to a common cause. And the only way you can influence is being part and parcel of them. You share your vision with them, you win them, and they will be willing to follow you and support you." Today, he has come to share his vision for the future of Kenyan water management with NAWACOMP stakeholders.

Like many who have spoken here today, Harrison begins with a biblical reference that underscores the critical importance of his work and the divine will that guides his efforts. "Before everything, when the world was created, the world was empty, only covered with water. Water is life." He points to the bottled water we are drinking, bought with funds from the grant that has enabled NAWACOMP. I recall the way that, under other circumstances, farmworkers poke fun at wealthy tourists and white farm owners who carry bottled water and tiny bottles of hand sanitizer. Bottled water is a privilege afforded by wealth, but it is also a symbol of the failure of public infrastructure. Harrison immediately differentiates his agency as a branch of government that stands apart from others. "You can find me in the district office, next to the register of persons." He laughs. "But my agency is kind of semiautonomous. We are both parts of government but with different mandates."

With a healthy measure of confidence and bravado, Harrison explains some of the changes that the restructuring of water law will bring to resource management in the near future. Provoking laughter from the audience, he lists some of the problems that have plagued water management in the Naivasha area. Landowners dig pit latrines downhill from or immediately next to wells. The municipal council cannot pay its employees and is "always coming to the Ministry of Water for help." Private well owners pay nothing for the water that they pump onto their fields. Thanks to the new Water Act of 2002, the WRMA is in a position to change all of these things.

Harrison proclaims, "We are really looking forward to having some sanity in water resource management. You can't dig a well wherever you please. Now we will work with the public health officer to close these latrines. Money from the water sector [collected by the council] is not plowed back into water services. Now we are allowed by law to revoke the council[members] and put in new people if services are not provided." He pauses and then continues: "And we are really zeroing in on private [land]owners. Your time is up. You are going to pay for that water. Effective first October 2007, water is no longer free. The money collected from these fees will go to the catchment areas, not to the central government. It will go to Community Forest Associations, the Water Resource User Associations. These are your organizations."

He pauses to allow this promise to sink in. No more will fees and taxes disappear into central government coffers; they will remain under local control and will be accessible to their community-based organizations. He asks for their support as both private citizens and influential local leaders and public servants. "WRMA cannot do this alone. We need partners." He holds aloft a copy of the new Water Act, and he opens the document to an ear-marked page. "According to rule no. 92, we are mandated by law to work closely with the provincial administration and local authorities to write orders to landowners, to insist that they comply with the law. I urge you all to buy a copy of these rules and inform yourselves of the letter of the law. If you build a latrine too close to a well, you are the enemy of yourself. We have no choice; we have to be part and parcel of water management. This is something we will all do together."

He explains that WRMA employees are not like the civil servants of old, the "corrupt" officials who "like to eat" and never seemed accountable to the public. He explains, "This is an era of performance contracts. Even me, I have signed a performance contract that binds me to perform my duties well. No wonder we have so many NGOs coming in [in the past]. They're saying, 'It's not working!' And we're saying, 'Now, it's working.'"

A murmur of approval comes from the audience. Another young man, a close colleague of Harrison's who works for a local environmental organization, laughs and says, "Kazi endelea" (The work continues). This is President Mwai Kibaki's campaign slogan, which urges Kenyans to allow him to continue his work, to see his policies come to fruition. In recent months, Kibaki has portrayed his first five years in office as a time of important policy changes designed to improve the economy, reduce or eliminate corruption, and simultaneously cultivate Kenya's important relationships with NGOs to demonstrate the nation's capacity for self-governance. It is no coincidence that the new Water Act was passed in 2002, Kibaki's first year in office.

Whether or not those in attendance today assign Kibaki credit for generating these kinds of policy changes, Harrison's statements resonate with many of the NAWACOMP stakeholders. According to Harrison's vision of the near future, NGO- and community-based-organization project officers can now partner with a new breed of civil servants who will do more than funnel fees back to their Nairobi ministries and into their own patronage networks. Private-sector entities will be *willing* to follow the law because it will bring "sanity" to water resource management and because any funds generated by fees and taxes will remain under their control. His rhetoric here echoes that of the black Kenyan farm managers who play a lead role in enforcing international and Kenyan policies in floriculture. Harrison's image of Kenyan professionals telling the international community, "Now it's working," is powerful and deeply satisfying to some members of this audience. Many of them would benefit directly from the devolution of authority and financing from international NGOs and the central government to community-based organizations and local institutions.

There is also a profound generational element in Harrison's rhetoric. While older civil servants and Kenyan elites have proven "the enemies of themselves," he suggests that he and his contemporaries will respect the letter of the new law, perform according to their contracts, and abstain from graft and "irresponsible" behavior. The NAWACOMP audience included many of the civil servants, elected officials, and private landowners that Harrison was openly accusing of nonperformance and/or graft. His speech was a warning to them: their behavior would no longer be tolerated. Although he spoke of the incentives involved in regulatory compliance, he also spoke of the forms of (mainly financial) punishment that awaited those who disobeyed.

Harrison's description of himself as both powerful and accountable point to the ways that members of a postcolonial generation born in the 1970s and 1980s understand what it means to be upwardly mobile young Kenyans. Like other members of his generation, Harrison values self-control, reflected in his careful diet, his exercise regimen, and his consumer tastes (Spronk 2009). He is also hyperconscious of the gaze of an external international community, and he desires access to forms of education and international connection that, for previous generations of Kenyans, were accessible only to the extremely wealthy and politically powerful. Although he is critical of previous generations of civil servants, he still sees the Kenyan state as the most legitimate source of regulatory authority in Naivasha. The work that Harrison believes should continue involves improving Kenyan *selves*, as well as Kenyan policies and institutions.

In separate conversations, I asked Harrison to elaborate on whether he thinks the LANAWRUA will meet with success in Naivasha. Like Stone, he framed the potential benefits of the LANAWRUA approach in contrast to the LNRA-led efforts of the recent past. He argued,"The *[LNRA] Management Plan* is not a bad document. The issue is just mistrust. A plan is more legitimate if it's a government project, a plan drawn with the leadership of a government agency that is specifically mandated to deal with that resource. [The Lake Naivasha Management Committee] can't manage that plan without the support of the farmers. They'll start to pester them, and they'll ask, 'Who are you and what mandate do you have?' They'll just laugh at you and call you a pretender."

Harrison recognized that, to some extent, these changes in water policy were being used by Naivasha flower farms to protect their investments and restrict the entrance of new competitors. He insisted, however, that despite the industry's ulterior motives, all of the WRUA's activities would be subject to the oversight and approval of the WRMA, and that the organization's leadership "is really reaching out to all the stakeholders." He argued that the broader Kenyan populace has become "enlightened to their rights" to participate in grassroots policy making, and he saw civil servants like himself as intermediaries between the public and private sectors: they would work with members of the public to ensure that the industry did not "hijack" the policy process. Other black Kenyan professionals involved in the LANAWRUA expressed a similar satisfaction with the ways that this new cooperative environmental management initiative shifted local power relations. Participants described the LANAWRUA as an "open" and "participatory" process, spoke highly of the attempts that flower growers had made to respond to their concerns, and stressed the importance of the state's central role in mediating the effort and enforcing new policies.

Although this confidence in the LANAWRUA might erode over time, its existence for the moment spoke to the aspirations of Harrison and his contemporaries. In one of our last conversations before I left the field in 2008, Harrison emphasized again his satisfaction over the restoration of the power of the state (and civil servants) to govern natural resources in Kenya: "We have become a threat to most of the NGOs now. They are not happy. They were claiming that it's not working. Now that it's working, we are taking their livelihoods. Someone led us from the wilderness to the desert. Now someone else has to take us to Canaan." In his view, NGO intervention had helped bring about an end to the Moi era and institute critical processes of reform, but the final section of the road to paradise would consist of strategic public-private partnerships that recognized the authority and right of the Kenyan state (and its agents) to steer the direction of national development. At least at the policy level, things were "working"; in practice, however, the LANAWRUA remained as potentially unwieldy and conflict-prone as the efforts at community-based resource management that preceded it.

When I asked Harrison to elaborate on his future aspirations, he surprised me by explaining that he hoped his work for the WRMA would lead to employment with an international NGO. He explained, "I've had enough of water, and I want to work with natural resources at another level." Surprisingly, Harrison did not see a contradiction between his critique of the power of NGOs in Kenya and his desire to work for one. He explained that NGOs play an important role in "collecting the data" necessary for resource management. Working for an NGO would allow him to further his education, earn a higher salary, and engage in research that would inform the policies that the WRMA would implement. He believed that the state should play the lead role in managing water resources, but civil service jobs were still entry-level positions that afforded the type of "exposure" necessary for upward mobility in a global system, without providing the structural opportunity to do so. He viewed his potential for *self*-actualization and professional growth within the agency itself as limited; in order to play a more important role in research or policy generation, rather than implementation and enforcement alone, he might need to leave the WRMA.

Harrison's encounter with floriculture had thus far proven relatively empowering and lucrative. He viewed himself as an "accountable" figure and a critical intermediary between the public and the private sectors partnering to manage water resources in Naivasha. His employment with the WRMA, a new agency created during the rollout phase of neoliberalism, had (at least momentarily) allowed him to escape accusations of corruption and mismanagement that plagued past generations of civil servants. Armed with his performance contract and a printed copy of the new water act, Harrison was eager to demonstrate that "now it's working," and that he and his contemporaries could be the ones to "lead [Kenya] to Canaan." Harrison's desires for personal advancement and enrichment were coconstituted with a desire for the state to remain the center of gravity in matters of national development and for Kenya to have a greater degree of control over its future.

During our conversations, both Harrison and Stone were speaking in an official, as well as a personal, capacity. They did their best to convince all who would listen that changes in Kenyan water policy would bring "sanity" to resource management in Naivasha. Despite the polished and polemical aspects of their rhetoric, the confidence in their own ability and authority to produce change was genuine. The amount of time that WRMA employees invested in their work, and the considerable financial resources that flower growers invested in the policy process, suggest that these were not empty gestures. The rollout phase of neoliberalism had provided them with an opportunity to make Kenyan institutions work, and both flower growers and agents of the Kenyan state genuinely desired to protect water quality and quantity in Naivasha. Flower growers played a central role in shaping the development of new policies; but as Naomi noted, they needed the state to enforce and cooperatively implement these policies.

In 2007, LANAWRUA meetings, Brand Kenya discussions, negotiations for economic partnership agreements, and the Grown under the Sun campaign served as spaces where powerful actors were (re)negotiating the relationship between state and corporate sovereignty during the rollout phase of neoliberalism. Although branding initiatives may seem superficial, they helped Kenyan growers exert very real influence in horticultural commodity chains frequently characterized as "buyer driven." When floriculturalists and state agents partner to strategically "brand" Kenya, they use neoliberal discourses to capture the attention of foreign investors with the capital necessary to help stimulate the nation's economic growth. This partnership is especially helpful in times of crisis, when either the image of the industry or the Kenyan state itself has been tarnished. Each works to protect the other from critical voices in the international media. The state has become the manager of the Kenyan brand under which Naivasha flowers are marketed, a role that helps the state remain the center of gravity in export horticulture. However, it has done so with the consent of a powerful flower lobby theoretically capable of avoiding these entanglements in statemaking and nation building.

Recent changes in Kenyan water policy also define new roles for the state in natural resource management and environmental regulation. These developments have often taken place at the behest of the horticulture industry, rather than as a proactive result of the state's own development agenda; but nevertheless, they suggest that both the industry and the Kenyan state have become increasingly codependent when it comes to the control and allocation of natural resources at sites of flower production. The Water Act of 2002 established a new institutional framework for water management that serves as a prime example of the type of strategic public sector (re)construction that Peck and Tickell (2002) see as central to the rollout phase of neoliberalism. Influential flower farm managers like Stone shared Harrison's conviction that the regulatory process put in place by the Water Act of 2002 would allow them to more effectively manage local water resources through a process best described as state-mediated self-regulation. However, the confidence that state agents and flower growers expressed in the LANAWRUA process was informed by both neoliberal ideologies *and* postcolonial desires and sociopolitical processes not specific to this historical moment.

CHAPTER FIVE

White Kenyans and Expatriates

Belonging and Control

With the growth of floriculture, the makeup of Naivasha's white community has expanded and diversified. White Kenyans, whose families have been in the country since the colonial era, have been joined by expatriates from Europe, especially the United Kingdom and the Netherlands. Although they hail from diverse generational, cultural, and class backgrounds, these elite actors' experiences of floriculture have been profoundly shaped by their whiteness. Whether they are descended from Kenya's colonial settlers or not, they must negotiate discourses that associate whiteness in Africa with imperialism, dispossession, and structural privilege. Life in this nerve center requires them to confront difficult questions about how and why they belong in Kenya; and like white actors elsewhere in contemporary Africa (Hughes 2010), many cite their achievements in floriculture or environmental conservation as evidence of their committment to this particular place and their right to live, work, and prosper in Naivasha.

The white actors whose lives and experiences are examined here were all intimately connected to Naivasha floriculture in some way. Many were upper-level flower farm managers, and others operated smaller mixed farms and tourist ventures in the lake area. Even those who did not make a living directly from floriculture were deeply entangled in the economic, social, and political changes this industry has brought to Naivasha. Their family members or close friends worked in the industry, and they were centrally involved in local social and environmental governance initiatives. Although they shared the need to negotiate a racialized "problem of belonging" (Hughes 2010) in Kenya, their viewpoints on floriculture and the future of Naivasha often differed considerably.

Expatriate farm managers often expressed a profoundly neoliberal faith that floriculture could contribute positively to Kenyan development and help generate more effective approaches to resource management. White Kenyans, including those with a considerable financial stake in floriculture, were more ambivalent about the industry's transformative effects on the environment and local power relations. They viewed some flower farm owners as "fly-by-night venture capitalists" with no long-term commitment to Naivasha, and they were reluctant to share responsibility for managing the lake with expatriates who did not share their perspectives on Naivasha's history and their aspirations for its future. Like elite black Kenyans, these white actors saw Naivasha as a place where Kenyan institutions could be productively reconfigured to make global industries more responsible (or sensitive) to Kenyan communities and environments. However, they disagreed about who should control these institutions and how they should function.

THE SPEECH: "NO ONE HERE IS INNOCENT, ESPECIALLY YOU AMERICANS"

While most midlevel farm managers welcomed my presence in Naivasha and eagerly invited me into their professional and personal lives, my interactions with white Kenyan and expatriate upper-level farm managers and owners often started on a much rockier footing. Many expected me to represent them as what anthropologist Susan Harding (1991) calls "the repugnant other," a group whose perspectives would provide a foil for the more enlightened, modern, and progressive viewpoints expressed by everyone else.

Just as black Kenyan professionals were clearly negotiating a broader corruption/anticorruption discourse as we spoke of their work in floriculture, white actors in Naivasha were troubled by discourses equating floriculture with oppression, exploitation, or neocolonialism. Many of my conversations with white expatriate flower farm managers began with a version of what I came to call "the speech," a preemptive, defensive attempt to reframe my perspective on Kenyan floriculture, a perspective they assumed had been colored by "all that bollocks in the BBC."

In its many versions, the speech had four distinct elements. First, I was reminded of the incredible economic gains that floriculture had brought to Kenya, specifically the creation of jobs for women. Most of these managers were young men from the Netherlands, the United Kingdom, and South Africa, and there was also an assumption that, as a woman, I might also be invested in accusing them of gender-based forms of exploitation.

Second, I was warned that my "interference," defined as anything that I might do to "harm" the industry by "misinforming" consumers in a way that led to boycotts or a drop in flower sales, would result immediately in the sacking of tens of thousands of workers overnight.

Third, I was asked to consider my own positionality as an American. The United States, I was informed, is in fact an occupied colonial territory, and American agriculture is more chemical-intensive and environmentally destructive than "anything that we do here in Kenya." I was then asked to justify why I wanted to study Kenyan floriculture when there were such pressing problems at home.

The fourth element of the speech involved complaints about the international media—the tendency to focus only on "tragedy" in Africa, the "unethical" means by which journalists conducted research on Naivasha floriculture (many managers had apparently been lied to by "undercover" journalists posing as students)—and a recitation of some of the egregious factual errors they had encountered in the press. The same global stage that their black Kenyan counterparts viewed with enthusiasm, they loathed as a forum where they would be caricatured as the new faces of empire.

The "speech" was often delivered with visible signs of anger and frustration—clenched fists, red faces, and crossed arms. The common arguments and consistency in language suggested that managers had discussed these matters in depth. They found these accusations personally insulting, and they took solace in "correcting the facts," "considering the bigger picture," and reminding themselves that white journalists, researchers, and activists had benefited from the same forms of privilege and structural violence as they. "No one here is innocent, especially you Americans," quipped one manager.

I rarely said anything to provoke "the speech," short of introducing myself and mentioning that I was pursuing research on floriculture. In engaging in this rhetoric, managers were talking through me to a larger audience, which they saw as antagonistic to both their personal and professional selves. Much to my relief, the speech was not always a conversational dead end. As long as I listened, expressed an intention to move beyond the "BBC version" of Kenyan floriculture, and asked a follow-up question that elicited information on some "benign" aspect of how floriculture actually works (e.g., "What do you use as a bedding medium?"), we could continue speaking. As our discussions became more congenial and I showed an interest in subjects other than worker pay and pesticide application rates, their relief was as palpable as my own. Not all of these managers chose to work with me, but some did.

On one occasion, a white Kenyan friend intentionally provoked "the speech" by telling a manager that I "was there to tell them how to fix floriculture." His goal was to "take the piss" out of the Dutch manager, but he also wanted to show me how easy it was to "wind up" a flower farmer. The particularly vitriolic version of "the speech" that his actions provoked entertained him to no end but left me feeling drained. He laughed, saying, "I set you up for that one, Megan. Sorry." This kind of provocation speaks to the antagonism that sometimes existed between white Kenyans and expatriate managers.[1]

Like expatriate farm managers, white Kenyans also engaged in defensive tactics designed to justify their place in contemporary Kenya and their control of resources. Some argued that, before white settlement, Naivasha was a no-man's-land, to which no indigenous group could lay a real claim. They pointed out the enduring elements of colonial infrastructure, including roads, airports, and bridges, that made life in contemporary Kenya possible and comfortable. If the colonial period was so awful, how was it that their forebears had done so much to "improve" infrastructure and connect Kenya to the world? However, they also poked fun at their parents' and grandparents' "kitchen Swahili," engaging in long, playful conversations in which they lampooned their forebears' aristocratic airs and their abuse of African staff. Part of the fun to be had in "winding up" expatriate, especially Dutch, farm managers was that it provided the opportunity for them to demonstrate a superior "sense of humor about the whole thing"—the "whole thing" being the rather serious matter of what anthropologist David Hughes calls "the tenuous and exclusionary nature of [white] privilege" (2010, 43), the drastic material inequalities that separated them from the majority of Kenya's population.

When white Kenyans engaged in something similar to "the speech," it involved two distinct elements. First, they stressed their deep roots in the country and their advanced knowledge of Kenya's peoples. Some had made extensive studies of Kenya's ethnographic history, and nearly all had read the memoirs of their forebears. Anthropologist Janet McIntosh explains that white Kenyans cite their relationships to colonial ancestors in a manner that "indexes a bloodline on Kenyan soil, a version of autochthony that some hope will establish entitlement to land or broader legitimacy as cultural citizens" (2015, 251). White Kenyans in Naivasha took great pride in their history in this place and the insights into Kenyan culture and politics that had accreted in their families over generations. As one young woman working in public relations at one of Naivasha's largest flower farms put it to me, "I knew nothing about horticulture except that flowers looked good, but I knew the language and I knew the people."

The second element of a white Kenyan version of "the speech" involved a critique of "two-year wonders"—NGO workers, Peace Corps volunteers, graduate students, and some farm managers—who came to Kenya for only a short time and then provided lofty prescriptions for stimulating progress. By contrast, they viewed their efforts to live and belong in Kenya as infinitely more genuine and more permanent. After all, they were in fact *Kenyan*; this was also their nation to build. For expatriate managers to be accepted into the white community in Naivasha, they were required to demonstrate an intention to remain here indefinitely and actively participate in environmental and social management strategies that respected white Kenyans' prior claim to this space and recognized the importance of livelihood activities other than floriculture.

Anthropologist Janet McIntosh argues that white Kenyans exhibit an "embryonic double consciousness" that they find "morally confusing." She explains, "Most of them had been raised to think that their settler families were good, giving people who lived bravely and sacrificed much, and that the colonial endeavor had been engineered to uplift Africa. Now they are informed that their forebears were oppressors, and that perhaps in some fashion they are too—and while they don't have to internalize this view of themselves, it has made inroads into their awareness" (2016, 7). As a result of this deeply frustrating and challenging positionality, white Kenyans have adopted a subject position McIntosh calls "structural oblivion." She defines this as "a state of ignorance, denial, and ideology that emerges from an elite structural position, and . . . is constituted by the refusal of certain implications of social structure" (10). Structural oblivion allows white Kenyans to "shake off" the identity crisis caused by their moral double consciousness.

Both white Kenyan and expatriate actors in Naivasha engaged in the systematic "denials, amnesia, selective narratives, and self-sustaining ideologies" (214) that McIntosh sees as indicative of structural oblivion. However, they never really reached a state of "oblivion." They remained permanently aware of their privileged structural positionality. The speech was a threat intended to dissuade me from pursuing my research, but it also contained nuanced arguments about how and why popular depictions of whiteness in Africa might obscure more than they reveal. Although they shared aspects of racialized structural privilege, not all white actors in Naivasha shared the same ways of belonging in this place.

EXPATRIATE PERSPECTIVES ON FLORICULTURE

Although South Asian farm owners and managers were growing in number in Naivasha in 2007, especially after the sale of Sher Agencies to a firm based in India, most expatriate managers still hailed from the Netherlands, the

United Kingdom, and southern Africa (South Africa, Zimbabwe, and Zambia). When low-level flower farmworkers and black Kenyan professionals spoke of the group of investors who controlled these farms, these were the faces that they pictured. Workers were eager to establish personal relationships with these managers, the vast majority of whom were men, in the hopes that they might yield greater access to the wealth generated by floriculture. Among farmworkers, some were described as villains and some were characterized as warm exceptions to the "colonial mind-set" that gripped other white actors in Naivasha.

These managers were drawn to Naivasha for many reasons. For some, working in Kenyan floriculture provided a means of escape from a "modern" life elsewhere that they found unappealing. For others, especially those from the Netherlands, floriculture was a family venture. Expansion within a global system provided a way for them to remain major players in the flower trade or to make their own mark on the family business. Some expected to work in multiple equatorial locations over the course of their professional careers. Others had "fallen in love" with Kenya and planned to stay indefinitely. Some would marry Kenyan women and start their own farms or businesses, no longer content to work as employees for larger companies.

Expatriate managers insisted that they were not heirs to a colonial legacy, and they attempted to set themselves apart from their white Kenyan colleagues by exhibiting more liberal behavior in their relations with African staff. Many described Naivasha as a showcase for business-led development in Africa, and they were proud of their roles in helping Kenya "solve its own problems." They insisted that they were not here to exploit but to help build Kenya's own infrastructural and regulatory capacity.

Garritt: "Some People Say You're Bitten by the Africa Bug or You Found the Love of Your Life"

The most striking thing about Garritt is his obvious youth. At thirty, he has already spent several years working in floriculture in Africa and in the Netherlands. He has been in Naivasha for only a few months, and he has already undertaken an ambitious plan to squeeze more productive area from the small farm where he works as a senior manager. The operation sits on a small lot, with little room for outward expansion, and he has instructed workers to construct new beds on every available inch of space. He wants to increase the farm's productivity immediately to make a favorable impression on his employers.

Garritt was raised in a part of the Netherlands known as "the glass city," where 50 percent of the nation's greenhouses are located. His mother worked for a major flower auction, and his father worked as a financial advisor in the industry. He chose to follow in their footsteps at a young age and focused on horticulture in secondary school. As a young teenager, he completed a three-month internship in "tropical horticulture" at a white-owned farm in Zimbabwe. "The farm is no longer in existence," he reminisces. "But I knew that I would return to Africa when I finished my degree." When I ask him to explain what attracted him to tropical horticulture, he laughs. "Probably the adventure at first. But it's very difficult to describe. It's not the weather. It's not only the people. It's not only the way of working. Some people say you're bitten by the Africa bug or you found the love of your life, things like that."

Garritt explains that starting a new flower-growing operation in the Netherlands requires an incredible amount of capital. "Think of all the equipment you need, the heating systems, the artificial lighting. It's so extremely expensive that if you choose the wrong variety [to plant initially], you're finished," he says. "European companies really want to expand in Africa, but it's scary." The company that built Garritt's farm devised a strategy to help entice nervous Dutch investors to Africa. They purchase (or lease) the land, build the greenhouses and grading halls, hire the workers, and then lease or sell the new operation to investors as a ready-made package. Garritt laughs and says, "In roses, you can arrange everything with [this Dutch company], and you just come from Holland with scissors [to cut the ribbon on opening day]. They will plant everything, so you only have to come when everything is there." Garritt's farm was an early experiment in this business strategy, and the company was now building ready-made farms in Ethiopia.

When he finished his university degree, Garritt initially pursued a position in Ethiopia, which he describes as a "new frontier" in floricultural development. A chance encounter with a farm manager at the Dutch International Horti Fair led him to Kenya. "The business is small," he tells me, laughing again, "and with the Dutch, it's even smaller. You meet one person, and soon enough you are connected to everyone. I mentioned that I needed a job, and [the manager] passed the word on to the right people here in Kenya." Garritt and his Dutch colleagues see themselves as working within a *global* floriculture industry: they may move between several sites of "tropical" production over the course of their careers. When I ask Garritt if he plans to remain in Kenya permanently, he answers, "Hopefully. But the last time I said that, I was back in Holland in a year. The work that you do determines that."

In the meantime, he is very invested in understanding what he calls the "Kenyan context" for flower production—the laws, the politics, and the agronomics. Reflecting on the growing pains evident in Ethiopian floriculture, he remarks, "At the moment, Kenya is more promising. The problem [in

Ethiopia] is government mainly. . . . Nobody can make decisions, only the higher people, so it's really slow. It's very difficult. Government in Kenya is far more business-minded." He also sees the floriculture industry in Kenya as more technologically advanced. He explains, "The way they're doing flowers here is not that different from the sixties until now. . . . They're trying in Ethiopia. They're still having problems to let loose, to let the economy do it."

I ask Garritt about his new life in Naivasha. He explains that finding community in Naivasha is "actually very easy" for him because five members of his university fraternity had also found work here as sales representatives, upper-level farm managers, and marketing specialists. Establishing relationships with other members of the white community, however, has been more difficult. He explains, "The English people—it's very difficult to break in. They're also very closed. The good part is that I have some friends working for companies where there are also English involved; . . . and in the compound where I'm living, it's all KCs [Kenya cowboys[2]]." Garritt says nothing about the ease of integration into black Kenyan society. At least initially, he has invested in cultivating relationships within a residential and professional community primarily composed of members of Naivasha's white population.

Like all expatriate farm managers, Garritt finds the negative press that the flower industry attracts frustrating. He explains, "In Holland, the press is also really negative. I think here it is more the press, and maybe the middle class, that are doing the actual articles. . . . I don't really know if the people, the general workers, Kenyans themselves, are really interested in it." He argues that neighboring landowners also contribute to the industry's media troubles. "In Holland you see a lot of people who are living close to horticultural production areas; they're also fighting the horticultural sector itself." He admits that working conditions need improvement, but he thinks change should happen slowly. "Labor laws cannot just change overnight. It would be economically irresponsible. People need to be patient. I think of Holland during the Industrial Revolution. Things changed gradually, over a long period, to become what they are today."

Garritt was not alone in denying that "Kenyans themselves" are behind the political pressure to reform floriculture. Farm managers often argued that labor unrest and negative press were generated by exogenous forces, especially foreign journalists and Dutch growers who want to slow the overseas expansion of floriculture. Like Garritt, most expatriate farm managers also described Kenya as undergoing a "revolution" best understood by drawing on the example of Europe's past. They argued that "gradually, over a long period," Kenyans would benefit from the same teleological process of development that had improved the quality of life in western Europe. Rather than protesting, they argued, Kenyans should exercise patience and accept that rapid change would be "economically irresponsible." Although he could not leverage structural change "overnight," Garritt was proud of his reputation among farmworkers as someone who was "free" in his interactions with his employees; like many expatriate managers, he consciously avoided behaviors that he thought would be construed as colonial.

An Employee Appreciation Party hosted by a Dutch-owned farm illustrates the tensions and confusion that arise when farmworkers openly criticize management strategies and counter the self-congratulatory narrative that floriculture is "the best form of development aid" for Kenya. This party also provides insights into the ways that black Kenyan farmworkers and professionals conceptualize the racialized and gendered power dynamics at work in the industry.

An Employee Appreciation Party: "You'll Give Me Speed, and I'll Give You Pay"

I meet Collin, a black Kenyan farm manager, at the Railways Club in Naivasha Town. He and his two colleagues, Steven and Justus, are on their way home from a day spent at the horticultural fair on the grounds of the Naivasha Country Club. All three are wearing new hats advertising a name brand fungicide and carrying bags of literature collected at the fair. Collin has taken a number of pamphlets advertising new pesticides and irrigation equipment. Steven, who works as a technical manager, dips a piece of roasted meat in salt. "I did not see much that was new this year, but it is nice to meet with colleagues and discuss things." Justus, a chemical manager, agrees: "There was a lot of talk of some of the new pesticides, but the representatives have already come by to market these things to us."

All three are looking forward to tonight's event, their farm's annual Employee Appreciation Party, which will feature a performance by a well-known Luo musician. In this election year, the musician's performance is a political as well as a social event. A close friend of Collin's, who works as an opposition-party campaign organizer, had helped arrange the musician's performance, and many of those involved are hoping to gain political favor with the farm's workforce. Collin hopes to showcase his ability to use farm resources to cater to Naivasha's Luo-speaking community. For one night only, the farm will give workers access to a form of entertainment that most cannot find, let alone afford, in Naivasha.

We take the *matatu* back to the farm to get ready for the party. Every employee has been given two tickets, each of which entitles the bearer to five beers or six sodas. My escort is a twenty-year-old black Kenyan supervisor who recently moved here from Nairobi. He found employment quickly thanks to a certificate in computers and a family connection. We stand in line outside the farm gate for thirty minutes. Anticipation is high, but most workers are quiet, exhausted from a long day spent in the greenhouse heat. Occasionally, someone sprints out of line to grab a ticket passed through the gate by a worker who has already been admitted.

A guard takes our tickets and waves us inside the farm's packhouse, which has been rearranged for the event. A makeshift stage with audio equipment stands in the corner. There are three long tables at the rear of the room. Two are reserved for senior staff and assistant managers, all of whom are black Kenyan. The last is reserved for the farm directors and upper-level managers. Everyone at this last table is Dutch, with the exception of a senior manager's Kenyan wife and a young American manager who just transferred here from a sister farm in Columbia. Rather than sitting at tables, workers sit on black plastic crates arranged in neat lines in front of the stage.

When dinner is served, the assistant managers line up at one buffet table, while general workers line up at another. Staff members deliver dinner plates and Tusker Malts to the farm directors and upper-level managers, who remain seated.[3] Workers wait in separate lines to exchange their tickets for beer or soda. Most of the women choose to drink soda. Lillian, who works as a quality inspection supervisor, explains, "They have to report back to the job very early, and besides that, they may be living here away from their husbands. They don't want people to see them drinking and just start talking."

We pass through the buffet line and take our seats among the senior staff. Collin points at the farm directors and whispers to me, laughing, "You have to marry a director to sit at that table." He speculates on the age of the newest manager: "I hear that he is just a child! You should talk to him and discover his age." He laughs again. "The workers are sitting here on crates like cattle, but they're good to us here, the Dutch. They're so free compared to other whites." He rushes over to get his photo taken with his general manager on a digital camera borrowed from a friend for the occasion. "When the music starts, you'll find them here dancing. Except for that lady [the senior manager's Kenyan wife]; she is too proud to leave that table."

Collin recognizes (and laughs about) a management hierarchy that places young, white expatriates at the helm of the company, while older, more experienced Kenyan employees rarely advance beyond midlevel positions. This is not the first time that I have heard from a farmworker that the Dutch are "free" compared to other white farm managers. Although Collin is critical of the senior manager's wife for being "too proud," the tendency for Dutch managers to marry or date Kenyan women contributes to this sense that they are more "free." Parties like this are opportunities for expatriate managers to solidify this reputation; they hope to interact "freely" with farm employees in a way that they will defy workers' expectations. In practice, however, the seating arrangement reflects the racialized and gendered hierarchies at work within floriculture. Dutch managers socialize with workers in a limited manner, taking pictures and chatting with them when they approach the "high table," but they cannot allow their professional authority to be undermined or their elite status to be forgotten.

The awkwardness of this exercise becomes clear during a series of after-dinner speeches. The general manager welcomes us and introduces the farm's longest-serving employee, Patrick, to talk about the history of the farm. "When I first came here thirteen years ago, we called the [labor] camp Jerusalem," Patrick recalls. "We were living so many people to one house, and there was no water. I commend the company for reforming these conditions." He pauses as the audience applauds, and then continues: "Despite these improvements, we still have a problem with pay. We need higher pay." His request elicits nervous applause and sounds of approval from the general workers. The farm directors smile and raise their eyebrows. Patrick allows the tension to stand for a moment and then breaks it with a joke, "You should also create a way for workers to watch Premier League Football." His final suggestion meets with laughter and thunderous applause from all.

The Dutch production manager takes the microphone next and asks the workers for a round of applause for their past managers and a list of supervisors. He pauses afterward, saying, "If you want higher salaries, you have to give me faster picking rates. That's a promise!" Lillian shifts in her seat and whispers to me, "They can't go any faster without making so many mistakes. If he demands speed, quality will fall, and they'll end up getting sacked. It can't work." The production manager repeats his promise again in an attempt to rally the tired audience, "Are you hearing me? I've just made a promise! You'll give me speed, and I'll give you pay. OK?" The workers applaud this time, and he seems satisfied.

The emcee, a popular radio host, takes the stage, and the concert finally begins. True to their reputation, the farm directors dance with the workers for a while and then begin slipping out one by one. At 2 a.m., the production manager takes the stage again and announces that the DJ will play one last song and then "security guards will clear the premises." He delivers this last line with too much force, and a few in the audience cluck in disapproval. He announces it three more times: "I repeat. Security will clear the building." The party has ended and authority and order are forcibly reestablished.

Despite the threats, the remaining workers leave the building in good spirits, grateful for the night of "appreciation." Most workers went home earlier, exhausted from a hard day's work and anticipating an early shift the next morning.

In a sense, this show of "appreciation" for workers is part of how these managers search for belonging in Africa. As they would in the Netherlands, they wish to express an appreciation for the labor that has enriched their companies, and they gamely adapt the format of the party to fit the tastes of the African workers. In practice, however, these efforts are awkward, and essential hierarchies remain firmly in place. Their speeches challenge laborers to work harder and faster, suggesting that they are underperforming and costing the company additional possible profits. The managers also expect to be "appreciated" in return, and they are nonplussed by workers' brazen demands for higher pay and better living conditions.

Workers look forward to and enjoy events like this, especially because they provide an opportunity to observe managers' attempts to "be free" with them, which they regard as humorous. However, mutual "appreciation" does not necessarily help employees and managers belong in the same social, racial, and economic spheres. Black Kenyan senior managers, especially women, know that they have little chance of sitting at that big table, and Dutch managers sense that they are regarded as enigmatic potential patrons. At the end of the day, they call security to clear the building and retreat to a more comfortable white space, while workers retreat to their homes to catch what little sleep they can before returning to the greenhouse.

Dirk: "Us Dutchmen, We Are Grown Up to Be a Very Liberal-Minded Society"

The perspectives of another Dutch farm manager, Dirk, who came to Naivasha in 1995, provide insight into both Garritt's observation that the English community seemed "closed" and the reasons why some prominent white Kenyans in Naivasha characterized Dutch expatriates in particular as "fly-by-night venture capitalists."

I first met Dirk in 2004, when his farm was embroiled in a protracted argument with the Lake Naivasha Riparian Association (LNRA). In 2001, the LNRA commissioned an aerial survey to locate permanent structures built illegally in the lake's riparian reserve. Based on the aerial survey, the LNRA informed several landowners that they were in violation of the 1931 Riparian Agreement. Naivasha's two largest flower farms, Oserian and Homegrown, agreed to remove all greenhouses and permanent structures built in the riparian reserve, with the exception of their pump houses, which are allowed under the conditions of the agreement. Both of these farms had large landholdings that included acreage on the opposite side of South Lake Road. This gesture reduced their productive capacity, but they were able to shift cultivation to other spaces. They cited their voluntary compliance with the LNRA's demands as evidence of their deep commitment to social and environmental responsibility.

In the case of Dirk's farm, the LNRA insisted that the general manager's private residence and several blocks of greenhouses needed to be demolished. Dirk and his colleagues considered the LNRA's demands unreasonable, inconsistent, and illegitimate. They demanded that they not be "singled out" and argued that all of Kihoto, one of Naivasha's villages, had been built below the riparian line. The farm's owners also noted that the deeds to their lakeside plots, which they purchased in 1992, did not technically include a riparian reserve. The LNRA argued that these title deeds were illegal under the terms of the 1931 Riparian Agreement and viewed this as a clear case of "land-grabbing" facilitated by "corrupt" government officials.

Government officials agreed that the title deeds were "irregular," but stopped short of ordering Dirk's farm to comply with the LNRA's demands. The LNRA leadership saw this as a spectacular "failure" on the part of the government; they feared that the LNRA was losing its ability to enforce the conditions of the Riparian Agreement, an outcome they regarded with despair. They accused Dirk and his Dutch colleagues of coming to Naivasha to make as much money as possible and then "run away with the profits," and they alleged that someone in Dirk's company had bribed government officials to avoid having to remove the structures. They paid for an advertisement in the *Daily Nation* that "named and shamed" Dirk's farm and publicly criticized government officials for failing to uphold the terms of the Riparian Agreement.

When we met again in 2007, Dirk's farm had been sold to new owners, who had inherited the still broiling controversy. LNRA members and employees of Naivasha's other major farms saw this as evidence that they had been correct all along. The investors in Dirk's company had always intended to maximize short-term profits. After twelve years, they had sold the company and, it was rumored, shifted their investments to Ethiopia. Dirk decided to stay in Kenya and continue working for the company, but he was "not treated too gracefully" by the new owners and quit after helping with the transition. A few weeks before our conversation, he sold his shares and moved to a Nairobi suburb to start his own small floriculture venture.

Dirk looks slightly uncomfortable as he sits on the porch of La Belle Inn, smoking and squinting out at the dust that swirls down Naivasha's streets.

"I'm not too happy to be back in Naivasha [for our interview]," he tells me. "Life here is not very exciting, I'm sorry to say." He laughs and relaxes a bit when the waiter brings us a pair of cold Cokes. "I've been here twelve years, and that's enough. . . . My youngest is ready to start primary school. I don't want to put her in boarding school. Moving closer to Nairobi is the obvious choice." Dirk is married to a Kenyan woman and intends to raise his family in Kenya.

Like Garritt, Dirk was "born into" floriculture. His father started a small vegetable and flower farm in Holland in the late 1940s. He laughs when I ask why he decided to come to Kenya. "No reason in particular." He pauses and then says, "It was on my list. I could go to Brazil. I could go to France. Kenya was at the bottom of my list, and all of a sudden, I turned around, and Kenya was at the top of my list." He takes another drag on his cigarette and answers the question more seriously. "I was waiting to see whether it [the rose farms that had been established] was going to work. If it's not going to work, within a year, I go somewhere else. But I've been here twelve years now, so I must like it in one way or another."

Although he seems ambivalent about remaining in Kenya, he explains that he no longer feels at home in the Netherlands. "In the beginning, I was still eager to read some Dutch newspapers, but now I don't bother with that at all, because what they're talking about in the newspapers is so pathetic. It's so far from the reality of life." He provides an example. During a contest to establish a domino chain of world-record length, a bird kept knocking over the tiles. The organizers shot the bird, causing enormous public outcry. "Can you imagine? For shooting an old bird. They get so annoyed by such petty things. And then here, in Kenya, of course, there are people that are really fighting for their lives day in and day out." He continues: "I've experienced so many more things than I ever could have experienced if I'd stayed in Holland, and also my point of view about things has changed dramatically." This sense of gradual alienation from "home" was common within Naivasha's expatriate population.

Like Garritt, Dirk, too, sees Kenya as a more supportive, business-friendly operating environment for floriculture, and he laments the environmental and social regulations that make it difficult and expensive to remain in Holland. He explains, "If I wanted to start a flower farm today in Holland, and I discovered a frog with an orange spot, the whole thing would be stopped. The interests of ten people obsessed with a frog come before the interests of thousands who might benefit from the employment." Although he is sympathetic to the cause of environmental sustainability, he relishes the fact that development in Kenya is still human-centered and "free of the bureaucracy" (or, more accurately, participatory democracy) that tangles entrepreneurial ambitions in the Netherlands.

We chat a bit about his new farm, but he is guarded about the details. Limited competition is critical to the success of small, start-up flower businesses, and growers are often secretive about the varieties they intend to cultivate. "It's a small farm," he says, "and what we're growing has never before been done in Kenya. It's a seasonal flower in Europe, so we're offering a consistent supply and quality. Already, I have four major players that have expressed an interest in signing a contract that we supply only them." He has leased land near Nairobi, and the farm will be irrigated using borehole water. After years of fighting with the LNRA about water resources in Naivasha, he sees this as a distinct advantage of farming near Nairobi. "We won't have all the problems [with resource management] that we had here."

I ask him if he considered starting his own venture in Naivasha. He shook his head vigorously. "I would not start [a new farm] in Naivasha. There is, of course, a lot of pressure on Lake Naivasha, on its resources. . . . I do believe that—and it needs to be initiated by the government—that any further development in Naivasha should be stopped or very much restricted. Leave it the way that it is. There is already more than enough strain on the natural resources that are there." He sees his new farm as chance to expand the benefits of floricultural development to a new region. He explains, "I'm now starting this farm, and there is a whole estate of houses; maybe there are a few thousand people living there. I don't know. But those people don't have a job. For me, starting over there [means that] those people will have a prospect for income, and that community will, hopefully, financially prosper—small *dukas* [shops], people buying things."

Dirk describes himself as "a capitalist with a realistic worldview." He expresses disgust with the system of foreign aid and subsidies that has rendered African commodities worthless on the global market or left African nations entirely dependent on only a few crops. He explains, "Everyone is talking about globalization; but in one way or another, it's a lot of crap." He lists examples of unfair practices: price-fixing, tax-dodging, and the subsidies that influence where he sources his inputs (e.g., chemicals) and where he markets his products. He continues: "[We talk about] globalization and a free market economy, but only when it suits the Western world. I consider myself a Westerner, but it's not something to be proud of. . . . It's World, Incorporated. One hundred multinationals control everything." Surprisingly, Dirk views floriculture as a potential exception to his "World, Incorporated" vision of globalization. He argues, "They're all pointing fingers at the African continent, saying that it can't solve its problems, but the continent has never been put in a position where it can solve its problems. In one way or the other, [floriculture] is the best form of development aid."

Dirk staunchly denies that his farm's disagreements with the LNRA influenced his decision to leave Naivasha. He reacts strongly to this question. "Oh, no. Absolutely not," he says. "No, no. Because at the end of the day, I still believe that we are right." However, he admits that white Kenyan authority in Naivasha made this place unpalatable to him. He explains, "Kenya is a former British colony. . . . [H]ere in Naivasha, there are still many of them, the former colonials, and they still believe that they are some kind of an authority that you have to listen to." He argues vehemently that foreign investors should have to answer only to the government. "If we come over here, and we invest in Kenya[,] . . . [t]o who are you answerable? To a self-proclaimed group of people that want to say that they're in charge, or to the government of the country? . . . In my opinion, that should be the government[,] . . . regardless of how people might look at the government being corrupt. Yes or no; that's not an issue."

He refers to white Kenyans in Naivasha as "the establishment," and he views his own Dutch cultural values as antithetical to theirs. He explains, "Us Dutchmen, we are grown up to be a very liberal-minded society, a very liberal-minded people, which completely contradicts British society." When I ask him to explain what he means by "the establishment," he offers a damning caricature of white Kenyans in the lake area: "The British settlers. The first generation that came over here made the money; the second generation spends the money, and they never learned how to work; and the third generation isn't shit at the moment. Because the money's finished. They don't know how to work." He contrasts his willingness to "get dirty myself" with what he sees as laziness and dependency on the part of white Kenyans in Naivasha.

By invoking the extremely unflattering stereotype of white Kenyans as "old colonials" and the "established unemployed," Dirk was engaging in a fundamentally *political* act designed to undermine the legitimacy of LNRA members' claims to represent the interests of a diverse group of stakeholders in Naivasha. Dirk's views were extreme, and his anger was fresh. Few expatriate farm managers shared this polarized sense of the differences between being "Dutch" and "being colonial" in Naivasha. However, many Dutch farm managers described themselves as "more liberal" than their white Kenyan counterparts and shared Dirk's sense that power needed to be strategically reconfigured in Naivasha in order to optimize the possibilities inherent in floriculture. They viewed white Kenyan claims to "authority" in Naivasha as politically and socially problematic; and like Dirk, they preferred to work with black Kenyan professionals and government officials to establish guidelines for regulating floriculture and governing local communities and landscapes. They negotiated the "problem of belonging" in postcolonial Kenya by exhibiting (at least rhetorically) a greater level of "trust" and "faith" in the Kenyan capacity for self-governance and development.

WHITE KENYAN PERSPECTIVES ON FLORICULTURE

Historian Dane Kennedy describes Kenya's initial white settlers as "refugees not from capitalism, but from industrialism and its corollaries" (1987, 47). Following the agricultural depression of the late 1800s, the value of their land and investments in Britain had been considerably reduced. They came to Kenya out of a sense of "revulsion against these changes, against the allied forces of industrialism, urbanism, democracy, and egalitarianism that were transforming the whole of British life, reorganizing social relationships and remodeling cultural values" (47). In the early decades of colonial rule in Kenya, these settlers developed strict social codes designed to insulate the white community from the "threats" posed by indigenous peoples and environments, both of which were viewed as potentially hostile. They cultivated social and regulatory insularity and independence while, paradoxically, negotiating economic interdependence with a much larger native population. Kennedy describes settler communities in colonial Kenya as "islands of white" insulated from both African and European society. He characterizes white settlers as "a body of people who, even at the height of their power, were curiously anachronistic, largely at odds with the major currents of their time" (8).

Although popular depictions often cast white Kenyans in Naivasha as direct heirs to both "colonial" wealth and cultural attitudes, the reality is, of course, much more complex. A few white Kenyan families living in Naivasha have held title to local land since the colonial era, but many purchased their properties in the 1970s and 1980s. Some did so with capital earned from the sale of land in other parts of Kenya, especially coffee-growing regions, where their families had held title since before independence. Others purchased land using income derived from nonagricultural businesses in Kenya.

Regardless of their length of residence in Naivasha, they found the history of the area fascinating. They frequently showcased their knowledge of Naivasha in the era before floriculture, describing it as a "sleepy" rural community where residents engaged mainly in very limited forms of mixed farming focused on livestock and dairying. A third-generation white Kenyan explained this oft-articulated perspective: "Naivasha was an amazingly lazy backwater. . . . It was really an absolutely amazing, peaceful paradise." They acknowledged that Maasai pastoralists grazed cattle here seasonally, but they argued that "no one lived here permanently." In the words of one white Kenyan farmer, "This was supposedly a Maasai area, but it was never used extensively. They watered here in times of drought, and that was it. Now, of course, they're all saying, 'It's our land, and how dare you take it from us?' I'm sure you'll hear a lot of that. . . . Most Maasai have no claim to this area."

Many also stressed that, when they purchased land here in the 1970s and 1980s, "no one was interested in Naivasha." A white Kenyan farmer, who relocated here from Kitale after selling his family's coffee farm to a Kenyan-owned cooperative society in 1977, explained, "Put it this way: this was one of the areas which was not developed, and land was available. And, you know, there wasn't any politics. It was a place to come to. Although, at that time, there was no farming, per se. It was just ranching." He described Naivasha as essentially empty, *terra nova*, a good place for his family to enjoy a new life in a beautiful, lakeside setting, free from politics and the development pressures that characterized other parts of Kenya. He concluded: "If you can imagine this place with absolutely nothing. No buildings, a really bad dirt track. You've seen how powdery the soil is; everything was covered in dust. The town was just tiny. There was a bit of tarmac down the middle. There was nothing really. It was wide open, covered in game. There was just nothing."

These memories of Naivasha as a "peaceful paradise" where "there wasn't any politics" suggest that, in the 1970s and 1980s, this place became a new "island of white" as settler families sought to reestablish a relatively insular existence in independent Kenya. However, the need to generate enough capital to remain in Kenya, the desire to provide their children with a suitable education, and (starting in the late 1980s) the growth of the flower industry rendered insularity elusive and impractical.

I interviewed second-, third-, and fourth-generation white Kenyans, many of whom had been educated in, or had spent significant periods of their adult lives in, the United Kingdom, Europe, South Africa, Australia, or other locations far and wide. They considered themselves principally white Kenyan, but many had established dual citizenship by living, working, and/or studying elsewhere. In other words, they had left the proverbial island, and their perspectives on life in Kenya had been greatly influenced by these experiences and by the events and processes that have shaped Kenyan history since independence.

Given the opportunity to remain abroad, these white Kenyans had decided to return home to Kenya, partly because they valued an agricultural lifestyle and forms of self-determination and independence not possible in the populous, hyperregulated, postindustrial West. They came to Naivasha because they wanted to live in a peaceful place characterized by mixed farms, dairy operations, hotels, and campgrounds. This vision of Naivasha's past and future sat firmly at odds with Naivasha's present. For many white Kenyans in Naivasha, floriculture was a paradox. They associated the rise of floriculture with many forms of loss: of personal security, of environmental quality, and of power. However, floriculture also allowed them to diversify and solidify their economic fortunes and look forward to a future in which their children might also choose to remain in Kenya.

In an attempt to render floriculture less paradoxical, many white Kenyans in Naivasha became heavily involved in the initiatives designed to create a plan for comanaging the lake. Some agreed with the LNRA's restrictive approach to matters of riparian development. Others favored the LANAWRUA's primary focus on water resources, describing this approach as the more reasonable of the two initiatives. Despite disagreeing about how lakeside development should be controlled, white Kenyans agreed that, as a group, they should play a central role in devising these strategies. They felt strongly that those with intentions to remain permanently in Kenya, and those with a broader perspective on the area's history and potential, should steer its future. Their attempts to control and direct regulatory matters, and their tendency to stress their "deeper" attachments to this place, sometimes alienated their expatriate and black Kenyan counterparts.

White Kenyans living in Naivasha, and the expatriates with whom they formed the closest relationships, viewed floriculture as one of *many* possible pathways to development in Kenya. Drawing on their understanding of local and national history, they often sought to preserve or restore what they viewed as the ideal local environmental state—a Naivasha characterized by mixed farming and tourism. Their personal and professional lives revolved around their long-term commitment to this particular place and their desire to protect Kenyan landscapes from the aspects of floriculture that they viewed as most troubling. Having seen the fortunes of many Kenyan industries rise and fall, they suspected that floriculture might also boom and then bust. They viewed their environmental efforts as a means of protecting the value of their land, the security of their investments, and the potential for Naivasha to thrive within and beyond this moment.

Barbara: "The Conditions Are Way above the National Standard, and It Creates an Imbalance in the Whole Economy"

I arrive at the farm gate, and the guard radios the farm office to verify my appointment with Barbara, a third-generation white Kenyan who works as a senior farm manager. Barbara grew up in the Naivasha area and returned after attending university and completing a postgraduate degree abroad. Although she returned to Kenya with other aspirations in mind, the horticulture sector was hiring, and her higher degrees in a related field allowed her to secure a job. She explains, "I came back to Kenya, and [a now defunct horticulture firm] were looking for someone to start a laboratory—and I had the laboratory background. A lot of people [working in this industry] aren't horticulturalists per se."

I ask her to describe how Naivasha has changed since her youth, and she begins by highlighting two changes that run counter to expectations. "The lake is actually a lot higher than it was when I was a kid," she says. "And there were more trees. At independence, I gather, all of the trees by were cut down by fishermen to make charcoal. There was no control. I've got aerial photos somewhere. [It was] completely bare. . . . Of course, it could also have been the lake level, which largely determines the tree line. If the lake goes too low, the trees die." She also recalls that the lake water was much clearer and covered in water lilies. "There was also quite a bit of marina activity at the time—boating, sailing, and water-skiing."

She argues that, as a flower farmer, she has to stay up to date on the research concerning the lake. She explains, "Invariably the flower farms are accused of absolutely everything that goes wrong with the lake, so we've done a lot of research [on the problems facing Naivasha]." Based on her research, she argues that the primary threats to the lake are invasive species, sedimentation from smallholder farming in the upper catchment basin, and sewage runoff from the unplanned shanty settlements surrounding the lake. "Not runoff from flower farms," she emphasizes.

She argues that the need for pesticides in Kenyan floriculture is actually driven by European regulations that require all imported produce to be free of any and all insects. "Europe at the moment has zero tolerance for insect pests, so we have to be very careful. If we happen to send something overseas with an insect in it, we have to pay for the crop to be destroyed, and if we do it three times in a year, we lose our license, lose our export status. If consumers don't want us to use pesticides, then they'll have to deal with a few benign insects on the flowers," she says.

She continues her defense of floriculture, framing flowers as an environmental improvement over previous crops grown in Naivasha. "Agriculture here has moved from fodder to vegetables to flowers. . . . Covered flowers are much more environmentally friendly than outdoor vegetables. They're not necessarily more environmentally friendly than fodder crops, but fodder crops are much more water-intensive, so there's an improvement in terms of water-use efficiency." This was a common perspective among flower farm owners and managers in Naivasha. For instance, an expatriate farm manager explained, "As water is a limiting resource, the land use needs to be optimized. Looking at what is the most water-efficient crop, . . . which crops have the higher output for unit of water? [It's f]lowers. . . . We've got the highest profit margin, highest employment, and all sorts of things which . . . [contribute] to the local economy. . . . If the lake level drops, . . . it shouldn't be us who are the ones shut down."

Although Barbara agrees that flowers are more water-efficient, she, like many of her white Kenyan counterparts with longer historical roots in the area, stops short of arguing that floriculture should have priority access to water. She explains, "Everything gets more expensive, and you have to be able to evolve to survive. . . . If the center-pivot vegetable growers had restricted access to water twenty years ago, then none of the flower farms would even be here." The key to success in Naivasha agriculture is the ability to evolve and experiment with new crops. She views regulation as critical but rejects the notion that flower farming will necessarily remain the "highest, best" use of land in Naivasha.

Barbara argues that, unlike the owners of Dirk's farm, the majority of flower farm owners and managers in Naivasha are responsible and environmentally conscious. "Most of us are here to stay. There's been a tremendous amount of time and money invested in these farms. We intend to be here long-term," she explains. She argues that many of the improvements introduced to Naivasha flower farms in recent years were actually the products of internal processes, rather than external pressure from consumers and retailers. "Even before there was any pressure from outside, [our farm directors] have always been interested in the environment and conserving it. They're tied here. They want their kids to grow up here, their grandkids, and they also want to improve land. They're traditionally wheat farmers. [With wheat farming,] you have to be there a long time; you have to use good farming practices and try to improve your soil."

As evidence of the farm directors' commitments to ecological sustainability, Barbara highlights several features of the farm's design and the specific production strategies that she employs. "Over 50 percent of the land is uncultivated. The closest thing to the lake is fifty meters out, and our water comes from a sump, which is nowhere near the lake. . . . It means that we leave the papyrus fringe and everything intact. So we're not disturbing the lake edge at all." From her point of view, the real test of a farm's commitment to ecological sustainability lies in its willingness to leave large areas of extremely valuable land in an "undisturbed" state.

She also argues that the farm actively works to protect the lake from poachers who frequently trespass on riparian land. She explains, "The main thing is just to leave the entire bottom of the farm undisturbed, and these days it's also important to protect it. We have a lot of people coming in and stealing trees and papyrus and all sorts of things. Poaching the wildlife. . . . We keep a security guard down there with a radio; and if there are any problems, he calls us and we get the police. We don't actually confront them because it could be dangerous." She is aware of local complaints that flower-farm fences and gates prevent "public access" to the lakeshore; by invoking these images of wanton destruction of vegetation and wildlife by poachers, she seeks to justify enclosure as necessary for protecting the ecosystem. She contrasts this with the "free-for-all" that followed independence, when trees were indiscriminately cut for charcoal and there was "absolutely no control."

Behind Barbara's desk stands a shelf lined with binders labeled in black marker: "KFC Gold Standard," "Milieu Programma Sierteelt" (which translates from Dutch as "Environmental Program Floriculture"), and "EuropeGAP" (Good Agricultural Practice). These binders outline the policies that the farm must follow to ensure access to the European market. Barbara expresses a characteristic ambivalence about the utility of these codes. She recognizes that they help create a baseline for social and environmental practice and limit the market access of noncompliant farms. However, she views the scrutiny placed on Naivasha farms in particular as unfair and bristles at the fact that these codes are often derived from European laws and standards, which she argues have much less relevance in Kenya. She explains, "Definitely in the lake area here, it's a lot of proactive [policy making]. A lot of the codes have been in place [since] long before the consumers got involved, and we still get a lot of negative press even though we've had the systems in place for years. It really doesn't matter, because the consumers will listen to what they want to hear."

Rather than blaming the floriculture sector for the extreme population buildup in Naivasha, she describes this as an unfortunate by-product of their extreme vigilance and adherence to European codes. "Where I get upset—but maybe that's just me—is, we abide by all these European regulations, and the working conditions on the farm are much more enticing than the conditions on most other agricultural or horticultural farms, which means that people all over Kenya think that a good place to come to work is Naivasha." She continues: "The conditions are way above the national standard, and it creates an imbalance in the whole economy; and all those people come from miles away looking for work. . . . The standards in this industry are evolving much faster than other industries in Kenya. . . . We here in the lake area are held to a much stricter standard than anyone else, including farms in Europe."

The idea that floriculture had created an imbalance in the Kenyan economy was a common theme in my interviews with white Kenyans living in Naivasha. Another third-generation white Kenyan espoused this theory in starker terms. Staring out at the lake from his veranda, he spoke of a time when the lake water was clear, the road was unpaved, and the population of the lake basin was manageable. "All of these people from western Kenya are here because they bloody well destroyed their local environment, and now they've got no choice but to come here and destroy ours. What we need to do is invest in making their place livable again and get them to go back home."

A second-generation white Kenyan who managed a small flower farm also expressed frustration about being held accountable for "creating too much of a good thing." She argued, "They say that the farms are responsible for bringing all of these people here, but we haven't really brought them. They've come on their own. . . . In retrospect, it would have made sense to pump a lot of money into the reserves to keep them from flooding here. . . . There was no way to know how quickly this would all develop and the degree of control that would be lost."

Although white Kenyans disagree about whether the flower industry is entirely responsible for Naivasha's rapid unplanned development, they feel overwhelmed by the influx of people from other places. Because Kenya's contemporary social and economic geography bears the mark of colonial era engineering, they often express a paternalistic sense of responsibility for ensuring that Kenyan development occurs in an even manner. Naivasha was never meant to be a "reserve," they say, where the native labor pool would reside permanently. Operating on the assumption that most Naivasha migrants would rather be living somewhere else, they regret that they have not done more to invest in workers' "home" places. White Kenyans view themselves as having cared for Naivasha well; but in trying to secure their own livelihoods, they have made Naivasha irresistible to people who do not have the same capacity to care for the lake, or the same environmental ethics. A sense of regret about "the degree of control that would be lost" was common in my interviews with white Kenyans in Naivasha.

Barbara's defense of floriculture is rooted in her sense that farm owners and managers like herself are "proactive," "environmentally conscious," and fundamentally committed to the long-term health of the lake. Her comments suggest that farm owners are more capable of good environmental practice than the "local people," who regard riparian land as a place to hunt, fish, and cut trees for charcoal. Without the security and oversight provided by these farms, there would be no "controls" in place. Far from destroying the lake, the farms play a key role in protecting it. She argues that white Kenyan farm directors and managers have helped set high standards, especially for environmental practices, and that, by working together, Naivasha flower farms can force other "noncompliant" farms to improve their practices.

Like other farm managers, Barbara counters popular depictions of the negative "effects" of floriculture that she sees as inaccurate and unfair. However, she also reminds flower farm managers and owners that floriculture must not expand in a way that stifles flexibility, innovation, and evolution in the agricultural sector.

Oliver: "If You Want Money, You Plant Flowers. . . . If You Want What's Best for the Land, You Do a Mix of Dairy and Tourism"

Oliver, a third-generation white Kenyan, describes himself as primarily a dairy farmer, although he also grows baby corn and French beans for export. He explains, "My main source of income is the dairy operation. It's very good money, but we have a lot of overhead, perhaps because we're horrible managers." He laughs, and continues: "We don't have much profit, but we produce a thousand liters of milk a day." Like many "mixed farmers" in the area, Oliver has invested in horticulture as a way to subsidize his other agricultural and business activities. He explains, "I've devised a system where the fodder crops pay for themselves. I plant a baby corn variety in a rotation with French beans and sell these for export as an outgrower on a contract basis." He uses the by-products from the export vegetables as fodder for his dairy cattle, and he uses the money from the contract arrangement to buy fertilizer and other inputs.

Like Oliver, other white Kenyan farmers and business owners consistently downplayed their profits. A senior flower farm manager argued, "We could make a higher rate of return if we put the money in a savings account." Another white Kenyan mixed farmer explained, "[Small-scale horticulture] is bread and butter. Our pumping costs and labor costs are fairly high. Generally it makes ends meet, but we don't get much out of it—especially now, because the costs have gone up. We are barely able to pay for our wages and the electricity." The owner of a local tourism business warned me that he might not be in Naivasha for much longer. When I asked why, he answered, "As it turns out, we might not be able to afford to stay here."

Whether or not these statements reflected the true state of their financial affairs, white Kenyans argued that rumors of their "wealth" were overstated, and they characterized their profits as precarious and unpredictable at best.

More so than expatriate farm managers who had only recently arrived in Naivasha, white Kenyans understood that, as land- and business owners, they were patrons; they claimed that they immediately reinvested their profits in "the people" through wages, business contracts with local suppliers, and charitable pursuits.

Like Barbara, Oliver expresses a keen interest in preserving the ecological integrity of the lake and making environmentally responsible business decisions. He argues that he is involved in export horticulture only "because of the cows." He explains, "If I was in it for the money, I would cut down the all the trees and intensify my operation. [Horticulture is] a way of growing food for the farm. This farm is built for cows." He gestures toward the riparian area that borders his farm. "No, if you want money, you plant flowers. In my opinion, if you want what's best for the land, you do a mix of dairy and tourism. And maybe if you get the tourism right, you make more money than you can in horticulture. I don't know." Like many white Kenyan landowners in Naivasha, especially those with riparian land, Oliver believes that, if he can find the "right" mix of ranching, horticulture, and tourism, he can balance his livelihood activities with his desire to "leave the rest of the farm as a natural area" that will provide a refuge for wildlife. In order for this to work, in an economic sense, "tourism is necessary so that the wildlife pays."

Oliver's grandfather purchased this lakeside farm in the early 1980s. Oliver explains that "he was looking to buy a farm and wanted one that was the right size so he could run dairy cattle." Although he was born in Kenya, Oliver was educated abroad and returned "home" when his father got too old to manage the farm. In retrospect, he laments the missed opportunity to create a park here. "This really is a beautiful area. It's a shame that it wasn't made into a park like Nakuru. It's really a great shame that Naivasha didn't end up like that." He sees the gradual destruction of riparian land and wildlife habitat as a disturbing process that may, ultimately, be inevitable. "What I object to most is the clearing of land, but I guess this can't be avoided. I mean, soon enough, England will be one giant slab of concrete. I'm more interested in keeping the farm like this, simple farming."

Although he is critical of floriculture and its effects on Naivasha, he also recognizes that his farm exists in what he describes as a "symbiotic relationship" with floriculture. He sells his milk locally to hoteliers, farm canteens, and grocers. This market exists because of the population boom driven by floriculture. "I don't know. Maybe without them, I would be selling to the KCC [Kenya Cooperative Creameries]; or maybe there would be more hotels, and tourism would really be blossoming. There's no way of knowing." He thinks about it a bit more and seems to reconsider some of his more critical viewpoints on floriculture. "Look, the flower farms have been amazing for Kenya," he says. "I think the country is now the second-largest producer in the world. It's been fantastic for government employment and government revenue. It's fantastic from the economic point of view, but not particularly good for the environment."

Like many white Kenyans in Naivasha, he defends his right to "belong" here by citing his intimate knowledge of the land, his desire to protect his workers, and his concern for the wildlife that seek refuge on his farm. "I have fish poachers come onto the farm here. I confront them, and they tell me, 'You're white. You don't belong here.' And I tell them it's not true. I know this land better than you." He is clearly hurt and angry in response to this particular accusation. He continues: "I have no desire to stop them from fishing. That's between them and the fisheries department. But the problem is the trespassing. I have expensive equipment here and workers who hang a coat on the fence with a phone in the pocket. I can't just have people wandering the property."

Oliver argues that the local environment "needs to be protected from unscrupulous developers," and he agrees that "some kind of management plan is very necessary." However, he does not think that the LNRA-led efforts will ultimately succeed. He explains, "The problem is that the LNRA is really white landowners and a few Africans. They really don't have the teeth to enforce anything, and they're perceived as wealthy, bigger landholders. In the past, they really didn't have the support of the community in developing the plan. It's a very difficult issue." He argues, "What is needed is an efficient organization that's backed by the government. Efficiency is critical. It could even be part of NEMA." Other white Kenyan mixed farmers in the lake area also argued that the LNRA had "polarized" the community. They viewed the LANAWRUA as a hopeful alternative that would be less burdened by its perceived roots in Naivasha's "colonial" history, a damning label from which they were also actively trying to distance themselves.

Barbara's perspectives represent those of a growing set of white Kenyans who chose to work "within" the floriculture industry to promote the adoption of better environmental practices. Like many flower farm managers, she felt strongly that flower farms played a larger role in protecting the lake than they did in destroying it. Oliver's more ambivalent narrative reflects the perspective of many white Kenyan mixed farmers in Naivasha who, somewhat reluctantly, chose to participate in export horticulture. They kept their investments relatively small and insisted that their main goal was to funnel the returns into other forms of agriculture or tourism initiatives that were less profitable but more environmentally suitable to the area. A few white

Kenyan residents adopted a more radical stance and played a role in creating external forms of pressure designed to force flower farms to adopt more responsible environmental and labor practices. A story from my fieldwork introduces one such actor—Peter, a third-generation white Kenyan—and illustrates what this pressure looked like in practice.

Peter: "What Do You Think Would Happen If All of These Farms [Went] Belly Up Today?"

I am sitting on a tire well in the rear hatch of an ancient Land Rover, straddling a dead goat. Joseph sits across from me paging through the *Daily Nation*. His phone rings and he speaks in short bursts of his Maa dialect. The truck hits a deep rut in the tarmac and the goat slides forward, its stiff legs knocking against a can of petrol. The goat smells not like death but like grass and mud and sweat. One of Joseph's two males, it died just this morning after a short illness. He claims that eighty-six of his goats, a small fortune on the hoof, have died after drinking poisonous water from a ditch adjacent to a flower farm.

A local journalist has already visited Joseph's home and taken photographs of the piled carcasses. He brought along a German colleague, who took water samples from the ditch and asked Joseph to wear a red wool *shuka* (blanket) for the photograph. But now three days have passed. The story has not been printed, and Joseph has received no word regarding the water samples. He wants to be compensated for his losses, and he needs something that will give him leverage with the farm's general manager, who has already turned him away once. The farm manager insists that, in compliance with the KFC's code of practice, his farm has strict wastewater management strategies in place. He himself inspects the farm daily to ensure that there are no illegal discharges, and an accidental poisoning event would be impossible. He accuses Joseph of attempted extortion.

We have enlisted the help of Peter, a white Kenyan campground owner, to take Joseph's goat to be autopsied. Peter's grandfather came to Kenya before 1910. Peter's father helped found Hell's Gate National Park and worked diligently to document Naivasha's history. Peter prides himself on his understanding of Kenyan social and political relations and his intimate knowledge of local history. He often shares stories of how Naivasha has changed since his family first established residence here.

As a self-identified "radical environmentalist," Peter has little use for the more than fifty flower farms that now line the shores of Lake Naivasha. He is a member of various committees that address environmental issues in the lake area, and Joseph's accusations would attract significant attention to his cause. When we discuss the effects of floriculture in the lake area, Peter often argues that "these farms are missing a fantastic opportunity to go completely green." At other times, he fantasizes about what would happen if the industry collapses. Many of his acquaintances are farm managers, and he listens eagerly for news that flower farming is no longer profitable in Kenya or for them to "honestly admit" their culpability in the radical changes under way in Naivasha. Until he begins to see signs of either of these outcomes, he has dedicated himself to applying pressure on these farms by other means.

It is sometimes unclear what he hopes this pressure will achieve. To some extent this is an exercise in making flower farm practices visible to an international community he thinks has been duped into believing that floriculture in Naivasha is sustainable. He would prefer a future in which Lake Naivasha becomes a renowned destination for ecotourists. He reckons that his difficult stance on floriculture has made him "persona non grata" among other white Kenyans. He is proud of this status, and argues that he does not regret this outcome. Membership on various environmental committees helps him regain some of this lost sense of community. Behind the wheel of the Land Rover, Peter swerves to miss a particularly nasty pothole.

The steady inflow of dust subsides as we pull to a stop in Naivasha Town. Peter arranges for the goat to be dissected by a friend, a veterinarian with a strong antifloriculture bias who would relish evidence of poisoning. "This is really quite fortuitous," says Peter, explaining that he ran into the veterinarian's husband at the supermarket. "She'll literally spend hours on this." Peter's friend calls the next day with the autopsy result. Joseph's goat succumbed to pasteurella, a communicable bacterial infection that spreads through mucous deposited on grass as an animal grazes. The goat had suffered a double lung collapse. The veterinarian found both lungs deflated and plastered against the interior of the rib cage. The disease is one of a few that affects goats more acutely than sheep, which explains why Joseph's other animals were not affected. There were no signs of poisoning. He advised that Joseph should vaccinate what remains of his herd with a common antibiotic. Peter gives me the name of the medication to pass on to him. I walk up to Joseph's *manyatta* (group of houses occupied by his family members), which rests just over Peter's property line on what is technically government land, a corner of Hell's Gate National Park on which Joseph and several other Maasai families are tolerated as "squatters." I deliver the news of the autopsy. Joseph asks me to repeat the information twice and then thanks me as he rushes down to the *matatu* stage to buy the necessary medicine in town. We do not discuss whether Joseph might have known that his livestock had a communicable illness. Nothing in his behavior signals that this was a deliberate attempt at extortion. He had been upset when the manager dismissed his accusations out of hand.

The matter rests until three months later, when Joseph's story finally appears in the *East African*, a prominent regional newspaper, as the lead-in for a feature article on the impacts of flower production on Lake Naivasha. The article garners elevated status for Joseph within the Maasai community, and several influential peers applaud him for drawing attention to their struggle for access to land and resources enclosed by flower farming.

Peter laughs as he reads the article, "It's completely unbelievable isn't it! But I think I'm rather happy about it." Peter's close friend Otieno, a safari guide and human rights activist who has worked on previous campaigns to improve working conditions in the flower industry, explains, "The scientific explanation [the autopsy result] is irrelevant because the problem is still there." Joseph, Peter, and Otieno define "the problem" of floriculture in very different terms, but in this instance, they settled on the same "solution."

For Joseph, this was a means of demanding rights to a confiscated ancestral territory. However, it was also a way of accessing the profits generated by this lucrative industry. Whether this was blatant extortion or a genuine claim for compensation, Joseph made strategic use of his Maasai ethnicity to amplify the legitimacy of his claim. He wore his *shuka* for the reporters and argued that, ultimately, this problem was a result of the enclosure of grazing land in Naivasha. His handling of this situation also garnered him recognition within the local Maasai community.

For Otieno, this was a project of making the industry more responsive to the needs of Kenyan workers and environments. His mother worked for twenty years for a local flower farm, and he remained appalled by the living and working conditions on these farms. He saw himself as responsible, as an educated Kenyan professional, for ensuring that "the problem" of floriculture remained a subject of debate and political action.

For the farm's general manager, this was an injustice, a false accusation not worthy of his attention. He dismissed Joseph because he was confident that this problem had *not* resulted from his farm's negligence. He viewed Joseph's claim as a typical case of "extortion," an example of the kinds of "corruption" that threaten Kenya's "best opportunity to develop itself." The *East African* article will become another of the unfair and inaccurate "smear pieces" cited by managers in "the speech" as evidence that "none of what you read about floriculture is true."

For Peter, this was a way of protecting a fragile ecosystem, an environment in which his livelihood in tourism and his family's history were deeply embedded. Like his father before him, he served as an advocate for conservation and the keeper of historical memory related to white Kenyan occupation and stewardship of this space. Like Joseph, he also viewed floriculture as a threat to his birthright and his way of "belonging" in Naivasha.

Nearly every time I visited Peter, he asked me some version of the same question. "Tell me, Megan," he would say, "as an anthropologist what do you think would happen if all of these farms go belly up today? Would all of these people bugger off back home and leave this place deserted? I need to believe that is what would happen." Peter saw his environmental activism as a way of protecting Naivasha's future, one that he was not willing to share with anyone who did not value the local environment and understand the "proper" ways to exist within it.

Anthropologist Katja Uusihakala argues that white colonial history in Kenya is "a dialogue between displacement and commitment" (1999, 27). For white Kenyans living and working in Naivasha, floriculture is a double-edged sword that allows them to act on their commitment to Kenya but also furthers processes that could lead to their displacement. They see incredible potential in floriculture, but they also view it as a form of development that has undermined existing forms of social and environmental control in Naivasha, especially the authority vested in them by the 1931 Lake Naivasha Riparian Agreement.

As has been the case in white Zimbabwe (Hughes 2010), environmental conservation has become central to the ways that white Kenyans establish a sense of belonging in Naivasha and signal their commitment to postcolonial Kenya. White Kenyans like Barbara, who are deeply invested in floriculture, argue that they are working from within to make the entire industry more environmentally responsible. Others, such as Oliver, embrace floriculture as a necessary part of a mixed farming strategy, but insist that they use the capital to subsidize other types of farming that they view as more "appropriate" for the local environment. Some, such as Peter, hope that flower farms will either go "radically green" or go "belly up" and allow Naivasha to flourish as a place devoted to other, more sustainable, livelihood pursuits. They use the tools available to them, especially the international press, to remind a global community that Naivasha is a place with *many* possible development futures.

White Kenyans' viewpoints on floriculture are centered on collective memories of Naivasha's past, a lost social and environmental landscape for which many feel nostalgic. However, they also object to the loss of alternative development possibilities in Naivasha. If floriculture comes to be regarded as the only legitimate and desirable form of agricultural production in Naivasha, what will become of their livelihoods in dairy ranching? Tourism? Open-air vegetable horticulture? If all of Naivasha's resources are earmarked for floriculture, what will remain of this place when and if the industry collapses (as so many have before)? As white Kenyans participate in the (re) negotiation and (re)construction of environmental and social governance strategies in Naivasha, they remind expatriate farm owners and managers that, no matter how successful floriculture is now, *sustainability* means maintaining the possibility for alternative futures and the capacity for innovation and change.

As white Kenyans narrate their perspectives on floriculture, they stress their long-range historical perspectives, their long-term commitments to this place, and their extensive knowledge of both the local environment and Kenyan peoples. Many cooperate closely and productively with their black Kenyan and expatriate counterparts as they work, from within and without, to make floriculture more responsible to Kenyan environments. However, their cooperative efforts are sometimes hindered by a tendency to view others, especially the population of general flower-farm laborers, as recent immigrants who lack the same capacity or desire to care for this place. Although they express concern for the local environment, they often cast the growing human population of Naivasha as a problem that can best be solved by creating opportunities for people in their home communities far away from here. They view the growing local population as a security issue, a burgeoning threat to the lake and to their own personal safety. By keeping the public away from the lake, they argue, they are protecting wildlife and their fixed assets in floriculture. What they see as legitimate means of protecting their security and private property, local land rights activists frame as problematic forms of enclosure that extend colonial-era practices into the present.

Expatriate farm managers are also proud of their efforts to behave responsibly in Naivasha, and they seek to counter popular discourses characterizing them as neocolonial actors bent on exploiting African communities and environments. They view floriculture as the "best form of development aid" for Kenya, and they frame Kenya's present as an evolutionary stage that resembles a moment in the European past. They believe fervently that business-minded policies will help the nation progress, and they see themselves as helping reengineer Kenyan institutions and governance structures so that the "economy can do the work" of development. Many form close personal and professional relationships with white Kenyans;

but in 2007, relationships between Dutch and white Kenyan farm managers were especially strained by the protracted struggle between Dirk's farm and the LNRA.

All white actors in Naivasha are keenly aware that their claims to political authority, responsible behavior, and belonging in this space are tied to contemporary discourses about colonial heritage, white privilege, and global inequality. Accusing one another of colonial or exploitative behavior could be used to advance their own claims to land and resources. Younger expatriates sometimes describe themselves as more liberal in their approach to life in Kenya, but the enduringly hierarchical aspects of the floricultural workplace reinforce the racialized and gendered inequalities they aspire to undermine.

At the top of the cut flower commodity chain, expatriate and white Kenyan flower-farm managers also discovered that floriculture may be more slippery than it seems. Most firmly believed in the industry's development potential, and they genuinely saw themselves as contributing in productive ways to processes of environmental and social reform in the industry. However, they were also aware of the many ways that their rosy aspirations for personal economic prosperity, regulatory control, and regional development might slip away. Their power to develop and protect Naivasha might be limited by factors beyond their control and outside of their comprehension. White Kenyans hedged their bets by diversifying their economic portfolios and working to preserve Naivasha's ecological integrity; expatriates remained prepared to move to other sites of tropical horticultural production. In the meantime, they did all they could to profit from floriculture, establish a sense of belonging in Naivasha, and shape ongoing conversations about what constitutes responsible behavior in this industry.

Conclusion

A Changing Naivasha

NAIVASHA is a nerve center in a triple sense. It is a politicized space with a contested history that touches nerves, sparking moral concern and debate about the ethical dimensions of global trade and export-led development. It is also a transnational space of interconnection, where wealth, power, and opportunity are concentrated. Lastly, it is a creative space where new strategies for social and environmental governance are developed, tested, and (potentially) expanded. Viewing Naivasha as a nerve center helps us see the many forms of agency and resistance at work in floriculture and prevents us from dismissing the aspirations of people living and working here as hollow ambitions. It also helps us understand the appeal (at least initially) of the rollout phase of neoliberalism in this postcolonial context. As they tend roses, advocate on behalf of workers, perform audits and inspections, or travel to international trade shows, these actors are participating in an ongoing process of nation building and statemaking. People living and working here attempt to catalyze change at a personal and structural level using the opportunities and resources concentrated in this industry.

The experiences and perspectives of specific individuals inform this ethnographic portrait of what life is like in Naivasha, how this place became a transnational nerve center, and why these changes are significant. Their aspirations and "dreams of flowers" help us understand the ways that Naivasha both aggravates moral economic and political sensibilities and innervates change in contemporary Kenya. Their aspirations matter, regardless of whether they are actualized, and their dreams are located within broader development discourses, political and economic processes, and the social and environmental history of this particular place. Different categories of actors dream differently in this space, and through their attempts to collaborate, this nerve center has the potential to "become something other" in the near or distant future.

Although the actors discussed here are profoundly dependent on floriculture, their ambitions often have little to do with cultivating flowers. They are interested in harnessing the forms of wealth, connection, and power concentrated in this industry in the service of dreams that predate and extend beyond this temporal moment. Some desire to preserve the potential for Naivasha to be a less densely populated space for nature-based tourism, mixed farming, and rural residential estates. Others envision Naivasha as a potential hub for energy generation and industrial development. Actors living and working here fundamentally disagree about who should have the right and the power to direct matters of development in Naivasha; but in the rollout phase of neoliberalism, they all see a compelling new role for the Kenyan state in this process. In this nerve center, roses are a complex means to many different ends. Conflicts over social and environmental regulation in Naivasha floriculture are also conflicts over how (and by whom) *Kenya* should be governed.

Too often in ethnography, we introduce key actors, explore their lives, and then leave them frozen in time, their stories paused in a single moment. Humanizing a commodity chain also means continuing to examine how these actors' perspectives and experiences change over time. To this end, I offer another glimpse into the lives of some of the people whose stories and voices I share in the preceding chapters.

RECONNECTIONS: "I AM STILL HERE; I AM STILL ALIVE"

When I last visited Eunice in person, in 2014, she embraced me at the Kamere *matatu* stage, smiling at me and laughing, "I am still here. I am still alive. I am not dead." We walked from the road to her one-room house, the same residence where I found her in 2007. She still worked for the same company, but in 2010 she was moved from the packhouse floor into a new position washing buckets. "My speed had reduced too much," she explained. Her salary was not altered, but she was now ineligible for the piece-rate bonus awarded for packing flowers quickly. "I don't mind the work," she said. "Now I report to the job at the same time every day at 8 a.m. instead of the earliest hours."

She had finished paying for a very small (one-eighth-acre) plot in Molo, and she was still paying for a second one. Her son explained, "She was cheated a bit. She thought that she was buying a plot adjacent to her first one so she would have a quarter-acre. When the papers came, it was another plot from the same subdivided property, but it was far from her first plot." She had recently taken out another loan to pay secondary-school fees for her daughter, and she planned to retire after her daughter completed her schooling. During our visit, a niece stopped by to chat as we prepared the afternoon meal. They discussed a neighbor who had recently been laid off from a nearby farm. Eunice whispered, "She is just staying in the house and not telling anyone." Although Eunice's position seemed secure, the specter of unemployment always loomed near.

In December 2018, Eunice formally retired after nearly thirty years of continuous employment in floriculture. She is still raising funds to pay for the construction of a small house on her plot and plans to relocate to Molo in 2019.

Tony, the low-level farm manager who dreamed of *maisha bora* ("the good life") and a career with KenGen, the electricity generating company, no longer works in floriculture. After losing his job as a production manager in 2008, he found a position at a flower farm in Uganda. "I worked there for one year," he explains, "but the pay was too low despite my title as a manager." He returned to Kenya, and a relative helped him find contract work at KenGen. In December 2011, he was given a position as foreman supervising the drilling of new geothermal wells.

The small flower farm where Tony's wife, Priscilla, worked as a supervisor was taken over by another company in 2011. Priscilla was laid off, and she and Tony no longer qualified to live in on-farm housing. They moved with their children into a one-room house in one of Naivasha's villages. Priscilla quickly found a job working as a general laborer at another farm, but by 2014 the company had been placed in receivership. The farm's fate was unclear, and she was once again looking for work. When I visited them not long after this, our conversations were steeped in sadness as we spoke of both the uncertainty surrounding her employment and the loss of their oldest daughter, who had recently died of a congenital disease. Priscilla and Tony were using loans against their salaries to educate their oldest son, who was enrolled in a technical degree program at the University of Nairobi. Tony's contract employment sustained them, but the strain of losing a child and the possibility of losing Priscilla's income stressed them financially and personally.

In 2018, Tony was hired by KenGen as a permanent, full-time employee, and he and Priscilla moved into a freestanding, multiroom home that fit his 2008 vision of "the good life." Priscilla did not find another job in floriculture and stopped working because, in Tony's words, "the flower industry in Kenya is not doing so well." Their oldest son graduated with his university degree, and their second-born son was studying for a degree in natural resource management, hoping for a career in the civil service. By transitioning from floriculture to the geothermal sector, Tony and Priscilla managed to find some success in a changing Naivasha.

Kasaya, the welfare officer who was not afraid "to be a bit political," is no longer employed by Zawadi Flowers. In 2010, after Zawadi was acquired by new owners, a human resources consultant hired by the company invited him to lunch at an upscale lakeside hotel. "I didn't know what it was about," he explained. "We sat down to eat, and they just said, 'We appreciate your work, but we are very sorry that we will not be able to keep you on the payroll.' They offered me the opportunity to resign honorably now, keep my benefits, stay in the house, and keep the kids in school. They said if I did not take the offer, they would do everything possible to make sure I went." He chose to resign. "I viewed it as a godsend. I had already decided to quit the next week. They didn't want to spend any money on welfare, and I was the only one bringing them problems. I was ready to involve government agencies. They gave me a banker's check and dismissed me that very day."

Since 2009, he has been working with a group of labor advocates to establish a new labor union, the Kenya Export Floriculture and Allied Workers Union, which will exclusively serve export-flower-farm workers. He explained the need for an alternative to the Kenya Plantation and Agricultural Workers' Union, which previously represented floricultural workers. "The union representing workers was founded in the 1940s during the colonial period, before flowers and vegetables, and they targeted only general workers. There were no supervisors and managers in the union. What could they do when they were sacked?" Kasaya and his colleagues applied to officially register the new union in 2009; but Francis Atwoli, who serves as both the general secretary of the Kenya Plantation and Agricultural Workers Union and the secretary general of Kenya's Central Organization of Trade Unions, opposed the registration, arguing that a separate union for the flower sector was unnecessary. In 2011, Kasaya and his colleagues filed a lawsuit with the Employment and Labour Relations Court to win the right to register the union, and in February 2014 the court ruled in their favor. Atwoli and the Central Organization of Trade Unions appealed this decision, but in May 2017 the Kenyan Court of Appeals again ruled in favor of the new union (Sherman 2017).

When I spoke with Kasaya after he won the right to register the union, I asked him about the next steps in this process and how the new union would benefit workers in floriculture. He argued, "Anybody who is for the good of his workers will allow them to join our union. What employer wants his workers to be oppressed? Pray for us. This union is the savior of the workers, and if it succeeds we will be talking a different language. We won't have to fight the employer. We will be able to negotiate and improve productivity." Although he no longer worked in floriculture, he was still agitating for change and making strategic use of the reputation and connections he forged while at Zawadi to fight for improved working conditions and better employment security for laborers and managers.

Isaiah, the human resources manager who ran for a seat in Parliament in 2007, made good on his promise to ascend to national political prominence. In 2017, he was elected to national political office. I leave the details intentionally vague here to help protect his identity, but Isaiah's path to power speaks to the role that Naivasha plays as a political nerve center in Kenya. Isaiah's "exposure" here helped him demonstrate his legitimacy as an advocate for Kenyan workers, members of his regional ethnolinguistic community, and the Kenyan political class. The power and prominence that he cultivated in Naivasha helped him defeat several candidates with impressive connections and political pedigrees.

Tom, the founder of the small NGO focused on gender equity, who hoped to "make changes and get access to central funds and resources," also met with success. His work on gender and environmental issues in Naivasha captured the attention of an international NGO focused on conflict management, which offered him a job working on national-level issues. He no longer lives in Naivasha, but in 2014 we were able to reconnect when his team stopped in Naivasha for a meeting with some local community partners. "I've moved away from gender and workers' issues," explained Tom. "My focus now is on resource conflicts and land politics." He was satisfied with his new position. He was paid well, and the organization had greater power, prominence, and funding. In 2018, he was still employed with the same NGO. He felt passionately about the topics he addressed through his work but noted that grants had been scarcer in recent years.

REORGANIZATIONS: "WE'RE STILL FUNCTIONING, AND WE'RE STILL FUNDED"

When I reconnected with figures centrally involved in environmental politics and regulation in Naivasha in 2014, I found the same set of influential actors working diligently on similar projects; but in most cases, their major funders and partner organizations had changed. In the intervening years, the Lake Naivasha Riparian Association had become less active. After stepping down as chairman, Andrew Cole sold his lakeside property and relocated. His immediate replacement served as chairman for a short time and then stepped down. A new chair had been elected, and the group still met annually, but my research collaborators argued that the organization's leadership role in local environmental initiatives had been reduced.

Although the LNRA-led management plan process was never successfully revived, two subsequent multistakeholder initiatives did generate integrated management plans for the lake basin. In 2011, a set of organizations secured a two-billion-shilling grant (about $23.5 million USD) to restore Lake Naivasha by creating a new community-based management initiative, called Imarisha Naivasha. This initiative was spearheaded by Raila Odinga during his short time as Kenya's prime minister, a position negotiated as part of the "power-sharing" agreement that ended the postelection crisis in 2008. In Swahili, *imarisha* means "to strengthen, repair, and renew." Through a multistakeholder process, Imarisha Naivasha developed a Lake Naivasha Basin Integrated Management Plan and a five-year Sustainable Development Action Plan, 2011–16. These plans relied heavily on tools and concepts that flower growers deemed business-friendly and realistic. The plans focus on water-use regulation and planning as the cornerstone of sustainable development in the catchment basin. In January 2013, the embassy of the Kingdom of the Netherlands in Nairobi provided funding for yet another multistakeholder water resource planning initiative, the Integrated Water Resource Action Plan program. This program was coordinated by the World Wildlife Federation in cooperation with Imarisha Naivasha, the Water Resources Management Authority (WRMA), and the Kenya Flower Council.

Many of the black Kenyan professionals in charge of implementing these initiatives were centrally involved in the LNRA-led Lake Naivasha Management Plan process in the past. They joked that they "had to please new masters" every time their donor funds expired, but they also viewed the Integrated Water Resource Action Plan program and Imarisha Naivasha as a continuation of their earlier work. These management plans helped bring some of their long-term aspirations to fruition, and these initiatives provided them with employment as well as continued exposure to new ideas, project partners, and training opportunities.

Flower farmers involved in the Lake Naivasha Water Resource Users Association (LANAWRUA) initiative in 2007 and 2008 also saw Imarisha Naivasha as a productive extension of their efforts, in part because they now viewed the WRMA as too poor to implement and enforce the policies recommended by the LANAWRUA. Mr. Stone, the senior farm manager who showed me the photo of the earth from space, was now a member of the Imarisha Naivasha leadership team. He explained, "WRMA still needs assistance to do its job properly. Its capacity is limited. Imarisha Naivasha helps coordinate implementation. We find those with money and expertise, and our work supports WRMA." He admitted that the dissolution of the prime minister's office in 2010 placed Imarisha Naivasha "in a lacunae," but he stressed that, despite the shifting national political terrain, "we're still functioning, and we're still funded."

Harrison, the charismatic young civil servant who enthusiastically embraced his new mandate in 2008, was still employed with the WRMA. Unlike Mr. Stone, he viewed Imarisha Naivasha as a distraction. He explained, "Why should the government pay Imarisha for work that the WRMA is doing? What LANAWRUA is doing?" The enthusiasm that he expressed for his work in 2008 had waned considerably by 2014. He alleged that the government had also misappropriated the WRMA's funding: "WRMA salaries come from water use fees, but only 15 percent of this goes back to WRMA. How can I write a report about how we used the hundred million shillings we received, when I never saw the money?" He still believed strongly in the WRMA's mission, and he argued that something should be done to ensure that water use fees actually come back to the WRMA. He hoped that the 2014 Water Bill, which was still being debated in Parliament, would "capture" the lessons learned since 2002. Despite his disappointment with his career, he stressed that "the best part of the job is being exposed to all sorts of people, German, French, US, name them." He also argued that WRUAs had generated tangible environmental improvements in the upper catchment, where "enlightened and informed" farmers no longer engaged in environmentally destructive practices.

As was the case in 2007 and 2008, those who were given (or who retained) authority, power, and access to funding through these partnerships viewed them with great enthusiasm. Those, like Harrison, who had seen their authority and access dwindle as these institutions evolved, were more pessimistic about whether these initiatives would help prevent further environmental degradation in the area immediately surrounding Lake Naivasha.

RENEWABLES: DREAMING OF (GEOTHERMAL) POWER

In recent years, the Kenyan government has fast-tracked geothermal development in the Naivasha area, creating new challenges and opportunities, new aggravations and innervations. By 2030, Kenya plans to generate five thousand megawatts of geothermal energy (Geothermal Development

FIGURE C.1 Newly constructed pipelines carrying steam to a geothermal power facility. In the last five years, geothermal development has expanded rapidly and aggressively in Naivasha, solidifying the area's status as a Kenyan nerve center.

Company 2015). With monetary infusions from the World Bank and private sector investment, Kenya has constructed new geothermal wells and power plants throughout the Rift Valley.[1] Most of this development is centered on the Olkaria region near Lake Naivasha.[2] In October 2014, President Uhuru Kenyatta opened a new geothermal power plant in Naivasha, declaring that this occasion represented "a milestone in our country's journey to self-sufficiency, competitiveness, and prosperity" (Rojas 2014). His comments underscore Naivasha's status as a nerve center, a perennial focus for Kenyan aspirations for development, global connection, and (this time quite literally) power (figure C.1).

In 2014, many local actors viewed geothermal expansion with excitement, but they also expressed concern about the pace of this development and the level of secrecy surrounding it. Harrison, for instance, worried that the geothermal sector was beyond the reach of critique. He explained, "Geothermal has impacts you cannot report. That one is a national government project, and there is no way to say, 'No.' With these government projects, you come to the table, you discuss, but you have no powers." When I asked him if he thought the industry was likely to have any negative impacts, he replied, "We will see an impact. There are more than three thousand more wells planned, and there are many fault lines. Maybe they will strike a fault line, and then the lake is gone." Many local actors shared Harrison's concern that geothermal wells might affect the quantity and quality of local water resources.[3]

When I spoke with the chairman of the LANAWRUA in 2014, he indicated that he was "not at all" concerned about the challenges posed by geothermal development in the lake's basin. He explained, "We have to look at it from the broader perspective. It brings employment to the area. I'm not aware of any large environmental effects. They're drilling at deep depths with no direct impact on groundwater. They will draw some water. We'll certainly need to look at what can be developed without causing harm to other water users." I followed up by asking if the major players in geothermal power were currently participating in the water resource users group. "Not at the moment, but I am confident that they will come to the table. From a private-sector perspective, this is about managing risks. They can't risk running out of water, and they can't risk conflicts with other stakeholders. The whole idea is that we work together to get enough water to do what you want to do. We need to engage with one another to manage risks and fulfill our strategies regarding sustainability."

Among those who worked in floriculture or for nongovernmental organizations involved in advocating for environmental causes in Naivasha, there was recognition that geothermal development was proceeding rapidly, and that all or most forms of environmental governance in Naivasha were designed explicitly to regulate floriculture. However, most viewed this phase of uncontrolled expansion as temporary, and they expressed confidence that the geothermal sector would "come to the table" in good time.

REFLECTIONS: POWER, PLACE, AND POSSIBILITY IN A CHANGING NAIVASHA

For the majority of low-wage laborers in Naivasha floriculture, the benefits of this industry are slippery. By using loans against their salaries, many workers are able to at least partially fund some long-term projects: they pay school fees for dependent children, make small payments to land brokers, and help family members recover from unexpected accidents and illnesses. However, these investments may prove precarious, their employment may be unstable, and their debts may be unserviceable. Floriculture offers more robust and enduring benefits to members of the educated Kenyan middle class—midlevel managers, technical professionals, and social and environmental advocates. These actors are best-positioned to take advantage of the forms of access and exposure that their work in floriculture provides.

Although monetary wealth certainly does not "trickle down" from this managerial class to general laborers, these professionals occupy important positions as intermediaries who lobby farm directors for social welfare reforms. Many are also influential patrons who use their positions in floriculture to redistribute resources throughout their social networks and establish political power and legitimacy by serving the interests of members of their ethno-regional communities. Their experiences and perspectives remind us that Naivasha is a space of political performance, a place where powerful actors make and deliver on campaign promises in exchange for votes and other forms of political allegiance and support. As they audit compliance with social and environmental standards on Naivasha flower farms, middle-class technical professionals seek to make this practice more virtuous and less virtual. They attempt to close loopholes, and they take seriously their role in enforcing these regulations.

White actors living and working in Naivasha are subject to (and exercise agency within) contemporary discourses linking race, privilege, and colonialism. Through their work in floriculture and in environmental conservation, they seek to solve the problem of (white) belonging in postcolonial Africa by demonstrating their commitment to Naivasha and to Kenya more broadly. White Kenyans and European expatriates approach this problem of belonging differently and cultivate different senses of place in Naivasha. Expatriates emphasize the positive economic development associated with floriculture, their role in advocating the responsible use of precious water resources, and their freer social relations with black Kenyan workers—relations that, in practice, still reflect profound power differences. White Kenyans often express broader concerns for the Lake Naivasha ecosystem, their "deeper" knowledge of the history of this place and of Kenyan communities, and their support for a hybrid landscape characterized by mixed farming and tourism. White actors see Naivasha as a place where Kenyan institutions can be productively reconfigured to make global industries more environmentally and socially responsible; however, they often disagree about who should control the institutions and how they should work.

The relationship between the cut flower industry and the Kenyan state is an evolving one. Journalists point out all the ways that the Kenyan state seemingly allows the cut flower industry to "cheat" by selectively enforcing tax, labor, and environmental laws. However, the state also benefits in profound ways from the many diplomatic and regulatory services provided by the Kenya Flower Council and the floricultural sector more generally. In 2007, the Brand Kenya campaign, the Economic Partnership Agreement negotiations, and the new LANAWRUA initiative served as spaces where powerful actors (re)negotiated the relationship between state and corporate sovereignty during the rollout phase of neoliberalism. Flower industry representatives served as co-opted agents of the state, negotiating the terms of international trade, fighting to preserve the nation's image as a safe place for foreign direct investment, and rewriting Kenyan water law to "rationalize" access to precious (and possibly dwindling) water resources. The expansion of the geothermal industry in Naivasha, however, highlights an important shortcoming in the forms of governance associated with the rollout phase of neoliberalism in Naivasha. Industrial self-regulation in the flower industry (e.g., the Kenya Flower Council and Lake Naivasha Growers Group codes of conduct) and management plans created through collaboration between local stakeholders (e.g., the LANAWRUA) have resulted in regulatory strategies that are very specific to floriculture. If a new land use suddenly becomes dominant and the "players" responsible for this industry are not at the table, they are not necessarily subject to any of the agreements currently in place.

The Kenyan state's overall development strategy has become increasingly focused on energy production, industrial development, and deepening connections with non-Western (especially Chinese) investors, corporations, and governments. In this new era, Naivasha will remain a place where large-scale changes in economic relationships and geopolitical alliances become uniquely legible, triggering micro- and macro-level social and political responses. The expansion of the geothermal industry will likely inspire the collaborative creation of a new set of flexible, neoliberal regulatory processes in Naivasha. Floriculture has shaped local lives, the practice of politics in Kenya, and approaches to environmental and social governance at multiple scales. However, the rise of floriculture was not inevitable, and its future prominence is not guaranteed. The expansion of geothermal power in Naivasha provides a stark reminder that this place has always had the potential to become something other. Alternative trajectories have always been (and will always remain) possible in this nerve center.

The perspectives of these different actors help humanize the cut flower commodity chain, revealing the conflicting emotions and ambitions that everyone in Naivasha brings to the cultivation of flowers. These actors frame their work and aspirations in floriculture in very different ways, but all are cultivating much more than roses. They are also carefully and consciously cultivating an interlinking set of dreams for national development, environmental and social control, and socioeconomic security and prosperity. Like many sites of concentrated global production, Naivasha is a synergistic nerve center. It is one where many actors seek to solve broader Kenyan social and environmental problems using the global flows of people, information, and money generated by floriculture. In doing so, they seek the opportunity, the power, and the right to participate productively and equally in the creative and collaborative construction of Kenya's future.

NOTES

INTRODUCTION

1 See, for example, Besky 2014; Leissle 2018; Lyon 2011; Reichman 2011; and West 2012.

2 See, for example, Basso 1996; Gupta and Ferguson 1997; Ingold 2000; and Kahn 2011.

CHAPTER 1: SITUATING NAIVASHA

1 Cole inherited a formal title in the Peerage of Ireland and is also known as Lord Enniskillen.

2 The organization was originally called the Lake Naivasha Riparian Owners Association (LNROA). In 1995, the organization revised its bylaws, removing the requirement that members own riparian land, as well as the stipulation that they be white. The name was also officially changed to the Lake Naivasha Riparian Association (LNRA). In this book, the acronym LNROA refers to the organization before 1995, and the acronym LNRA refers to the organization during and after 1995.

3 The historical narrative presented here is based on uncatalogued correspondence, meeting minutes, and special reports held in the LNRA's private archives. I also examined documents stored at the Kenya National Archives in Nairobi and the Public Records Office in London, especially colonial-era correspondence related to the founding of the LNROA and the organization's changing role in the management of Lake Naivasha and its environs over time. Self-published memoirs and local histories also helped me piece together a general timeline of events and compare multiple perspectives on patterns of environmental and social change in Naivasha over the last century. My interviews with people living and

working in contemporary Naivasha also explored historical subjects, especially perceptions of how the lake area had changed (socially and environmentally) with the advent of floriculture.

4 Africans and Asians were explicitly barred from owning land in the White Highlands. South Asians had been among the first non-African migrants into the region; they followed trade routes and the railroad in from the coast, where they had a long history of commerce and settlement (Bates 1989).

5 The Kikuyu are Kenya's largest ethnic group, comprising about 17 percent of the nation's contemporary population. Large parts of central Kenya, especially the Mount Kenya region, are recognized as traditional Kikuyu territory. Before and following colonization, the Kikuyu depended heavily on agriculture. British colonial officials targeted Kikuyu communities in particular for agricultural labor recruitment, assuming that their skills and experience would be useful to white settlers who intended to establish farms.

6 This correspondence is on file in folio AG/43/39, "Foreshore Rights: Lakes—Naivasha, Elementeita, and Nakuru: General (1928–1944)," in the Kenya National Archives.

7 Official colonial correspondence regarding foreshore rights and access points on Lake Naivasha between 1925 and 1928 can be found in folio BN/44/1, "Foreshore Rights—Lake Naivasha (1925–1929)," in the Kenya National Archives. These letters reference a recent district survey that delineated four riparian "outspans" conducive to public access. Ritchie suggested that the colonial government officially retain three of these outspans, one of which adjoined property owned by J. D. Hopcraft.

8 These concerns are documented in official meeting minutes, arbitration records, and letters stored in the private records of the LNRA.

9 Correspondence regarding the introduction of a sport fish to the lake, including Dent's survey and recommendations, can be found in folio KP/4/8, "Lake Naivasha (1927–1935)," in the Kenya National Archives.

10 Correspondence between British Museum trustees and Kenyan colonial officials regarding the introduction of both bass and tilapia to Lake Naivasha can be found in folio CO533/388/2, "Proposed Introduction of Specimens of the American Black Bass into Lake Naivasha (1929)," in the Public Records Office, London.

11 Ritchie's letters to colonial administrators, draft policies and ordinances regarding "control measures" on Lake Naivasha, and correspondence between officials and Lake Naivasha residents regarding Fisheries and Game Department proposals can be found in folio KP/4/8, "Lake Naivasha (1927–1935)," in the Kenya National Archives.

12 This report can be found in folio CO533/549/4, "European Settlement, Squatters, 1947," in the Public Records Office, London. Records in the

private collection of the LNRA indicate that the organization was less active during this period and reflect members' concerns about absentee land ownership.

13 These letters are on file in the LNRA's private archives.

14 These reports can be found in folio DC/NVA/1/1, "Naivasha District Annual Reports, 1952–1960," in the Kenya National Archives.

15 Correspondence regarding whether lakeside landholders might sell their properties at the end of colonial rule, including C. T. Todd's letter, is on file in the LNRA's private archive.

16 This correspondence can be found in folio KP/4/1, "Lake Naivasha (1949–1976)," in the Kenya National Archives.

17 Records related to this fish-packing plant can be found in folio KP/4/8, "Lake Naivasha (1927–1935)," in the Kenya National Archives.

18 These events and perspectives are documented in the LNRA meeting minutes for 1971 and letters on file in the LNRA's private archive.

19 DCK also purchased a second small farm near Nairobi, which it intended to use as a nursery. The Nairobi farm was later incorporated as a separate company and sold to an influential set of Kenyan investors. Development analyst Stephen Jaffee argues that this was "driven primarily by political considerations" (1994, 121). The goal of the scheme was "to expand Kenyan participation in an expanding industry that was almost totally controlled by European expatriates." The new company developed an outgrower scheme and contracted with small farmers in the area to produce carnations and statice. Farmers grew the flowers using inputs, expertise, and credit supplied by the company, which paid them when they harvested and delivered the cut flowers to designated collection sites. The venture was initially very successful. By 1978, 425 small farmers had contracted with the firm, and another 1,200 had been placed on a waiting list to join the project. According to Jaffee, however, the initiative collapsed later that year when the company was acquired by the Agricultural Development Corporation, a government parastatal, and expatriate managers were replaced.

20 Before DCK purchased the property, it was owned by two men with the surnames Sullivan and MacDonald. The name Sulmac is derived from the combination of their names.

21 This proposal is dated February 13, 1967, and can be found in folio KP/4/1 "Lake Naivasha (1949–1976)" in the Kenya National Archives.

22 See, for example, Wangui 1998; Mbaria 2001; Green 2002; Kamau 2002; Lusha 2002; Majtenyi 2002; Okoth 2002; Wamalwa 2002; Wang'ombe 2002; and Rich 2003.

23 See, for example, Blowfield and Dolan 2014, as well as Dolan 2005a, 2005b, and 2007.

24 Established in 1971, the Ramsar Convention "is an intergovernmental treaty that embodies the commitments of its member countries to maintain the

ecological character of their Wetlands of International Importance and to plan for the "wise use," or sustainable use, of all of the wetlands in their territories" (Ramsar Convention on Wetlands 2011). The benefits of Ramsar designation include international attention, access to funds earmarked for wetlands conservation, and the networking opportunities that accompany attendance at conventions, working groups, and other transnational forums.

25 Mungiki, literally meaning "a multitude" in Kikuyu, is the name of a complex organization that functions as a youth movement, a Kikuyu ethnic revival sect, and an organized crime syndicate. Some members of the sect see themselves as heirs to the Mau Mau legacy, conducting similar oathing rituals and promoting their activities as a means of reviving Kikuyu traditions subverted by colonialism. In practice, however, the group functions as "both a rural religious sect and an urban political militia" (Anderson 2002, 537). The group allegedly operates a "protection racket" in Nairobi, collecting significant funds from *matatu* operations; and self-identified Mungiki members sometimes orchestrate *matatu* stoppages, erect roadblocks, and engage in other threatening displays of their power in Nairobi's slums. Before the election violence, Mungiki had twice organized roadblocks in Naivasha Town during my time in the field; both were to protest the incarceration in the Naivasha Prison of Maina Njenga, who was recognized as the sect's "leader" in 2007. People living and working in Naivasha, including Kikuyu political and business leaders, alternatively described Mungiki to me as a loose collection of "dangerous thugs" and as a potentially powerful group that could be mobilized to protect Kikuyu ethnic interests. Accusations that the Mungiki attacks in Naivasha were planned at the State House, and that members were provided with arms and explicit instructions to retaliate in Naivasha, continue to animate political debate in Kenya (e.g., Kwamboka 2011; Mathenge 2011). Anthropologist Daniel Hoffman argues that in Sierra Leone, war can also be work for young men who join militias in the absence of other economic opportunities (Hoffman 2010). He describes these young men as a just-in-time labor force deployed to violent ends. Membership in Mungiki may also be a way for Kenyan elites to temporarily engage young men with few economic opportunities as short-term mercenaries.

26 Although the violence in Naivasha was deeply ethnicized, this was not a case of one ethnic community violently attacking another. Ethnic identity and heritage in Naivasha is complex, as it is in all Kenyan locales; many residents identify flexibly with multiple ethnic affiliations. Many ethnic minority residents shared stories of Kikuyu neighbors helping them escape to safety by distracting attackers, providing transport, or

lending them funds. Despite an atmosphere of fear and chaos, not all personal relationships were eroded by ethnic essentialism.

CHAPTER 2: LOW-WAGE LABORERS

1 Between April and May 2008, I interviewed 125 Naivasha flower farm workers and labor hopefuls (61 women and 64 men) with the help of a local research assistant. Seventy interview participants were current or former flower farm workers; the remainder were living with relatives or acquaintances while they searched for work in floriculture. Rather than accessing workers through farm management and interviewing them on-farm, we opted for a research design that would allow us to include a greater diversity of local perspectives (including those of labor hopefuls), let us learn more about workers' *off-farm* lives, and allow us to better safeguard their confidentiality. To recruit research participants, we visited each of Naivasha's six residential villages in turn. We did not move on to the next village until we determined that our data had reached saturation, in the sense that new interviews no longer yielded new types of answers (Bernard, Wutich, and Ryan 2017). We also received formal permission to interview workers living in the labor camp associated with one of Naivasha's largest flower farms. We spent two weeks interviewing workers in this labor camp. Farm managers did not accompany us as we conducted our research activities, and workers living here spoke with the same level of candor displayed by study participants living in the residential villages. All interviews were conducted inside participants' homes. We sought a gender balance in our sample so that we could better understand what both men and women experience in Naivasha and the ways that flower farm wages contribute to household or family income. Interview questions focused on why they had come to Naivasha, what they hoped to achieve through their work in floriculture, their progress toward their aspirations, their labor and living conditions, and their perspectives on a set of local social and environmental issues. Before and after conducting these interviews, I also established significant, long-term relationships with several farmworkers. I came to know these workers and their families very well, and I have followed their lives for over a decade. I also conducted participant observation activities on several smaller Naivasha-area farms, and I attended meetings organized by NGOs and community-based organizations where flower farm workers were invited to share their experiences and discuss strategies for improving their lives in floriculture. All names used to refer to farm employees are pseudonyms.

2 Many workers saw our interviews as opportunities to share painful memories of the postelection tension and violence that profoundly disrupted life in Naivasha in later 2007 and early 2008, as well as their general concerns

about the issues of ethnic identity and belonging in Naivasha. Ethnic identities in Kenya are socially constructed, constantly in flux, and frequently manipulated for strategic political ends (Lynch 2011). In each election cycle, politicians stoke "political tribalism" (Lonsdale 1994), the use of ethnic identity to create (or enhance) political competition between groups, by accusing leaders from other ethnic groups of benefiting unfairly from their access to state power and resources in the distant and recent past. Political parties in Kenya are closely associated with specific ethnic groups, and members of Kenya's elite political class intentionally cultivate competing senses of "ethnic nationalism" (Lynch 2011) to generate political support. Kenya's "winner-take-all" political system, which concentrates power in the hands of the president, heightens the sense that losing the presidential election also means losing access to state resources and the economic and political tools necessary for regional development in the areas that Kenyan ethnic groups view as "home." Patron-client relationships and elections in Kenya also hinge on "moral ethnicity" (Lonsdale 1994), the idea that people from the same ethnic group have a moral obligation to one another and are relationally interdependent in a deeper way than those outside of this imagined community. Before and after the December 2007 national election, political leaders strategically manipulated ethnic identity in order to create support for specific candidates and policies. In this chapter, when farmworkers discuss concerns about ethnic tensions and violence, these were rooted in the particular sociopolitical context generated by the December 2007 election cycle and its aftermath. However, political tribalism is a perennial source of vulnerability for farmworkers. Like Eunice, some workers migrated here following strategically ethnicized political "clashes" in other locales and earlier historic moments. In each election cycle, powerful actors with political ambitions court workers' support, promising to improve their lives and appealing to their senses of ethnic nationalism and moral ethnicity. Political tribalism is part of what makes life in this Kenyan nerve center especially precarious for workers, who rely on well-connected patrons to access the resources and opportunities that floriculture potentially provides.

CHAPTER 4: FLORICULTURE AND THE STATE

1 The concept that corporations should be "socially responsible" predates the neoliberal era. Ireland and Pillay (2010) note that this idea arose in the 1920s, and that, in the immediate post–World War II moment, government officials and members of a European and British public shared a more radical consensus that corporations should be public institutions with a responsibility to a broader set of stakeholders (rather than to

shareholders alone). However, in the neoliberal era, CSR became "essentially ameliorative, seeking to temper without unsettling or displacing the idea of the corporation as a private, exclusively shareholder- and profit-oriented enterprise" (78). This historically contingent, neoliberal understanding of CSR prevailed in Kenyan floriculture. Consumers, retailers, and the Kenyan state expected these farms to be "socially responsible" to a point. Social and environmental concerns needed to be addressed, but not in a way that would compromise the industry's contributions to Kenya's economic growth and development.

2 Although nation branding grew out of campaigns like Café de Colombia, which strategically linked the image of particular nations to particular products (e.g., Colombia's association with high-quality coffee), the eventual goal of nation branding is to create a positive image of the *nation* so that it will no longer be strictly dependent on any one signature product. Individual products of value to international consumers are a starting point for these campaigns, but the success of these products is meant to create an image of the nation as a safe, supportive environment for *other* types of foreign investment. If Colombia can support a high-quality coffee industry, what other types of commercial aspirations could be actualized here? Kenyan flower growers were mildly interested in place-based labels that would help consumers recognize roses as originating from Naivasha, but ultimately they worried that this attention to place might do them more harm than good. Since not all Naivasha flower farms shared the same CSR commitments and on-farm "best practices," one noncompliant farm could easily ruin a positive place-based image and undermine the value of such a label. Terroir labels (e.g., like those used to market Darjeeling tea or French champagne) are also a poor option for Kenyan flower growers. Although the flower varieties they cultivate have been bred for local environmental conditions, most were initially developed in Europe and none are strictly unique to Kenya or to Naivasha. Becoming part of a nation-branding initiative held great appeal for Naivasha-based flower growers because they could direct consumer attention toward the industry's critical role in Kenyan economic development and away from lingering social welfare and environmental problems associated with flower-growing in an environmentally sensitive space.

3 In a process designed to foster regional economic integration, the economic-partnership-agreement negotiations required African nation-states to form regional blocs. Kenya joined Burundi, Rwanda, Tanzania, Uganda, and South Sudan to negotiate as members of the East African Community.

4 The negotiation of an Economic Partnership Agreement between the East African Community and the European Union continued for more than eight years after my conversation with Naomi. EU and East African

Community delegates agreed on a draft Economic Partnership Agreement in 2014. When Kenya missed the October 2014 deadline to officially commit to the draft agreement, the EU began charging duties on Kenyan products. The Kenya Flower Council estimated that growers paid about three million euros in tariffs before Kenyan officials relented and signed the agreement in December 2015 (Moulds 2015). Only two East African Community countries, Kenya and Rwanda, had signed the agreement by the intended start date of October 2016. Tanzanian officials announced plans in July 2016 to pull out of the agreement completely, citing concerns that the nation's domestic industries could not withstand competition from European goods (Mkapa 2016). Since *all* of the East African Community member countries other than Kenya are classified as least-developed countries, the agreement provides no clear economic benefit to them in the short term (Vasey 2017). In September 2016, a Kenyan delegation led by members of the Kenya Flower Council convinced EU officials to sign an Economic Partnership Agreement with Kenya and Rwanda alone. The new Economic Partnership Agreement requires Kenya to gradually open 82.6 percent of its market to European goods over a twenty-five-year period. In exchange, a market-access-regulation provision "grants Kenya duty-free access to the EU market on a long-term basis and without any specific deadline for expiry," thereby saving Kenyan flowers from "disaster" (Middelburg 2016).

5 A draft of the new law was finalized in 2008, but it languished until a revised policy was adopted into law in 2013.

6 These dramatic changes in water governance are not unique to Kenya. Neoliberal policies transferring the responsibility for water management to local water resource user associations were introduced globally starting in the 1980s. A rich body of social science research has since examined the efficacy of these programs. For an excellent discussion of the contradictions and challenges posed by neoliberal water management strategies at a global level, see Furlong 2010. This chapter examines why Kenyan actors (especially flower growers and state agents) found these policies appealing at the moment of their inception and initial implementation, when it was still unclear whether these new strategies would actually prove effective.

CHAPTER 5: WHITE KENYANS AND EXPATRIATES

1 I showed a draft of this book to my white Kenyan friend. He corrected "sometimes" to read "virtually always."

2 The term *Kenya cowboy* refers to the descendants of colonial-era white settlers. The term plays on the fact that these are KC's, Kenya citizens, but it

also references a common stereotype of white settlers as rugged, adventurous, and independent.

3 Tusker Malt is manufactured primarily for export and is packaged in smaller bottles. Most Kenyans prefer the larger, one-liter bottles of standard Tusker. Drinking Tusker Malt signals an ability to pay more for less.

CONCLUSION

1 As part of its Sustainable Energy for All Initiative, the World Bank provided $336 million in support for geothermal development globally in 2012. The initiative is aimed at facilitating a shift to renewable energy sources and achieving universal energy access for all in the near future. Kenya is seen as a leader in the development of the African geothermal sector (World Bank 2012, 2013, 2015).

2 KenGen has operated geothermal power facilities in Naivasha since 1985. In 2007, KenGen's Olkaria plants generated 115 megawatts of power, about 15 percent of the nation's energy supply. Since then, Olkaria II and III have been expanded, and a new plant, Olkaria IV, came online in October 2014. Together, these plants contribute about 289 megawatts to the national grid. In April 2017, President Uhuru Kenyatta broke ground for the new Olkaria V plant, capable of generating 158 megawatts of power. Funded by the Japanese International Cooperation Agency, the plant will begin operating in 2019.

3 Compared to fossil-fuel-derived energy operations, geothermal power produces significantly less greenhouse gas and carbon emissions. Despite these clear benefits, however, geothermal power production can result in unintended environmental side effects, including geologic hazards (increased seismicity and ground deformation), surface or groundwater pollution from fluid and solid-waste emissions, depletion of water resources, atmospheric pollution from airborne emissions, and land-use changes that might affect biodiversity (Bayer et al. 2013). A team of Icelandic researchers describes the global effects of geothermal energy development as "unique, varied, positive, and negative." They argue that "the way in which a geothermal resource is utilized will ultimately determine whether or not the utilization is sustainable" (Shortall, Davidsgottir, and Axelsson 2015, 391).

BIBLIOGRAPHY

ARCHIVAL MATERIALS

Kenya National Archives, Nairobi

"Development Organization and Policy—Lake Naivasha (1963–1969)," KL/24/8.

"Foreshore Rights—Lake Naivasha (1925–1929)," BN/44/1.

"Foreshore Rights—Lake Naivasha (1930–1931)," BN/44/2.

"Foreshore Rights: Lakes Naivasha, Elementeita, and Nakuru: General (1928–1944)," AG/43/39.

"Lake Fishing Industry, Lake Naivasha, Lake Victoria Nyanza (1929–1932)," KP/4/9.

"Lake Naivasha (1927–1935)," KP/4/8.

"Lake Naivasha (1949–1976)," KP/4/1.

"Lake Naivasha (1970–1975)," KW/13/26.

"The Lake Naivasha Protection and Control Ordinance (1933) and Foreshore Rights: Lakes Naivasha, Elementeita, and Nakuru—General (1933)," AG/2/190.

"Naivasha County Council Minutes (1931–1960)," JA/1/170.

"Naivasha District Annual Reports (1952–1960)," DC/NVA/1/1.

"Naivasha District Intelligence Committee Summaries (1953–1962)," VP/2/19.

"Naivasha Farmer's Association (1912–1919)," MSS/128/13.

"Naivasha, Lake Naivasha Riparian Owner's Association (1931)," BN/1/31.

Public Records Office, London

"Agricultural Settlement Trust, Kenya, 1960–1962," CO822/2626.

"Agricultural Settlement Trust—Kenya (1963)," CO822/3169.

"Correspondence between Kenyatta and His Ministers Regarding Buy-Out of European Settlers (1963)," PREM 13/2179.
"European Settlement (1937)," CO533/484/2.
"European Settlement (1938)," CO533/497/7.
"European Settlement (1941–1942)," CO533/528/1.
"European Settlement (1948)," CO533/459/3.
"European Settlement in Kenya (1957–1959)," CO822/1506.
"European Settlement Purchase of Land Granted Free to Soldier Settlers (1939)," CO533/511/9.
"European Settlement, Squatters (1947)," CO533/549/4.
"Hut Tax in the Provinces of Kisumu and Naivasha (1902)," FO881/7715.
"Interview between Lord Delamere and Secretary of State Regarding Kenya (1963)," CO822/3274.
"Lake Fisheries Investigation—M. Worthington's Report (1931)," CO533/406/2.
"Land Commission Report: White Highlands, Position of Indians and Natives (1935)," CO533/453/4.
"Letter of Complaint Regarding Land Settlement Problems of Ex-Service Settlers in Kenya (1963)," DO 214/125.
"Naivasha Agricultural Research Station (1933)," CO533/436/2.
"Naivasha District Intelligence Reports (June–December 1953)," WO276/389.
"Naivasha Livestock Research Station (1940)," CO533/517/7.
"Naivasha Livestock Research Station (1941–1943)," CO533/524/16.
"Proposal to Establish an Animal Investigation Center at Naivasha, Kenya (1948)," CO927/96/3.
"Proposed Introduction of Specimens of the American Black Bass into Lake Naivasha (1929)," CO533/388/2.
"Recruitment of Women Labour (1929)," CO533/388/15.
"Regional Coordination of Agricultural Research—Naivasha Veterinary Research Station (1949–1950)," CO927/188/8.
"Report of the Rowett Institute Experimental Farm at Naivasha (1934–1935)," CO533/456/5.
"Rowett Institute Experimental Farm at Naivasha (1931)," CO533/406/15.
"Rowett Institute Experimental Farm at Naivasha (1934)," CO533/447/10.
"Rowett Institute Experimental Farm at Naivasha (1935)," CO533/456/4.
"Rowett Institute Experimental Farm at Naivasha, Audits and Expenditures (1938)," CO533/504/6.
"Rowett Institute Experimental Farm at Naivasha, Expenditures (1935–1936)," CO533/477/18.
"The Squatter Problem in the White Highlands (1957–1959)," CO822/1612.

"Trade in the Provinces of Kisumu and Naivasha (1902)," FO881/7811.
"Valuation of Land to Be Purchased under the Kenyan Land Settlement Scheme (1963)," T317/235.
"White Settlement—Fedritive Land Settlement (1935)," CO533/461/18.

Lake Naivasha Riparian Association, Naivasha

Uncataloged materials in this private collection include letters, meeting minutes, and other manuscripts related to the organization's activities in the Lake Naivasha area, 1927–present.

Other Sources

Abrahamsen, Rita. 2000. *Disciplining Democracy: Development Discourse and Good Governance in Africa*. London: Zed Books.
Adams, Prue. 2008. "Food to Go." *Landline*, November 23. www.abc.net.au/tv/programs/landline/old-site/content/2008/s2426086.htm.
Anderson, David. 2002. "Vigilantes, Violence and the Politics of Public Order in Kenya." *African Affairs* 101 (405): 531–55.
———. 2003. "Briefing: Kenya's Elections 2002: The Dawning of a New Era?" *African Affairs* 102 (407): 331–42.
———. 2005. *Histories of the Hanged: The Dirty War in Kenya and the End of Empire*. New York: W. W. Norton.
Anholt, Simon. 2002. "Foreword to a Special Issue on Nation-Branding." *Brand Management* 9 (4–5): 229–39.
Barrientos, Stephanie, Catherine Dolan, and Anne Tallontire. 2003. "A Gendered Value Chain Approach to Codes of Conduct in African Horticulture." *World Development* 31 (9): 1511–26.
Basso, Keith H. 1996. *Wisdom Sits in Places: Landscape and Language among the Western Apache*. Albuquerque: University of New Mexico Press.
Bates, Robert. 1989. *Beyond the Miracle of the Market: The Political Economy of Agrarian Development in Kenya*. New York: Cambridge University Press.
Bayart, Jean-Francois, and S. Ellis. 2000. "Africa in the World: A History of Extraversion." *African Affairs* 99 (395): 217–67.
Bayer, Peter, L. Rybach, P. Blum, and R. Brauchler. 2013. "Review on Life Cycle Environmental Effects of Geothermal Power Generation." *Renewable and Sustainable Energy Reviews* 26:463–63.
Becht, R., and D. M. Harper. 2002. "Towards an Understanding of Human Impact upon the Hydrology of Lake Naivasha, Kenya." *Hydrobiologia* 488 (1–3): 1–11.
Bernard, H. Russell, Amber Wutich, and Gery W. Ryan. 2017. *Analyzing Qualitative Data: Systematic Approaches*. Washington, DC: Sage.

Besky, Sarah. 2014. *The Darjeeling Distinction: Labor and Justice on Fair-Trade Tea Plantations in India*. Berkeley: University of California Press.
Blowfield, Michael E., and Catherine S. Dolan. 2008. "Stewards of Virtue? The Ethical Dilemma of CSR in African Agriculture." *Development and Change* 39 (1): 1–23.
———. 2014. "Business as a Development Agent: Evidence of Impossibility and Improbability." *Third World Quarterly* 35 (1): 22–42.
Boar, R. R., and D. M. Harper. 2002. "Magnetic Susceptibilities of Lake Sediment and Soils on the Shoreline of Lake Naivasha, Kenya." *Hydrobiologia* 488 (1–3): 81–88.
Brand Kenya Board. 2010. Homepage. Accessed June 6. www.brandkenya.co.ke.
———. 2017. Homepage. Accessed August 7. www.brandkenya.co.ke.
Carnelley, Mervyn. 1976. "Lake Naivasha: An Extended History." Unpublished manuscript in the private collection of the Carnelley family, Naivasha, Kenya.
Cege, Alex. 1993. "Fiery Birth Rose Farm Marks First Birthday." *Daily Nation*, May 3.
Collins, Jane L. 2002. "Mapping a Global Labor Market: Gender and Skill in the Globalizing Garment Industry." *Gender and Society* 16 (6): 921–40.
Cooper, Frederick. 2002. *Africa since 1940: The Past of the Present.* Cambridge: Cambridge University Press.
Cowell, Alan. 2003. "Letter from Africa: Beside Blossoming Fields, Where Poverty Grows." *New York Times*, June 4.
Cranfield University. 2007. "About Us." Accessed March 12, 2010. www.cranfield.ac.uk/about/index.html.
Crilly, Rob. 2007. "Kenya Farmers versus Euro Environmentalists." *Time*, November 9.
Daily Nation. 1976. "Traders Want Flower Power." March 3.
Delaney, David. 2005. *Territory: A Short Introduction.* Malden, MA: Blackwell.
Dolan, Catherine S. 2004. "On Farm and Packhouse: Employment at the Bottom of a Global Commodity Chain." *Rural Sociology* 69 (1): 99–126.
———. 2005a. "Benevolent Intent? The Development Encounter in Kenya's Horticulture Industry." *Journal of African and Asian Studies* 40 (6): 411–37.
———. 2005b. "Fields of Obligation: Rooting Ethical Consumption in Kenyan Horticulture." *Journal of Consumer Culture* 5 (3): 365–89.
———. 2007. "Market Affectations: Moral Encounters with Kenyan Fairtrade Flowers." *Ethnos* 72 (2): 239–61.

Dolan, Catherine, and John Humphrey. 2001. "Governance and Trade in Fresh Vegetables: The Impact of UK Supermarkets on the African Horticulture Industry." *Journal of Development Studies* 37 (2): 147–76.

Dolan, Catherine, Maggie Opondo, and Sally Smith. 2002. *Gender, Rights, and Participation in the Kenya Cut Flower Industry.* Natural Resources Institute Report No. 2768. Chatham, UK: Natural Resources Institute.

Donham, Donald L. 1999. *Marxist Modern: An Ethnographic History of the Ethiopian Revolution.* Berkeley: University of California Press.

Dupas, Pascaline, Sarah Green, Anthony Keats, and Jonathan Robinson. 2012. *Challenges in Banking the Rural Poor: Evidence from Kenya's Western Province.* National Bureau of Economic Research Working Paper No. 17851. DOI: 10.3386/w17851.

Elkins, Caroline. 2005. *Britain's Gulag: The Brutal End of Empire in Kenya.* London: Pimlico.

Ellis, Amanda, Jozefina Cutura, Nouma Dione, Ian Gillson, Clare Manuel, and Judy Thongori. 2007. *Gender and Economic Growth in Kenya: Unleashing the Power of Women.* Washington, DC: World Bank.

English, Phil, Steve Jaffee, and Julius Okello. 2006. "Exporting out of Africa: The Kenya Horticulture Success Story." In *Attacking Africa's Poverty: Experience from the Ground Up,* edited by Louise Fox and Robert Liebenthal, 117–47. Washington, DC: World Bank.

Everard, M., and D. M. Harper. 2002. "Towards the Sustainability of the Lake Naivasha Ramsar Site and Its Catchment." *Hydrobiologia* 488 (1–3): 191–203.

Fanon, Franz. 1968. *The Wretched of the Earth.* First Black Cat edition, translated by Constance Farrington. New York: Grove Press.

Ferguson, James. 2006. *Global Shadows: Africa in the Neoliberal World Order.* Durham, NC: Duke University Press.

Finch, Julia, and John Vidal. 2007. "Tesco Makes Green Pledge." *Guardian,* January 18.

Fox, James. 1982. *White Mischief: The Murder of Lord Errol.* New York: Random House.

Freidberg, Susanne. 2001. "On the Trail of the Global Green Bean: Methodological Considerations in Multi-site Ethnography." *Global Networks* 1 (4): 353–68

———. 2003. "Cleaning Up Down South: Supermarkets, Ethical Trade, and African Horticulture." *Social and Cultural Geography* 4 (1): 27–43.

———. 2004. *French Beans and Food Scares: Culture and Commerce in an Anxious Age.* Oxford: Oxford University Press.

Freidemann-Sánchez, Greta. 2006. *Assembling Flowers and Cultivating Homes: Labor and Gender in Colombia.* Boulder, CO: Lexington Books.

Furlong, Kathryn. 2010. "Neoliberal Water Management: Trends, Limitations, Reformulations." *Environment and Society: Advances in Research* 1:46–75.

Gallagher, Kevin P., and Lyuba Zarsky. 2007. *The Enclave Economy: Foreign Investment and Sustainable Development in Mexico's Silicon Valley.* Cambridge, MA: MIT Press.

Gardner, Katy. 2012. *Discordant Development: Global Capitalism and the Struggle for Connection in Bangladesh.* London: Pluto.

Geothermal Development Company. 2015. "Who We Are." Accessed March 8. www.gdc.co.ke.

Gereffi, Gary. 1994. "The Organization of Buyer-Driven Global Commodity Chains: How U.S. Retailers Shape Overseas Production Networks." In *Commodity Chains and Global Capitalism*, edited by G. Gereffi and M. Korzeniewicz, 95–161. Westport, CT: Praeger.

Gibbon, Peter. 1992. "A Failed Agenda? African Agriculture under Structural Adjustment, with Special Reference to Kenya and Ghana." *Journal of Peasant Studies* 20 (1): 50–96.

Gibson-Graham, J. K. 2006. *A Postcapitalist Politics.* Minneapolis: University of Minnesota.

Giddens, Anthony. 1990. *The Consequences of Modernity.* Stanford, CA: Stanford University Press.

Gordon, David F. 1986. *Decolonization and the State in Kenya.* Boulder: Westview Press.

Green, Maia. 2014. *The Development State: Aid, Culture and Civil Society in Tanzania.* Woodbridge, UK: James Currey.

———. 2015. Making Africa Middle Class: From Poverty Reduction to the Production of Inequality in Tanzania. *Economic Anthropology* 2 (2): 295–309.

Green, Matthew. 2002. "Valentine's a Thorny Issue for Staff at Flower Farms." *Daily Nation*, February 14.

Grown under the Sun. 2008. Homepage. Accessed March 12, 2010. http://grownunderthesun.com/index.html.

Gupta, Akhil. 1995. "Blurred Boundaries: The Discourse of Corruption, the Culture of Politics, and the Imagined State." *American Ethnologist* 22 (2): 275–402.

Gupta Akhil, and James Ferguson. 1997. *Culture, Power, Place: Explorations in Critical Anthropology.* Durham, NC: Duke University Press.

Guyer, Jane I. 1995. "Wealth in People, Wealth in Things." *Journal of African History* 36:83–90.

Hale, Angela, and Mary Magdalene Opondo. 2005. "Humanising the Cut Flower Chain: Confronting the Realities of Flower Production for Workers in Kenya." *Antipode* 37 (2): 301–23.

Harding, Susan. 1991. "Representing Fundamentalism: The Problem of the Repugnant Cultural Other." *Social Research* 58:373–94.

Harper, D. M., K. M. Mavuti, and S. M. Muchiri. 1990. "Ecology and Management of Lake Naivasha, Kenya, in Relation to Climatic-Change, Alien Species Introductions, and Agricultural Development." *Environmental Conservation* 17 (4): 328–36.

Haugerud, Angelique. 1993. *The Culture of Politics in Modern Kenya.* Cambridge: Cambridge University Press.

Hayes, Charles. 1997. *Oserian: Place of Peace.* Nairobi: Rima Books.

Hemsing, Jan. 1992. *Naivasha and the Lake Naivasha Country Club.* Nairobi: Modern Lithographic.

Hoffman, Daniel J. 2010. "Violence, Just in Time: The Future of War and Work in the Mano River Basin." Paper presented at the annual meeting for the American Anthropological Association, New Orleans, Louisiana, November 19.

Hubble, D. S., and D. M. Harper. 2001. "What Defines a 'Healthy' Lake?: Evidence from Lake Naivasha, Kenya." *Aquatic Ecosystem Health and Management* 4 (3): 243–50.

Hughes, Alex. 2004. "Accounting for Ethical Trade: Global Commodity Networks, Virtualism and the Audit Economy." In *Geographies of Commodity Chains,* edited by A. Hughes and S. Reimer, 215–31. London: Routledge.

Hughes, David. 2010. *Whiteness in Zimbabwe: Race, Landscape, and the Problem of Belonging.* New York: Palgrave Macmillan.

Hughes, Lotte. 2006. *Moving the Maasai: A Colonial Misadventure.* New York: Palgrave Macmillan.

Ingold, Tim. 2000. *The Perception of the Environment: Essays on Livelihood, Dwelling and Skill.* London: Routledge.

Ireland, Paddy, and Renginee G. Pillay. 2010. "Corporate Social Responsibility in a Neoliberal Age." In *Corporate Social Responsibility and Regulatory Governance: Towards Inclusive Development?* edited by P. Utting and J. C. Marques, 77–104. London: Palgrave Macmillan.

Jaffee, Eugene D., and Israel D. Nebenzahl. 2001. *National Image and Competitive Advantage: The Theory and Practice of Country-of-Origin Effect.* Copenhagen: Copenhagen Business School.

Jaffee, Steven M. 1994. "Contract Farming in the Shadow of Competitive Markets: The Experience of Kenyan Horticulture." In *Living under Contract: Contract Farming and Agrarian Transformation in Sub-Saharan Africa,* edited by Peter D. Little and Michael J. Watts, 97–139. Madison: University of Wisconsin Press.

Jansen, Sue Curry. 2008. "Designer Nations: Neo-Liberal Nation Branding—Brand Estonia." *Social Identities* 14 (1): 121–42.

Jones, Geoffrey. 2005. *Renewing Unilever: Transformation and Tradition.* Oxford: Oxford University Press.

Kahn, Miriam. 2011. *Tahiti beyond the Postcard: Power, Place, and Everyday Life.* Seattle: University of Washington Press.

Kamau, John. 2002. "Raw Deal for Flower Farm Workers." *Daily Nation,* August 27.

Kamau, Joseph Nyingi, A. Gachanja, C. Ngila, J. M. Kazungu, and M. Zhai. 2008. "Sediment-Water Fluxes of Selected Heavy Metals in Lake Naivasha: Anthropogenic and Seasonal Influences on the Dynamics of Selected Heavy Metals in Lake Naivasha, Kenya." *Lakes and Reservoirs: Research and Management* 13:145–54.

Kanogo, Tabitha. 1987. *Squatters and the Roots of the Mau Mau.* Athens: Ohio University Press.

Kaplan, Robert D. 1994. "The Coming Anarchy: How Scarcity, Crime, Overpopulation, Tribalism, and Disease Are Rapidly Destroying the Social Fabric of Our Planet." *Atlantic,* February 1.

Kasmir, Sharryn. 2018. "Precarity." In *The Cambridge Encyclopedia of Anthropology,* edited by F. Stein, S. Lazar, M. Candea, H. Diemberger, J. Robbins, A. Sanchez, and R. Stasch. www.anthroencyclopedia.com/entry/precarity.

Kennedy, Dane Keith. 1987. *Islands of White: Settler Society and Culture in Kenya and Southern Rhodesia.* Durham, NC: Duke University Press.

Kenya Electricity Generating Company. 2011. Homepage. Accessed April 1. www.kengen.co.ke.

Kenya Flower Council. 2009. Homepage. Accessed January 17, 2010. www.kenyaflowercouncil.org.

Kenya High Commission in the United Kingdom. 2007. "Grown under the Sun: Are Food Miles Fair Miles?" *Newsletter,* no. 5 (July): 15.

Kitaka, N., D. M. Harper, and K. M. Mavuti. 2002. "Phosphorous Inputs to Lake Naivasha, Kenya, from Its Catchment and the Trophic State of the Lake." *Hydrobiologia* 488 (1–3): 73–80.

Kwamboka, Evelyn. 2011." Mungiki, Arms, and the State House Link." *East African Standard,* August 20.

Lake Naivasha Management Committee. 2004. *The Lake Naivasha Management Plan.* Lake Naivasha Riparian Association Archives, Naivasha, Kenya.

Lake Naivasha Riparian Association. 2008. Homepage. Accessed April 3, 2011. http://web.ncf.ca/es202/naivasha.
Lawrence, Felicity. 2011. "Kenyan Flower Industry's Taxing Question." *Guardian*, April 1.
Leissle, Kristy. 2018. *Cocoa*. Cambridge, UK: Polity.
Little, Peter D., and Catherine S. Dolan. 2000. "What It Means to Be Restructured: Nontraditional Commodities and Structural Adjustment in Sub-Saharan Africa." In *Commodities and Globalization: Anthropological Perspectives*, edited by A. Haugerud, M. P. Stone, and P. D. Little, 59–78. New York: Rowman and Littlefield.
Lonsdale, J. 1994. "Moral Ethnicity and Political Tribalism." In *Inventions and Boundaries: Historical and Anthropological Approaches to the Study of Ethnicity and Nationalism*, edited by P. Kaarsholm and J. Hultin. Roskilde, Denmark: International Development Studies, Roskilde University.
Lusha, John. 2002. "Trapped in Squalor and Misery." *East African Standard*, March 18.
Lynch, Gabrielle. 2011. *I Say to You: Ethnic Politics and the Kalenjin in Kenya*. Chicago: University of Chicago Press.
Lyon, Sarah. 2011. *Coffee and Community: Maya Farmers and Fair-Trade Markets*. Boulder: University Press of Colorado.
Lyons, Rob. 2008. "Why There's No Mileage in Food Miles." *Spiked Magazine*, March 27. www.spiked-online.com/2008/03/27/why-theres-no-mileage-in-food-miles.
MacDonald, Peter. B. 1970. "Lake Naivasha—Centre of Crisis or Natural Asset?" *East African Standard*, December 2.
Majtenyi, Cathy. 2002. "Cut Flower Industry Accused of Human Rights Abuse." *East African Standard*, June 1.
Mathenge, Oliver. 2011. "Dossier Links State House to Chaos." *Daily Nation*, August 19.
Mbaria, John. 2001. "Flower Firms Up to No Good." *Daily Nation*, February 21.
Mbembe, Achille. 2001. *On the Postcolony*. Berkeley: University of California Press.
McIntosh, Janet. 2015. "Autochthony and 'Family': The Politics of Kinship in White Kenyan Bids to Belong." *Anthropological Quarterly* 88 (2): 251–80.
———. 2016. *Unsettled: Denial and Belonging among White Kenyans*. Oakland: University of California Press.
McKie, Robin. 2008. "How the Myth of Food Miles Hurts the Planet." *Guardian*, March 23.

Mekonnen, M. M., A. Y. Hoekstra, and R. Becht. 2012. "Mitigating the Water Footprint of Export Cut Flowers from the Lake Naivasha Basin, Kenya." *Water Resources Management* 26 (13): 3725–42.

Middelburg, Arie-Frans. 2016. "How the Kenyan Flower Industry Was Saved from a Disaster." *Floribusiness*, November 17. www.hortipoint.nl/floribusiness/archief-floribusiness/how-the-kenyan-flower-industry-was-saved-from-a-disaster.

Mintz, Sidney. 1985. *Sweetness and Power: The Place of Sugar in Modern History.* New York: Penguin.

Mkapa, Benjamin William. 2016. "East Africa: Economic Partnership Agreement Has Never Made Much Sense for Tanzania." *Tanzania Daily News*, July 28. http://allafrica.com/stories/201607280743.html.

Moore, Donald S. 2005. *Suffering for Territory: Race, Place, and Power in Zimbabwe.* Durham, NC: Duke University Press.

Morrison, E. H. J., and D. M. Harper. 2009. "Ecohydrological Principles to Underpin the Restoration of *Cyperus papyrus* at Lake Naivasha, Kenya." *Ecohydrology and Hydrobiology* 9 (1): 83–87.

Moulds, Josephine. 2015. "EU Trade Agreements Threaten to Crush Kenya's Blooming Flower Trade." *Guardian*, January 6.

Mugambi, Kaburu. 2007a. "Friday Deadline Looms for EU Agreement." *Daily Nation*, November 18.

———. 2007b. "EU Reaches Trade Deal with EAC." *Daily Nation*, November 28.

Muiruri, Peter. 2012. "Naivasha's Changing Fortunes." *East African Standard*, August 23.

Musangi, Pauline. 2017. "Women, Land and Property Rights in Kenya." Paper presented at the World Bank Conference on Land and Poverty, Washington, DC, March 20–24.

Museleku, Erastus, Mary Kimani, Winnie Mwangi, and Paul Syagga. 2018. "Drivers of Agricultural Land Subdivision in Drylands of Kenya: A Case of Kajiado County, Kenya." *International Journal of Innovative Research and Knowledge* 3 (6): 196–212.

Mwangi, Isaac Wachira. 2011. "Determinants of Access to Credit by Individuals in Kenya: A Comparative Analysis of the Kenya National FinAccess Surveys of 2006 and 2009." *European Journal of Business Management* 3 (3): 206–27.

Njururi, Blamuel. 1978. "Horticulture Exporters Owe Shs. 500m." *Nairobi Times*, August 5.

Okoth, Dann. 2002. "Wilham Tragedy: An Accident or a Mere Act of Negligence?" *East African Standard*, March 18.

Orvis, Stephen. 1997. *The Agrarian Question in Kenya.* Gainesville: University Press of Florida.

Oserian. 2008. Homepage. Accessed June 15. http://oserian.com.

Osterhoudt, Sarah R. 2017. *Vanilla Landscapes: Meaning, Memory, and the Cultivation of Place in Madagascar.* Bronx: New York Botanical Garden Press.

Peck, Jamie, and Adam Tickell. 2002. "Neoliberalizing Space." *Antipode* 34:380–44.

Peet, Richard, and Michael Watts, eds. 1996. *Liberation Ecologies: Environment, Development, Social Movements.* New York: Routledge.

Peluso, Nancy Lee, and Michael Watts, eds. 2001. *Violent Environments.* Ithaca, NY: Cornell University Press.

Perales, Monica. 2010. *Smeltertown: Making and Remembering a Southwest Border Community.* Chapel Hill: University of North Carolina.

Pigg, Stacy. 1992. "Inventing Social Categories through Place: Social Representation and Development in Nepal." *Comparative Studies in Society and History* 34 (3): 491–513.

Power, Michael. 1997. *The Audit Society: Rituals of Verification.* Oxford: Oxford University Press.

Ramsar Convention on Wetlands. 2011. "About Ramsar." Accessed August 11. www.ramsar.org/cda/en/ramsar-about-about-ramsar/main/ramsar/1-36%5E7687_4000_0.

Raphael, Arnold. 1976. "Kenya Wins Flower Fight." *East African Standard,* January 25.

Reichman, Daniel. 2011. *Broken Village: Coffee, Migration, and Globalization in Honduras.* Ithaca, NY: Cornell University Press.

Republic of Kenya. 2013. "National Environmental Policy, 2013." www.environment.go.ke/wp-content/uploads/2014/01/NATIONAL-ENVIRONMENT-POLICY-20131.pdf.

Rich, Bjorn. 2003. "How Kenya Is Cheated Out of Her Wealth." *Daily Nation,* March 11.

Rojas, Francisco. 2014. "President Kenyatta on the Impact of Geothermal Energy for Kenya." *Think Geoenergy,* October 20. www.thinkgeoenergy.com/president-kenyatta-on-the-impact-of-geothermal-energy-for-kenya.

Roy, Ishita Sinha. 2007. "Worlds Apart: Nation-Branding on the National Geographic Channel." *Media, Culture, and Society* 29 (4): 569–92.

"Salvinia Weed Could Cause an International Crisis." 1970. *Daily Nation,* November 27.

Scott, James C. 1976. *The Moral Economy of the Peasant: Rebellion and Subsistence in Southeast Asia.* New Haven: Yale University Press.

Sherman, Adulhakim. 2017. "Cotu's Atwoli Suffers Major Blow as Court Rejects His Appeal over Registration of New Workers Union." *Justice Now Online News,* May 16. http://justicenow.co.ke/2017/05/14/cotus-atwoli-suffers-major-blow-as-court-rejects-his-appeal-over-registration-of-new-workers-union.

Shore, Chris. 2008. "Audit Culture and Illiberal Governance: Universities and the Politics of Accountability." *Anthropological Theory* 8 (3): 278–98.

Shore, Chris, and Susan Wright. 1999. "Audit Culture and Anthropology: Neo-Liberalism in British Higher Education." *Journal of the Royal Anthropological Institute* 5:557–75.

———. 2015. "Governing by Numbers: Audit Culture, Rankings, and the New World Order." *Social Anthropology / Anthropologie Sociale* 23 (1): 22–28.

Shortall, Ruth, B. Davidsgottir, and G. Axelsson. 2015. "Geothermal Energy for Sustainable Development: A Review of Sustainability Impacts and Assessment Frameworks." *Renewable and Sustainable Energy Reviews* 44:391–406.

Sivaramakrishnan, K. 1999. *Modern Forests: Statemaking and Environmental Change in Colonial Eastern India.* Stanford, CA: Stanford University Press.

Smart, Andrew C., David M. Harper, François Malaisse, Sophie Schmitz, Stephanie Coley, and Anne-Christine Gouder de Beauregard. 2002. "Feeding of the Exotic Louisiana Red Swamp Crayfish, *Procambarus clarkii* (Crustacea, Decapoda), in an African Tropical Lake: Lake Naivasha, Kenya." *Hydrobiologia* 488 (1–3): 129–42.

Smithers, Rebecca. 2010. "Tesco's Pledge to Carbon-Label All Products Set to Take Centuries." *Guardian,* October 13.

Sorrenson, M. P. K. 1968. *Origins of European Settlement in Kenya.* London: Oxford University Press.

Specter, Michael. 2008. "Big Foot: In Measuring Carbon Emissions, It's Easy to Confuse Morality and Science." *New Yorker,* February 28.

Springer, Jenny. 2000. "State Power and Agricultural Transformation in Tamil Nadu." In *Agrarian Environments: Resources, Representation, and Rule in India,* edited by A. Agrawal and K. Sivaramakrishnan, 86–106. Durham, NC: Duke University Press.

Spronk, Rachel. 2009. "Media and the Therapeutic Ethos of Romantic Love in Middle-Class Nairobi." In *Love in Africa,* edited by J. Cole and L. Thomas. Chicago: University of Chicago Press.

Stone, M. Priscilla, A. Haugerud, and P. Little. 2000. "Commodities and Globalization: Anthropological Perspectives." In *Commodities and Globalization: Anthropological Perspectives,* edited by A. Haugerud, M. P. Stone, and P. Little, 1–32. Lanham, MD: Rowman and Littlefield.

Strathern, Marilyn. 1997. "'Improving Ratings': Audit in the British University System." *European Review* 5 (3): 305–21.

———. 2000. "Introduction: New Accountabilities." In *Audit Cultures: Anthropological Studies in Accountability, Ethics and the Academy*, edited by M. Strathern, 1–18. London: Routledge.

Tarafdar, Sujata, and David Harper. 2008. "Anti-persistence in Levels of Lake Naivasha: Assessing Effect of Human Intervention through Time-Series Analysis." *Physics A* 387:296–302.

Tesco. 2008. "Carbon Labeling and Tesco." Accessed November 12. www.tescoplc.com/plc/media/pr/pr2008.

Thomson, Joseph. 1887. *Through Masai Land: A Journey of Exploration among the Snowclad Volcanic Mountains and Strange Tribes of Eastern Equatorial Africa.* New and revised edition. London: Sampson, Low, Marston, Searle.

Uusihakala, Katja. 1999. "From Impulsive Adventure to Postcolonial Commitment: Making White Identity in Contemporary Kenya." *European Journal of Cultural Studies* 2 (1): 27–45.

Vasey, Conner. 2017. "Bloc to Bloc: Will the EAC Sign the European Union's EPA?" *Global Risk Insights*, March 2. http://globalriskinsights.com/2017/03/bloc-to-bloc-will-the-eac-sign-the-european-unions-epa.

Vaughan, Adam. 2012. "Tesco Drops Carbon-Label Pledge." *Guardian*, January 30.

Wamalwa, John. 2002. "Small Flower Growers Taken for a Ride." *Daily Nation*, September 16.

Wambalaba, Frances, and George K'Aol. 2006. "Is Corporate Citizenship Making a Difference in Horticultural Industry in Kenya? The Case of Homegrown Kenya Ltd." Symposium paper delivered in Ghana, November 20–22. www.imarisha.le.ac.uk/academic-report/agriculture-cultural-horticulture/648.

Wang, Chih-Kang, and Charles W. Lamb. 1983. "The Impact of Selected Environmental Forces upon Consumers' Willingness to Buy Foreign Products." *Journal of the Academy of Marketing Science* 11 (2): 71–83.

Wang'ombe, Florence. 2002. "Women Workers Are Underpaid, Sexually Molested, and Exposed to Bigger Health Risks." *East African Standard*, March 18.

Wangui, Kanina. 1998. "Flower Farms Not So Rosy!" *The People*, September 11.

wa Thiong'o, Ngugi. 1986. *Decolonising the Mind: The Politics of Language in African Literature.* Portsmouth, NH: Heinemann.

West, Paige. 2012. *From Modern Production to Imagined Primitive: The Social World of Coffee from Papua New Guinea.* Durham, NC: Duke University Press.

Williams, Adrian. 2007. "Comparative Study of Cut Roses for the British Market Produced in Kenya and the Netherlands." *Précis Report for World Flowers*, February 12. www.fairflowers.de/fileadmin/flp.de/Redaktion/Dokumente/Studien/Comparative_Study_of_Cut_Roses_Feb_2007.pdf.

Winter-Nelson, Alex. 1995. "A History of Agricultural Policy in Kenya." In *Agricultural Policy in Kenya: Applications of the Policy Analysis Matrix*, edited by S. Pearson et al. Ithaca, NY: Cornell University Press.

World Bank. 2012. "Kenya's Power Shortage Problem Meets Innovative Finance." April 5. www.worldbank.org/en/news/feature/2012/04/05/kenya-power-shortage-innovative-finance.

———. 2013. "Plugged in to Progress with Geothermal Energy in Kenya." January 11. www.worldbank.org/en/news/feature/2013/01/11/plugged-in-to-progress-with-geothermal-energy-in-kenya.

———. 2015. "Kenya's Geothermal Investments Contribute to Green Energy Growth, Competitiveness and Shared Prosperity." February 23. www.worldbank.org/en/news/feature/2015/02/23/kenyas-geothermal-investments-contribute-to-green-energy-growth-competitiveness-and-shared-prosperity.

Zwager, Hans. 2005. *The Flowering Dutchman: Horticulture in Harmony with Wildlife*. Kelowna, BC: Ehman Printworx. Self-published memoir.

INDEX

E

L

M

O

CULTURE, PLACE, AND NATURE
Studies in Anthropology and Environment

The Kuhls of Kangra: Community-Managed Irrigation in the Western Himalaya, by Mark Baker

The Earth's Blanket: Traditional Teachings for Sustainable Living, by Nancy Turner

Property and Politics in Sabah, Malaysia: Native Struggles over Land Rights, by Amity A. Doolittle

Border Landscapes: The Politics of Akha Land Use in China and Thailand, by Janet C. Sturgeon

From Enslavement to Environmentalism: Politics on a Southern African Frontier, by David McDermott Hughes

Ecological Nationalisms: Nature, Livelihood, and Identities in South Asia, edited by Gunnel Cederlöf and K. Sivaramakrishnan

Tropics and the Traveling Gaze: India, Landscape, and Science, 1800–1856, by David Arnold

Being and Place among the Tlingit, by Thomas F. Thornton

Forest Guardians, Forest Destroyers: The Politics of Environmental Knowledge in Northern Thailand, by Tim Forsyth and Andrew Walker

Nature Protests: The End of Ecology in Slovakia, by Edward Snajdr

Wild Sardinia: Indigeneity and the Global Dreamtimes of Environmentalism, by Tracey Heatherington

Tahiti Beyond the Postcard: Power, Place, and Everyday Life, by Miriam Kahn

Forests of Identity: Society, Ethnicity, and Stereotypes in the Congo River Basin, by Stephanie Rupp

Enclosed: Conservation, Cattle, and Commerce among the Q'eqchi' Maya Lowlanders, by Liza Grandia

Puer Tea: Ancient Caravans and Urban Chic, by Jinghong Zhang

Andean Waterways: Resource Politics in Highland Peru, by Mattias Borg Rasmussen

Conjuring Property: Speculation and Environmental Futures in the Brazilian Amazon, by Jeremy M. Campbell

Forests Are Gold: Trees, People, and Environmental Rule in Vietnam, by Pamela D. McElwee

The Nature of Whiteness: Race, Animals, and Nation in Zimbabwe, by Yuka Suzuki

Organic Sovereignties: Struggles over Farming in an Age of Free Trade, by Guntra A. Aistara

Caring for Glaciers: Land, Animals, and Humanity in the Himalayas, by Karine Gagné

Living with Oil and Coal: Resource Politics and Militarization in Northeast India, by Dolly Kikon

Working with the Ancestors: Mana *and Place in the Marquesas Islands,* by Emily C. Donaldson

Roses from Kenya: Labor, Environment, and the Global Trade in Cut Flowers, by Megan A. Styles